To
Elinor Ostrom, Eduardo Brondízio, and Leah vanWey
For their friendship and scholarly partnership
with me over many years

Contents

List of Illustrations

Figures

Plates

Preface

This book will synthesize the foundations for the emergence of a new cross-disciplinary enterprise that many scholars are calling environmental social science, and/or, human–environment interactions research (aka, sustainability science and coupled human natural systems research). The book, to remain coherent, cannot take on every topic under this broad umbrella. Thus, important areas in human environment research such as international environmental regulatory regimes (environmental treaties), environmental policy formation, public environmental concern and pro-environmental behaviors and valuation of environmental goods and services are not addressed here. The goal, instead, is to make accessible to both natural and social scientists the tools and the language that are used in this multidisciplinary type of work thereby facilitating the collaborative work across the natural and social sciences. The focus is very much on spatially explicit approaches to this area of research and how to use these approaches to bridge the divide between the social and natural sciences. One of the impediments to multidisciplinary research has been a lack of familiarity with the foundational theories and methods underlying the approaches used in the social sciences and the biophysical sciences. It is my hope that this book will assist those who wish to work across these boundaries. To do so we need to understand the underlying assumptions and theories, and which ones have been productive in past and current research.

In writing the book, on a topic that I have spent decades studying, researching and analyzing, I have turned to some of my earlier writings (particularly those from the past decade or so) and readers will find some of the writing here reminiscent of some of these earlier writings of mine. This is as it should be, since this book is an effort to take much of what I have learned from cross-disciplinary research and teaching, and leverage it now in this effort to provide a compendium of that experience as it applies to how to facilitate the interaction of social and bio-ecological scientists.

This is a continuing challenge, and one that this book will not solve. However, it is my sincere hope that the book will provide members of the community with resources to facilitate conversation, formulation of questions that are integrative in nature, and to result in better collaboration between scientists. The literature on this broad range of subjects is also all encompassing, and I have tried to be selective in providing an entry into these subjects, rather than try to be encyclopedic.

It is probably worthwhile here to make note that there are many terms used for this area of research which could cause confusion among those new to the subject. Each of the social sciences has an environmental component (i.e. environmental anthropology, environmental geography, environmental history, environmental sociology, environmental and ecological economics, environmental psychology), and one finds almost the same sort of detail in the bio-ecological sciences (i.e. plant ecology, human ecology (now a section of the Ecological Society of America), and ecosystem ecology to name just a few). If one moves to consider interdisciplinary approaches, the problem occurs again with names such as human ecology (which goes back to the early years of the twentieth century, and of which there are diverse branches such as the well-known program at Cornell University, where it referred to Home and Consumer Economics (but largely focused on nutrition), and to the Urban Ecology School at Chicago in the 1920s, and the physical anthropologists working on Human Biology and Adaptability). Stern (1993) has proposed the use of the term "second environmental science" to refer to this human environment area, and NSF has nudged the field by creating a program on "coupled human natural systems" (cf. Liu et al. 2007a, 2007b). While each of these terms has a history, and some distinctive context from which it came, they are mostly concerned with linking social and natural sciences in addressing the complex problems of the environment. While there are any number of recent edited volumes that try to introduce readers to this subject, this book is an effort to provide a more unified perspective wherein spatial approaches are viewed as a lingua franca or integrative framework for this research area, and introduce both social and natural scientists to the tasks that we must undertake to make these types of complex systems approaches move forward. Depending on the training of instructors and what they view as missing here, it is presumed that this book will be used in conjunction with other books and/or a diversity of articles to provide advanced undergraduates and graduate students with the necessary breadth and depth to become informed participants in this interdisciplinary field of study.

I want to take this opportunity to thank the many colleagues who have for years stimulated me with their questions, reviews, critiques, and shared their experiences in this cross-disciplinary area. They are too numerous to mention individually. I was particularly stimulated by participation over many years in the National Research Council Committee on the Human Dimensions of Global Environmental Change, the Land Use and Land Cover Change Scientific Steering Committee, the Transition Team for the Global Land Project, and the Smithsonian's scientific committee of the National Museum of Natural History. The imprint from these interactions with superb scholars engaged in the issues raised by this book was always inspiring and has moved me to write this book. I also wish to thank the National Science Foundation (NSF), the National Institute for Child Health and Human Development at NIH, the National Aeronautics and Space Administration (NASA), the National Oceanic and Atmosphere Administration (NOAA) and the Tinker Foundation for support of my work over the years that has made possible my engagement with these research issues – and Indiana University for having provided a home in which I had the freedom to pursue these diverse tasks, centered at two research centers, the Anthropological Center for Training and Research on Global Environmental Change (ACT, www. indiana.edu/~act) and the Center for the Study of Institutions, Population, and Environmental Change (CIPEC, www.indiana.edu/~cipec). Readers will find many resources, including downloadable PDFs at these two websites, which complement substantively the broad ideas presented in this book.

I also want to thank my research assistants, Paula Sauer Dias, Melanie Knapp, and Kelsey Scroggins, for their dedicated work in finding the literature and preparing the book for publication. Linda Day helped coordinate their efforts and I also wish to thank her. I wish to thank Rosalie Robertson and Julia Kirk, from Wiley-Blackwell, for keeping just the right amount of gentle pressure to keep me writing even as I found myself engaged in multiple research projects that required my time as well. This book is dedicated to Elinor Ostrom, Eduardo Brondízio and to Leah VanWey – three colleagues with whom I have had a very productive partnership over the years (designing and writing proposals together, and then carrying out and writing up the results), and who have proven always stimulating scholars and loyal friends. I feel immensely grateful for having had the opportunity to work closely with them.

Bloomington, IN
July 1, 2009

1

The Challenge of Human–Environment Interactions Research

During the past decade there has been rapid development of research on the human dimensions of global environmental change. This growth has been a result of several factors. Evidence for climate change, loss of biodiversity, rapid deforestation in the tropics, and an impending crisis in availability of potable water have made scholars and policy makers aware of the need to address the causes and consequences of these global processes. Moreover, it is widely recognized that these cumulative processes vary in their severity from region to region, and from place to place. In order to understand these processes, research for the past decade has supported the breakdown of traditional disciplinary boundaries in order to understand in more systematic fashion the complexities of the current human–environment nexus. While interdisciplinary research is nothing new, there has been considerable progress in identifying some of the dimensions that speak to these contemporary environmental problems.

The chapter begins by examining the mounting evidence for the cumulative nature of global environmental change, and the requirements to begin to scientifically understand it. Scientists working on this issue have come to a nearly unanimous conclusion that we cannot begin to understand global environmental change without a concerted and unified effort that integrates both biophysical and social sciences (NRC 1997a; NSF 2003). Human agency (i.e. actions of individuals) is implicated in most of our current dilemmas, and must play a part in solving them. However, integrating the social sciences and the natural sciences has not been easy, nor has the cacophony of competing theories and paradigms helped to promote collaboration between the social sciences and the natural sciences. This chapter reviews the evidence for the nature of the changes, considers the difficulties in understanding these complex biogeophysical and social processes, provides some history of the development of this interdisciplinary area of study and of global environmental change, and lays the basis for the organization of the rest of the book.

The Evolution of Social Ecological Systems[1]

As a species we have relied on our capacity for sociality and communication in order to surpass our physical limitations (Richerson 1977). Our success as a species in spreading and colonizing the planet was through operating as relatively small groups of hunter-gatherers (HG). HGs' advantages were their behavioral flexibility, based on small-group trust and reciprocity, in response to opportunities and their highly mobile strategy of resource harvesting. This strategy served our species well for most of our time on the planet. However, as we grew in population size this strategy began to demonstrate its limitations in providing for an ever larger population. Hunter-gatherers knew about plant reproduction and carried out light management of plants of interest to them long before they began to sedentarize and turn into farmers (Smith 1989).

This first major transformation in social ecological systems, from hunter-gathering to farming, was a result of population increase, growing confrontation of HG bands over resources, and of rising costs and risks of moving into marginal environments. It took a couple of millennia for the transformation from a mostly HG landscape to one increasingly occupied by farming groups (i.e. in North America at least, Smith 1989). Whether famine played a role is not clear from the archeological record. Like many other transformations in social ecological systems, it probably had the shape of the diffusion of innovations (Rogers 1969) with a few adopting the change early, followed by a very slow adoption by others, and finally substantive adoption when the benefits were absolutely clear to most (and the price of nonadoption was dear). The greater density of farming communities allowed them to occupy preferred territories, and HGs increasingly were pushed into marginal areas which could not be cultivated. The keystone features of this new farming mode of production were the evolution of community institutions, shifts in the scope of reciprocity and trust, domestication of plants and animals, and sedentarization. The shift in reciprocity and trust led to features of social cooperation being associated at first with the settlement, and as settlements grew in size to kin-based groupings such as lineages, clans, and moieties. This reduced flexibility in HG systems since the common form of descent was bilateral, meaning that individuals traced their descent from either the paternal or maternal sides, and band membership was highly flexible.

In settled farming communities, control over land through inheritance grew over the years. In order to ensure control over the better land, and eventually over investments such as irrigation and homes, lineal descent

[1]   This section is based on an earlier discussion to be found in *People and Nature* (Moran 2006).

(through either father or mother) came into play in order to provide clear forms of inheritance, along with the development of rules of preferred marriage, and even endogamy, to ensure control over resources. Whereas exogamy had been preferred before, and indeed it is a preferable evolutionary strategy from a biological perspective, with the growing importance of land, and accumulated wealth, interest in keeping wealth intact among those already well-off favored intermarriage among favored families. This resulted in extreme cases in caste endogamy, and class consciousness in marriage choice. The deleterious biological impact of this strategy is well known in the genetic aberrations found in some European royal families in the past.

The evolution towards kin-based lineal systems also provided a more rigid form of passing on cultural values, identities, norms, and religious preferences. This process took hundreds of years to occur as groups developed their own combination of workable ways of controlling resources as a function of population density, competition, and resource availability. In areas with great resource patchiness, where control over favorable patches was key to success, the development of sophisticated forms of kin-based control was more rapid given the stakes, whereas in areas with widely distributed resources and patches it was often easier for resource competitors to just move elsewhere and maintain a more flexible and less restrictive set of community rules.

Over time, as agriculture moved from extensive production systems to more intensive systems based on irrigation and eventual mechanization, social stratification, ethnicity, and complex rules for resource use and exclusion came into being. Whereas in the former extensive systems it was a value to share accumulated resources with other less fortunate members of the community, thereby acquiring social capital and prestige, in the latter the amount of shared resources declines, prestige still goes to those capable of concentrating resources but those resources are more sporadically redistributed, thereby increasingly rewarding those who already have more resources and productive capacity or wealth. Control over land becomes the greatest source of wealth, and by extension this provides greater control over labor, as more and more people are not able to control access to land – especially in patchy environments such as semi-arid landscapes.

Boserup (1965) and others (Netting 1968, 1981, 1993) have shown that the most important driver of the intensification implied by the shift from HG to agriculture has been population growth leading to greater applications of technology to production in order to stave off famine and meet the basic needs of growing populations. It is associated with greater competition over resources and the growing need to store supplies for times of scarce resources. The need to store provisions, rather than move to find them, resulted in a shift in how labor was invested, and in the settlement pattern of peoples worldwide.

As these populations grew more numerous, chronic warfare ensued as groups competed for the best soils and the prime spots along the river or mountain, and sought ways to recruit more members to their communities. In a world of hand-to-hand combat, having strong and numerous men to field was the top determinant of success in holding onto territory. Over time, some groups developed from single village communities into networks of communities, and chiefdoms emerged that provided some capacity to mobilize larger social units when any of their member communities was threatened. The evidence is quite substantial that, as human communities grew more successful in production, the temptation was great for other communities to take away their accumulated wealth (often in the form of grain or animals). As in the shift from HG to extensive cultivation, the shift from extensive cultivation to intensive cultivation appears to have been driven by population growth putting too much pressure on resources (Boserup 1965; Netting 1993). One study showed that a given area of irrigated land could support 14 times as many families as it could under shifting cultivation (Palerm 1968; Spooner 1972). However, another explanation offered by scholars has been that this intensification was forced upon people either by external domination and colonialism (cf. Geertz 1963) or by internal domination brought about by elites wishing to control land resources for their own political and military objectives (Demarest 2004).

Associated with farming populations one often found pastoralists, occupying land unsuitable for cultivation. In some cases, they represented segments of ethnic farming populations, in other cases they represented other ethnic groups. Pastoralist social organization shows much greater flexibility than other forms of subsistence because of the flexible nature of managing animals. Sometimes it is possible to gather people and animals in areas when rain is abundant and pasture is rich, but for at least half of the year or more, the drying of the savannas results in scattering of people and animals. This scattering would put these populations at risk if it were not for mechanisms such as segmentary lineages that allow segments of large lineages to call upon others to come to their assistance in times of trouble. Thus, pastoral societies have developed an impressive capacity to field armed men to defend their animals and people – and then to return to a very scattered and apparently disorganized pattern of moving to find the best forage (McCabe 2004). It is a remarkable example of social self-organization that results in politically sophisticated outcomes. Farmers and pastoralists maintained an uneasy truce and trade relationship over the years, and there are well-documented cases of pastoralists becoming farmers and vice versa under favorable conditions.

It was just a matter of time, and opportunity, for people to have their growing villages develop into larger and more complex entities that we have come to call cities. Urban areas provided a site for trade, for the exchange of information, for specialists in a large number of skills to meet the needs of a more technologically intensive society, and for redefining the nature of social ecological interactions. The rise of urban centers is most commonly associated with irrigation and the rise of complex water control. As these systems grew in size and complexity, breakdown became more common and more costly. In time, when they had grown to pharaonic proportions, the systems could collapse when either information or climate, or both, were beyond the capacity of managers (Butzer 1976).

If the rise of cities and a growing network of linked villages into states proved to be a considerable source of disturbance in social ecological interactions, imagine what happened with the rise of that technological wonder that is the industrial revolution. Cities are symptomatic of human transformation of social ecological systems: they are creative centers where some of the best and brightest of every society are concentrated to develop the arts, technology, education, science, and commerce. Yet, they are also often chaotic, with erosion of social controls, and distant enough from day-to-day realities of environment to ignore environmental feedbacks for a very long time. That is because urban areas have too many layers of information between the environment and the decisions managers take – who are motivated by many other incentives than just ensuring good environmental management: political pressures, mis-valuation of the resources, self-interest, and corruption (see discussion of urban ecology in Moran 2007, ch. 10).

The industrial mode of production[2] is accompanied by major technical innovations that also result in a reorganization of the division of labor (Schnaiberg 1980). The industrial revolution's larger environmental impact is the product of discovering the use of fossil fuels. First, and for a very long time, this involved only the use of coal. Oil and natural gas came much later. In using fossil fuels humans did not have to compete with any other animal species to use the resource, as we had often had to do with the use of plants (herbivores) and animals (carnivores). This would seem to be a win–win situation, and it certainly allowed for an enormous increase in the amount of energy that humans could harness for productive purposes. Unfortunately, the exploitation of the huge amounts of fossil fuel materials stowed away for geologic periods of time in subterrestrial sinks and the launching of the by-products from their use into the biosphere, kicked off biogeochemical changes in the atmosphere that took a couple of centuries to be felt and which now threaten our planet. But these changes were not entirely surprising. Local and regional consequences of the use of

---

[2]   Mode of production is used in the anthropological meaning of the term, rather than Marx's usage.

fossil fuels were felt early on: the nineteenth century fogs of industrial cities like London, with serious health consequences for people living in these locations being the most recognized. While the rich could escape to their rural estates to breathe fresh air, the poor in the cities grew sick from the constant exposure to foul air. Social stratification, along with the use of police and power to maintain this mode of production with its high human and environmental costs, took place then and continues into the present, as developing countries industrialize with similar consequences (e.g. the current urban pollution in China's industrial centers). The result has been a growing loss of trust and the virtual extinction of reciprocity except in the bosom of families, growing disparities between people in wealth and access to resources, an increase in the amount of time spent working, and a growing emphasis on consumption to support the productive capacity unleashed on the planet (see Moran 2006 for an extended examination of this issue).

In short, over a period of 400 generations, or 10,000 years, the human population has grown from a few million to more than 6 billion. This growth has taken place quickly in recent decades, and has changed the nature of how we deal with each other (Raven 2002). The biggest shift has been since World War II and is connected to rising living standards and rising consumption levels for materials and energy. This compounding of population and consumption is recent and without precedent. Human populations do not respond in homogeneous ways to the environment, or anything else. Human society and culture is characterized by high diversity, and in the past this has gone along with biological diversity. The number of people who live by hunting-gathering today is shrinking, and most of them are connected to the global economy to some degree. Horticultural populations (i.e. extensive farmers using slash-and-burn methods mostly) still constitute significant populations in rural areas of developing countries – and among those in developed countries who seek to return our food production system to more organic methods. The latter is a fast and expanding movement that questions the industrial mode of food production and seeks to return to more organic ways to take care of the land and produce the food we need. Pastoral peoples have been under pressure for decades to abandon their migratory ways, but they still constitute an important component of how grasslands are managed, despite efforts to block the routes of their movements. Intensive farming is growing ever more intensive, now including genetic modification to a degree that has not been seen before. These shifts in the relationship of people to the environment constitute the fundamental questions that drive environmental social science and human–environment interactions research. With the growing recognition of the human dimensions of contemporary global environmental change this area of study has grown rapidly.

Characterization of Contemporary Global Environmental Changes[3]

The present condition of our planet is worrisome to those who pay close attention to the evidence. More and more species are becoming endangered or going extinct. Wetlands are disappearing at a rapid rate, endangering the migration routes of birds, and the maintenance of local and even intercontinental biodiversity. Unprecedented levels of CO_2 threaten our climate system, coral reefs, and the Greenland and Antarctic ice sheets. Pollution levels in a growing number of cities can only be called toxic for human health. The story goes on, giving cause for considerable alarm. There is very little evidence that governments are succeeding in implementing concrete strategic policies which ensure a sustainable earth system. Everyone talks about sustainability, but fails to implement measures to reduce our downward spiral, and we fail to even define what sustainability means or how we can begin to get on a sustainable path.

What is not widely recognized is that we have in the past 60 years changed nearly every aspect of our relationship with the environment. The Industrial Revolution began some 300 years ago, and since then, the impact and the pace of our impacts on the earth have been gradually increasing (Turner et al. 1990). Yet, the impact in the past 300 years pales by comparison with our impact in the past 60 years. We have no equivalent experience in our entire history or prehistory as a species.

Burning fossil fuels results in emissions of vast amounts of carbon dioxide and other earth-warming gases that are changing the atmosphere, the productivity of terrestrial vegetation, and are at the highest levels known over the past 400 millennia. More nitrogen fertilizer is applied in agriculture than is fixed naturally in all terrestrial ecosystems (Crutzen 2002). Fishing fleets have depleted the stock of many species, removing more than 25% of the primary production in upwelling ocean regions (Crutzen 2002), and the catches are collapsing. Irrigation and other alterations of surface and underground water are increasing the vulnerability of hydrologic systems and the people that depend on these precious water sources (Crutzen 2002). Agricultural activities have resulted in massive deforestation and alteration of land cover at huge scales – with the amount of land devoted to agriculture increasing fivefold over the past three centuries (Lambin and Geist 2006). In short, human activities are so pervasive that they are capable of altering the earth system in ways that could change the viability of the very processes upon which human and nonhuman species depend.

[3] This section is based on an earlier discussion to be found in *People and Nature* (Moran 2006) and Steffen et al. (2003).

Both data and information at global scale are now abundant in alerting us to the magnitude and seriousness of the processes we have unleashed. This evidence tells us of exponential increase in carbon dioxide, exponential rates of ozone depletion and nitrous oxide concentrations in the atmosphere, rapid losses in tropical rainforests, increases in the frequency of natural disasters and in the rate of species extinctions. The same can be said for fertilizer consumption, damming of rivers, water use, paper consumption, the number of people living in cities, and the number of motor vehicles (Steffen et al. 2003). There has also been a steady increase in the last 60 years in the incidence of armed conflict worldwide (Kates and Parris 2003:8062). In 1992, one third of the world's countries were involved in such conflicts, and in that year 40 million refugees and displaced persons were affected by armed conflicts (ibid). These figures do not include the growing globalization of both terror and crime beyond state borders. Some have described this growing conflict in terms of "the coming anarchy" and as a "clash of civilizations" (ibid.). These numbers have increased severalfold since then.

The exponential increase in all these measurable phenomena is tied to the increase in the human population, and to our consumption habits. Indeed, one must think of these two factors in tandem. One Euro-American citizen consumes 25 times the resources that one average citizen from India, Guatemala, or other less developed countries does (Redclift 1996; Wernick 1997). While birth rates have steadily declined to replacement level or even below in developed countries, these populations continue to impact the earth's resources far more than the larger populations in developing countries. Both developed countries and developing countries have a huge impact on the environment, the former through consumption, and the latter through population increases. Some developing countries have now succeeded in reducing rates of growth (e.g. Brazil is now at, or below, replacement).

In all societies one sees conflicting cultural values. Europe has similar traditions to the USA in a number of regards (e.g. democratic institutions, capitalism) but it does not value individualism above the common good. This has made it possible for Europe to accept more quickly than the US the proposed reduction of carbon dioxide in the atmosphere to 1992 levels and thus to support the Kyoto Protocol on the emission of greenhouse gases. A profound rift between the more advanced nations of Western Europe and the USA has developed over the willingness of the former to set limits on carbon dioxide emissions, and the unwillingness of the US to do so. (Nevertheless, we must remember that even West European countries have had difficulty meeting the Kyoto greenhouse gas emission targets.) The use, and misuse, of the earth's resources is at the very center of international negotiations, the global political economy, and the fate of nations. These negotiations require an understanding of both environmental science, and social science – and thus the need for integrative science that can address the biophysical and the social dimensions of human–environment interactions.

The Cartesian dichotomy between humans and nature is a peculiar notion in Western society. Most peoples in the world see humans as very much a part of nature. In its more extreme forms it takes the form of ideologies where we are reincarnated in forms other than human (i.e. plant, animal), and vice versa. Mythologies across the globe have always pointed to the close connection in both origin, and continuity, between animals in nature and us; between the plants in the landscape and our spiritual and material lives (Pretty 2002:13). Australian Aborigines' Dreamtime embodies these beliefs, for example, in how the land came to be, how closely they are still connected to these ancestors, and why the land must be respected – that it belongs to no one, but that it belongs to everyone. Today we even know that we are closely tied to our primate ancestors, with over 90 percent of our DNA shared with them, yet we insist in our philosophical stances, and behavior, to act as if we hold a place above the rules that govern the rest of the species on the planet.

One of the challenges we must face is rethinking how we view the environment. Dichotomous thinking led us to think of people as apart from nature, and charged with controlling nature for human purposes – and crucially, as distinct from the inherent dynamics of the earth system itself. It is from this error that a lot of our post-World War II spiral towards self-destruction comes. What happens to the air we breathe, the water we drink, and the land upon which we depend for our food matters. If we take care of it, it will nurture us – and if we damage its capacity to provide us with sustainable goods and services, and the comfort of aesthetic beauty, we will put ourselves at risk. We cannot do this alone, but it must be a partnership of trust in human communities bound by covenants that favor life over material accumulation, that favor dignity for members of the community and the pleasures of taking care of each other, and nature, as the highest good. We need to reconceptualize our relations with each other, and with nature – and to think of human agents as organic parts of nature (for more detailed discussion see Moran 2006).

Figure 1.1 illustrates what is happening in the realm of human process variables –and it raises a number of concerns. Population has been increasing rapidly since 1750 but it has gone exponential since 1950, and shows very little sign of leveling off in the next 30 to 40 years. In the past 60 years we have gone from 2.5 billion to 6 billion people. In less than 30 years the human population will be in excess of 10 billion. Total Gross Domestic Product, foreign direct investment, damming of rivers, water use, fertilizer consumption, urban population, paper consumption, and the number of motor vehicles, have all jumped exponentially since 1950, with no evidence of a turnaround in this upward increase. This increase would be enough

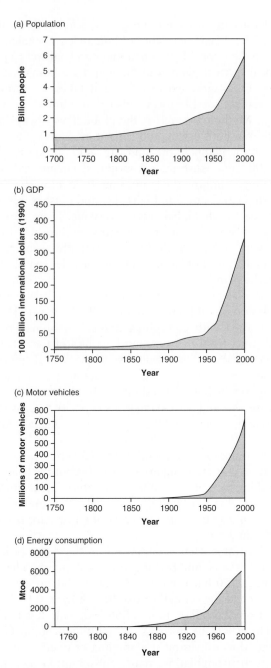

Figure 1.1   Rate of increase in several spheres of human activity for the past 300 years: a. population (US Census Bureau 2000); b. world economic GDP (Nordhaus 1997); c. motor vehicles (UNEP 2000); d. energy consumption (Klein Goldwijk and Battjes 1997)
Source: Steffen et al. 2003

cause for concern if it were happening in one or two of these measurable areas, but it is happening in all simultaneously.

As if this were not enough reason for concern, similar synchronous events are happening on the biophysical side (see Figure 1.2): CO_2 concentrations, N_2O concentrations, CH_4 concentrations (all three of them earth-warming gases), ozone depletion, Northern Hemisphere average surface temperatures, the number of natural disasters, the rate of loss of fisheries, the increase in nitrogen fluxes in coastal zones, the rapid loss of tropical rain forests and woodlands, and the number of species gone extinct have all gone exponential since 1950. While some might argue, for example, that there is evidence that CO_2 concentrations are actually beneficial to many plants and can result in enhanced productivity, experimental studies have shown that increases in productivity when CO_2 concentrations are up to a certain level (e.g. 56 Pa) can take place but that these gains are lost when concentrations go higher (e.g. to 70 Pa), at which time there is a steady decline in productivity (Granados and Korner 2002). There are also notable differences in how different species and types of forest vegetation respond to CO_2 enrichment (Norby et al. 2002). There is very little positive light that can be found in these measures going exponential. Are thresholds about to be crossed from which systemic collapses can ensue?

One of the most troubling changes in the planet has been the human alteration of the global nitrogen cycle. We know with a high degree of certainty based on available scientific evidence (a) that we have doubled the rate of nitrogen input into the terrestrial nitrogen cycle and that these rates are still increasing; (b) that increased concentrations of the greenhouse gas N_2O globally, and other oxides of nitrogen, drive the formation of photochemical smog; (c) that this nitrogen increase has caused losses of calcium and potassium from soils, essential for soil fertility; contributed to the acidification of soils, streams, and lakes; increased the quantity of organic carbon stored in terrestrial ecosystems; and accelerated losses of biodiversity, particularly plants adapted to efficient use of nitrogen (Vitousek et al. 1997).

Surface temperatures over the Northern Hemisphere at present are warmer than at any other time over the past millennium, and the rate of warming has been especially high in the past 60 years (Hurrell et al. 2001:603). Agricultural yields, water management, and fish inventories are affected by this warming – having as it does its origin in an upward trend in the North Atlantic Oscillation, dictating climate variability from the eastern seaboard of the US to Siberia and from the Arctic to the subtropical Atlantic. Changes in the North Atlantic Oscillation, in turn, affect the strength and character of the Atlantic THC. Climate changes can have profound effects on society as suggested by recent research suggesting that the lowland Maya collapse was associated with an increase in droughts in Yucatan resulting

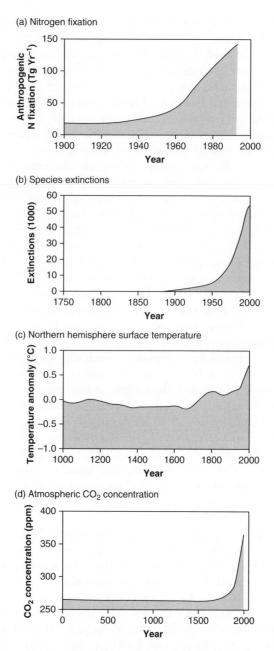

Figure 1.2   Rates of increase in several spheres of the earth system: a. nitrogen fixation (Vitousek 1994); b. species extinction (Smith 2002); c. northern hemisphere surface temperature (Mann, Bradley, and Hughes 1999); d. atmosphere CO_2 concentrations (adapted from Keeling and Whorf 2000)
Source: Steffen et al. 2003

from bicentennial oscillations in precipitation (Hodell et al. 2001). The Maya were dependent on rainfall and small water reservoirs for the sustainability of their agriculture, and these multidecadal and multicentury oscillations in precipitation probably exacerbated other challenges faced by the Classic Maya (Demarest 2004). One of the conclusions of recent climate change studies is not that it will be warmer everywhere but, rather, that we will see more extreme events more frequently, such as the occurrence of El Niño events – with drought in some places and flood in others (Caviedes 2001). In Brazilian Amazonia there is already serious concern with the increased frequency of devastating fires entering into Amazonian forests as a result of El Niño. In 1997 climate scientists and ecologists were in agreement that the droughts associated with that El Niño were responsible for a fire that consumed 13,000 square kilometers of forest in just one location. We know of similar vast fires during the 1982–3 El Niño over Borneo (Prance 1986:75–102) and of devastating fires in the Amazon 250–400 years ago (Sanford et al. 1985).

We know that climate change will increase the severity of population and species declines, especially for generalist pathogens infecting multiple host species. The most detectable effects relate to geographic expansion of pathogens such as Rift Valley fever, dengue fever, and Eastern oyster disease. While other factors are surely implicated, such as land-use change, there is very little doubt in the end that warming trends will affect crop and human diseases (e.g. potato late blight; rice blast; cholera, and Rift Valley fever) (Harvell et al. 2002). Climate warming is also expected to alter seasonal biological phenomena such as plant growth, flowering, and animal migration (Penuelas and Filella 2001). Some Canadian tree species (e.g. *Populus tremuloides*) show a 26-day shift to earlier blooming over the last century, and biological spring in Europe is about 8 days earlier from data for the period 1969–98 (ibid.). In the Mediterranean, leaves of deciduous plant species now unfold 16 days earlier and fall on average 13 days later than they did 60 years ago (ibid.).

In short, the simultaneous and interconnected nature of these changes in human and in environmental conditions since 1950 suggest that human activities could inadvertently trigger abrupt changes in the earth system with consequences that we can only faintly imagine. The most troubling of all is, of course, triggering a disruption in the "oceanic conveyor belt," as it is called, which regulates world climate (Broecker 1991). The increases in greenhouse gases can trigger changes in the North Atlantic circulation and computer simulation results have most of the scenarios resulting in rather dramatic collapses. We know already that the Atlantic Thermohaline Circulation (THC) can have multiple equilibria and multiple thresholds, that THC reorganization can be triggered by changes in surface heat and in freshwater fluxes, and that crossing thresholds can result in irreversible

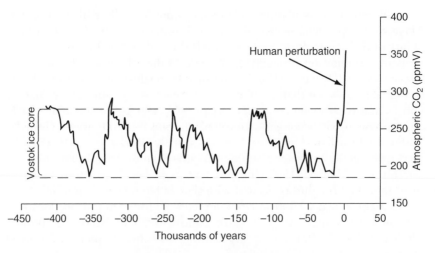

Figure 1.3   Vostock Ice Core provides the best current record of carbon dioxide changes for the past 420,000 years
Source: Petit, Jouzel, and Raynaud 1999 as modified by Steffen et al. 2003

changes of ocean circulation (Rahmstorf and Stocker 2003). Our current situation with regards to CO_2 alone, not to mention all the other earth-warming gases being emitted exponentially, is well above the experience of the past 420,000 years as recorded in the Vostock Ice Core (see Figure 1.3).

The evidence for the seriousness of climate change was affirmed at a meeting of members of 63 national academies of science from all parts of the world, affirming support for the work of the Intergovernmental Panel on Climate Change (IPCC) which says that it is at least 90 percent certain that temperatures will continue to rise by at least 5.8 degrees Celsius above 1990 levels by 2100, and urging prompt action to reduce emission of greenhouse gases (IPCC 2000). In their joint statement, the representatives of the 63 national academies of science concluded that "the balance of the scientific evidence demands effective steps now to avert damaging changes to Earth's climate." (Interacademies 2000).

The past 60 years have been devastating to the earth system's functions. These changes have been of sufficient magnitude to rival climate change in both environmental and social terms (Vitousek et al. 1997; NRC 1999a, 1999b). During the first 50 years of the twenty-first century, demand for food and other commodities by a wealthier and larger global population will be a major driver of global environmental change (particularly from the BRIC countries, Brazil, Russia, India and China). While some of this change may come from more intensive and efficient agricultural production, much of it will come from converting further land areas and natural ecosystems into agricultural fields. This will result, at least, in a 2.5 increase in the amount of nitrogen and phosphorus making its way into terrestrial fresh-water and near-shore marine ecosystems resulting in unprecedented eutro-phication and habitat destruction (Tilman 2001). Much of the nitrogen and phosphorus from fertilizers and animal wastes enters surface and ground-water untreated and unimpeded to any significant extent (Tilman et al. 2001). The result is eutrophication of estuaries and coastal seas, loss of bio-diversity, changes in species composition, groundwater pollution, and trop-ospheric smog and ozone. The projected conversion of up to 1,000,000,000 hectares of natural habitat to meet our expected demand for food is viewed as conservative.

For most of the 400 generations that we have been farming, production and consumption of food has been intimately linked to social and cultural systems, to systems of beliefs, and respect for the environment. Foods were given special meaning, and were surrounded with ritual. First crops harvested were treated with deference and gratefulness. We still see some of these practices in some ethnic rural populations, and even in an industrial super-power such as Japan, particularly in relation to traditions regarding rice. Japan's rice paddy fields are carefully maintained, even by those who hold other employment as their main means of support, and all special occasions include rice dishes as ways of connecting people to this basic staple and giving it importance. Rivers and mountains embodied the divine and the forces of creative and destructive nature that were respected. Over the past three gen-erations we have changed this respect for the environment in too many places. Industrial agriculture has steadily replaced family farms worldwide, and, while this seems to produce a lot more food in absolute terms, it does so at huge cost in terms of loss of soils, damage to biodiversity, pollution of the air and water, and negative impacts on human health through heavy use of chemicals (Pretty 2002:xii). Industrial agriculture, in an age of cheap fossil fuels, was able to ship produce across large distances and drive local produc-ers out of business. In a future world, where fossil fuel will be increasingly dear, we will need to redesign whole systems of food production, more directly linking those who grow food to those who consume it, using methods that have a lighter impact on the environment, and in which the land takes on, once again, the nurturing value that it had for most of human history.

In the past 35 years, we were able to double food production but we did so with a sixfold increase in nitrogen fertilization, a threefold increase in phosphorus fertilization, and a substantial increase in the area under culti-vation (Tilman 1999). Another doubling of food production would result in a threefold increase in nitrogen and phosphorus fertilization and an increase of 18 percent in cropland cultivated. These increases will further eutrophy fresh and marine ecosystems, leading to biodiversity losses, shifts in the structure of the food chains, and impairment of fisheries (Tilman 1999).

History of the Development of the Human Dimensions Agenda[4]

Until 1988, the study of global environmental change was carried out largely by earth science disciplines such as meteorology, atmospheric chemistry, atmospheric sciences, and geology. The focus of this work, under the aegis of the International Geosphere-Biosphere Programme (IGBP), was on documenting the extent of biosphere change and projecting at global scale the likely consequences of changing atmospheric conditions on the earth. Modeling, particularly global circulation models (GCMs), were heavily used given the absence of many important data points and the ambition of understanding the global environment – but scientists also identified, and lobbied for, research in areas needed to better run the GCMs. Among the many achievements of this effort, for example, was the creation of a vast network of buoys in the earth's oceans to measure changing temperatures. Over time they led to the current ability of atmospheric and marine scientists to forecast El Niño and La Niña events many months in advance of human populations feeling their terrestrial impact. Scientists accurately predicted the onset of the 2002–3 El Niño Southern Oscillation almost a year in advance, and farmers in many locations modified their planting behavior, thereby reducing economic losses and human misery. This is done by observing the warming or cooling of the waters over the northern Pacific and following its circulation around the globe. But something was missing. The coarse spatial scale of these early GCMs did not allow for any meaningful role for what human behavior does within the earth system, which ran at very coarse spatial (several degrees of latitude) and temporal (decades to centuries) scales with broad assumptions like what might happen if all tropical forest cover were removed and replaced by pasture. While the results of such models were informative, they rarely included adaptive behavior on the part of humans, who are likely to desist from the total elimination of tropical forest cover by information dissemination and feedback processes.

At the request of scientists associated with the International Geosphere Biosphere Programme (IGBP), the International Social Science Council (ISSC) was asked to consider assembling a working group to develop a human dimensions (social and economic sciences) agenda to parallel the ongoing work of atmospheric and climate scientists working on global environmental change. The ISSC met and recommended that it would be desirable to begin to create national panels to undertake such a discussion and write up research plans that would articulate well with the IGBP research. This led to the creation of a group parallel to the IGBP, named Human

---

[4]   This section is based on an earlier discussion in Moran (2005).

Dimensions Program (HDP), composed of a panel of social scientists from around the globe to discuss how best to proceed. In the USA, both the National Research Council (NRC) and the Social Science Research Council (SSRC) created expert panels of scientists to discuss research priorities for the human dimensions as well.

The obvious changes in our global environment led first to the creation of a network of scientists to address these globally scaled processes. The International Geosphere Biosphere Programme (IGBP) was started in 1987 because of the need for an international collaborative research endeavor on the phenomenon of global change. A Special Committee was appointed to guide the planning and initial implementation of the program. The planning phase ran from 1987 to 1990 and involved about 500 scientists worldwide. This community of climate and atmospheric scientists, in turn, turned to the social sciences in 1988 and asked them to join them in an effort to understand the human dimensions of global environmental change (NRC 1999a, 1999b). This agenda began to be formulated in 1992 with the National Research Council's book, *Global Environmental Change: Understanding the Human Dimensions* (NRC 1992), which set the early agenda for research in this area. The early research on global change had focused on climate change, biodiversity, pollution, and international environmental agreements driven by a growing awareness of global impacts such as accumulation of earth-warming gases, the appearance of an ozone hole changing the amount of ultraviolet (UV) radiation people receive, and documentation of glacier meltdowns. Current trends are expected to continue to have cumulative effects on the atmosphere and climate change (NRC 1998b; Hunter 1999; Potter 1999).

"Human dimensions research addresses the workings of social systems that manage environmental resources – markets, property rights regimes, treaties, legal and informal norms, and so forth – and the potential to modify those institutions through policy and thus to mitigate global change or increase adaptive capability" (NRC 1999b:5). The first issues identified in 1992 as needing urgent attention and research priority were: (1) understanding land-use and land-cover changes; (2) understanding the decision-making process; (3) designing policy instruments and institutions to address energy-related problems; (4) assessing impacts, vulnerability, and adaptation to global changes; and (5) understanding population-and-the-environment interactions.

A great deal was accomplished in the years that followed, focusing on the causes, consequences, and responses of human populations to global environmental change (NRC 1999b). Advances were particularly notable in the study of land-use and land-cover change which had been defined as the topic that the research community was most ready to undertake (see some of the syntheses produced from this effort in Gutman et al. 2004; Moran and Ostrom 2005; NRC 2005a) to understand human responses to climate events (NRC 1999c; Moran et al. 2006; Galvin et al. 2001; M. Guttman 2000). Human dimensions of global change became an important priority at the National Science Foundation (NSF), the National Oceanic and Atmospheric Administration (NOAA), the National Aeronautics and Space Administration (NASA), and the Social Science and Population Program at the National Institute for Child Health and Human Development (NICHD).

New priorities have been identified that place human–environment research even more at the center of research on global change. One important reason is that there is growing evidence that socioeconomic uncertainties are greater than biophysical uncertainties, for example in the study of climate impacts (NRC 1999c:1). Major sources of changes in the global atmosphere come from human activities, such as deforestation and energy consumption. Studies showing that tragedies of the commons are not inevitable but are, rather, the product of how humans organize themselves to respond to perceived threats to their well-being further strengthen the case for the importance of human–environment interactions research. Since 1992, the field has evolved and a new set of research priorities have emerged. For the first decade of the twenty-first century several research questions have been identified:

1 Understanding the social determinants of environmentally significant consumption (NRC 1997a; Moran 2006);
2 Understanding the sources of technological change;
3 Making climate predictions more regionally relevant and accurate (NRC 1999c);
4 Improving how human populations can better respond to environmental surprises;
5 Understanding the conditions favoring institutional success or failure in resource management (Ostrom 1998, 2005);
6 Linking land-use and land-cover dynamics to population processes, especially the role of human migration (Moran and Ostrom 2005; NRC 2005a; Lambin and Geist. 2006);
7 Improving our understanding of human decision-making (Moran et al. 2006; Brondizio and Moran 2008);
8 Advancing capacity to make social science data spatially explicit (NRC 1998a; Goodchild and Janelle 2004).

Interestingly, the SSRC, the NRC, and the HDP quickly came to agreement that the research area which would best articulate with the work of IGBP, and to which social scientists could make the strongest contributions in the short term, would be the study of land-use and land-cover change. The logic was that there was a preexisting community in the social sciences concerned with cultural ecology, agrarian studies, and agricultural and resource economics whose work approximated the likely areas of interest of a land-centric research program. This led to the creation of the Land-Use and Land-Cover Change core project (LUCC), a joint activity of IGBP and HDP, with support from groups such as SSRC and NRC. A panel of scientists began to meet that produced over the next several years a Science Plan to guide the work of the international community (Lambin et al. 1999). The Science Plan had several major science questions that they deemed central to the core project:

- How has land cover changed over the last 300 years as a result of human activities?
- What are the major human causes of land-cover change in different geographical and historical contexts?
- How will changes in land use affect land cover in the next 50 to 100 years?
- How do immediate human and biophysical dynamics affect the sustainability of specific types of land uses?
- How might changes in climate and biogeochemistry affect both land use and land cover?
- How do land uses and land covers affect the vulnerability of land users in the face of change and how do land-cover changes in turn impinge upon and enhance vulnerability and at-risk regions?

Similar but varying in some degree were research priorities defined by the NRC and SSRC. The first major guiding document to appear from these expert panels was the "rainbow book," *Global Environmental Change: the Human Dimensions* (NRC 1992). This book defined a broad set of priorities that identified land-use and land-cover change as the top research priority but that listed in detail other important questions that deserved attention, such as environmental decision making, integrative modeling, environmental risk analysis, and studies of population and environment. Many of the recommendations of this book served as guidance to funding agencies, and have since that time been implemented – such as the creation of human dimensions centers of excellence by the National Science Foundation, land-use and land-cover change research programs at NASA; human dimensions of global change programs at NOAA; and population and environment programs at NICHD.

The following year, the NRC published a smaller and more accessible document entitled *Science Priorities for the Human Dimensions* (1993). This document reaffirmed the priorities of the 1992 book and a couple of new areas of interest: land-use and land-cover change, decision-making processes, energy-related policies and institutions, impact assessment, and population dynamics. By 1995 the National Science Foundation announced a competition for national centers of excellence on the human dimensions of global environmental change.

Since that period considerable advances have taken place. These are summarized at some length in an NRC volume: *Global Environmental Change: Research Pathways for the Next Decade* (1999a). The Human Dimensions Programme became the International Human Dimensions Programme (IHDP) in 1996 when it moved from Geneva to Bonn, Germany. IHDP has played a growing role in coordinating the work of national human dimensions panels, and creating IHDP-based research groups on the Institutional Dimensions of Global Environmental Change, and the Environmental Security and Vulnerability group.

One of the important activities of the LUCC program has been to stimulate the generation of syntheses of what we know about LUCC processes, such as tropical deforestation (e.g. Geist and Lambin 2001, 2002; Lambin and Geist 2006), agricultural intensification (McConnell and Keys 2005), and urbanization, to provide input to a larger synthesis for earth system science (Steffen et al. 2003). These efforts at synthesis rely heavily upon the scholarly community working on issues of land-use and land-cover change.

Other interesting research areas in the human dimensions of global change agenda include: social dimensions of resource use; perception of environmental change; how people assess environmental changes and environmental risks; the impact of institutions; energy production and consumption; industrial ecology; environmental justice; and environmental security. In 2001 an expert panel from the National Research Council came up with eight *Grand Challenges in the Environmental Sciences* that defined key priorities (NRC 2001). The eight priorities share one common denominator: they require joint work by biophysical and social scientists. A similar recommendation came from the National Science Board which developed similar but not equivalent priorities and also gave multidisciplinarity across the biophysical and social sciences a strong nod.

Characteristics of the Research on the Human Dimensions

Research on the human dimensions differs from disciplinary research in a number of ways. Global change research must be inherently multidisciplinary given the complexity of factors that must be taken into account. No discipline offers an adequate array of theories, methods, and concepts to provide integrative modeling (see Chapters 2 and 3, this volume). Because it is global, the work must be multinational in scale, otherwise one is likely to erroneously think that what one sees as processes in one country applies to the globe. This forces an agenda oriented towards comparative research wherein one must collect comparable data in a number of nations and regions so as to sample the diversity of biophysical and social processes (Moran and Ostrom 2005). Because the earth is such a complex entity, this means that the work must be spatially explicit so as to be able to anchor the work precisely on the earth's surface and understand what is site specific from what is generalizable (see Chapter 4). Because the agenda is driven by a concern with changing dynamics, the work must be multi-temporal and have some historical depth. The depth will vary with the question and processes of interest, so that some scientists operate in temporal scales of millennia (paleoclimatologists and palynologists), while others work in terms of centuries and decades (e.g. historians, ecologists, social scientists). Because disciplines' methods vary, it is likely that processes examined vary not just in time and spatial scales but also in scale of analysis (from local to regional to national to global; see Chapter 5). It is well known but rarely analytically addressed that explanations for processes vary by the scale at which they are studied. Thus, specificity of what scale is being explained is essential, but also it is necessary for each analysis to make an effort to scale both up and down from the scale of interest so that the effort and investment is useful to other scientists in the community working at other scales. Finally, because the work is about an impending environmental crisis of global, and local, proportions, the work must keep in mind the relevance and importance of the research in informing policies which might reverse current negative outcomes and favor sustainability of human–environment interactions (see Chapters 6, 7, and 8).

Participation in human dimensions research offers a number of advantages to the advancement of theory, particularly theories on human–environment interactions. The questions posed by the human dimensions agenda are new questions that reach beyond traditional disciplinary concerns and thus extend the value of social science and natural science to all of society. The disciplines bring important theories to this kind of research: anthropology and geography have contributed cultural ecology and political ecology, which remain important paradigms in understand human use of resources. Biology and ecology have contributed ecosystem and evolutionary ecology. Political science has contributed theories about institutions and collective action. Unlike traditional disciplinary research, however, human dimensions research demands a multi-scaled approach. This is rarely the case with discipline-based research and is thus a broadening of the way the social sciences can contribute to the understanding of the world around us. The work on human dimensions links the biological, physical, and social sciences, thereby making social sciences centrally important not only to other social scientists but to the rest of the sciences. It is important to recall that it was the physical sciences that recognized the role of human actions and that felt the need to encourage the social science community to join them in an effort to understand global environmental changes. While a lot remains to be done to achieve this integration, there has been progress.

Work on human dimensions requires comparison and multidisciplinary approaches. This offers the potential for more robust tests of the applicability of site-, region-, or nation-specific findings. By testing things cross-nationally, cross-regionally, and cross-locally, the results are more likely to be robust and theory strengthened. The human dimensions research agenda challenges most of the social sciences (except geography, which already is sensitive to this) to develop new spatially explicit ways to select cases for comparative analysis, to determine sampling frames in a spatial context, and to model results that are spatially informed. This is true as much for the social sciences as for ecology, which only now, too, is developing spatial ecology as a field of study and thereby revolutionizing the way we think about population ecology and community ecology (see Chapter 4).

Undertaking these challenges is an awesome task. It requires that we work in large teams of scientists, rather than work alone as is more common in the social sciences. As noted earlier, the work should be multinational, multidisciplinary, multi-scale, multi-temporal, spatially explicit, and policy relevant. To be successful, it requires that we leave our "weapons" at the door, that we choose the right tools, theories and methods for the question that is being asked (without regard for what discipline it comes from). The goal is to pick the right one for the job at hand, even if it means that team members will need to learn all sorts of new approaches that were not part of their earlier academic training. It is a challenging and exciting task, one that ensures continuous growth in one's skills and perspectives, an open approach to research, without sacrificing rigor, and ensuring that the research speaks to the questions society needs answers to, and not just to the academic scientist.

The Way Forward: Integrative Science

In order to advance the state of the art, there is a need to engage all of the social sciences in multidisciplinary research, jointly with each other and with the biophysical sciences. In this enterprise, integrative science approaches have much to offer. Anthropologists and geographers bring to the analysis of global change two main contributions; first, both are committed to understanding local and regional differences. When looking at a satellite image, for instance, they search for land-use patterns associated with socioeconomic and cultural processes coming from local populations. Consequently, they strive to find the driving forces behind land-use differences and for land-use classifications that are meaningful in socioeconomic and cultural terms. Sociology and Economics bring a set of sophisticated skills to the study of demography which is integratable with both bioecological and spatially explicit approaches. Political science contributes institutional and cross-national approaches that address a variety of scales of interactions. Biological scientists and ecologists bring robust theories about evolution by natural selection and how environmental change occurs at a variety of levels of organization.

A second important contribution is related to data collection and methods. Anthropologists, sociologists, and human geographers using satellite images want to reveal the living human reality behind land-cover classes. Such a perspective requires methods that link local environmental differences to human behavior (Moran and Brondizio 1998, 2001; Rindfuss et al. 2003). Environmental social scientists pride themselves on the emphasis given to fieldwork, and they should take advantage of this preference to make important contributions to advancing the state of spatially explicit social science (Walsh and Crews-Meyer 2002; Goodchild and Janelle 2004; Moran and Ostrom 2005). Ecologists and biologists, too, give a very high place to fieldwork, and this is a very positive thing as this can lead them to respect one another and work together. On the other hand, there are many issues that require discussion across the disciplinary traditions with regards to selecting sample areas and study sites, how much detail to capture at each location, and how best to scale up from the "patch" to the larger units of social and ecological organization.

In several disciplines, emphasis is placed on one dimension over another. History traditionally places more emphasis on time and less on spatial aspects. Geography, on the other hand, emphasizes the spatial dimensions over the temporal one. Other disciplines, such as geology and ecology, contain a mix of both dimensions. Certain social sciences (e.g. political science, sociology, and anthropology) traditionally emphasize space or time when needed. For example, political scientists do, at times, undertake research that emphasizes the temporal aspects in longitudinal studies. The emerging interdisciplinary field of human–environment interactions must give attention to both spatial and temporal variability.

With the diverse vocabularies of separate disciplines, it is no wonder that human–environment interactions can appear extremely complicated. Aggravating this is a sense of urgency often felt by researchers, students, policy makers, and land managers because the state of the earth calls for immediate action, and a feeling that our understanding lags severely behind the processes involved. If our collective monitoring and understanding of human–environment interactions continues to lag severely behind those changes, how can humanity mitigate any negative consequences and try to prevent avoidable future problems?

How can this synthesis be accomplished? What strategies can we use to help integrate all the varying analytical "lenses" used by scholars from a variety of social and physical science disciplines? Can we make individual case studies more comparable and compatible with each other such that we can identify significant trends manifest across all cases? While each researcher moves forward in his or her individual research endeavors, the environmental research community as a collective group would probably benefit by becoming familiar with a common set of theories and methods that are mutually understood across the social and natural sciences. Studies that are well documented with respect to their spatial and temporal dimensions can inform and build on one another. Specific articulation of the spatial and temporal parameters in each study would significantly ease case-to-case integration and compatibility. While this proposition is simple, it is a collective action problem that may yield synergistic results that are critical for research to progress. Moreover, diverse spatial and temporal perspectives will help students and researchers understand how contrasting processes relate to each other and will help place a given case study in a broader context.

In order to have a robust interdisciplinary and multidisciplinary human–environment science it is essential that one consider how to overcome disciplinary biases, without losing rigor in theory and method. Theories and methods are developed to address specific questions, most commonly of broad scope but focused on specific scientific challenges, and on particular spatial and temporal scales of analysis. In Chapters 2 and 3, theories and methods that promise to aid the development of this new area, human–environment interactions research, are proposed. Clearly, no single set of theories and methods will address all questions posed by investigators in this broad and encompassing multidisciplinary field. The methods and theories are offered as a first approximation or baseline for multidisciplinary team participants. One of the challenges the area of human–environment research poses is that doctoral training is still largely disciplinary and thus, when investigators or students begin to work in teams, as they must to address complex socioenvironmental questions, they face a major obstacle in understanding the jargon from other disciplines present in the team. One response is simply to do one's small bit in the large project and not worry about the approaches used by others. This is not always a productive way to work, as it will surely lead to disappointment over the definition of the focus of the work to be done, and about the conclusions and recommendations. Instead, it is proposed here that by becoming familiar with a baseline set of theories and methods from "across the aisle," understanding and dialogue are facilitated, integrative questions rather than disciplinary ones can be asked, it becomes more possible to challenge one another in the field and in the lab, and to arrive at integrative analysis. It is in such a spirit that Chapters 2 and 3 present a set of theories and methods to facilitate a baseline dialogue across the social sciences and the natural sciences.

2

Theories and Concepts from the Social Sciences

This chapter reviews a set of theories from anthropology, geography, history, psychology, political science, and sociology that provide the foundations for addressing cross-disciplinary issues in global environmental change. The chapter will pay particular attention to the limitations of the theories in addressing multi-scaled problems, given that most theories have been generated with a given level of analysis in mind. In addition to helping social scientists appreciate the theories of other disciplines in the social sciences, this chapter may be particularly useful to nonsocial scientists who want to work with social scientists on environmental research.

Understanding environmental change and its underlying human dimensions in the early years of the twenty-first century is a major challenge. Research teams composed of scholars from multiple social and biophysical disciplines face the problem of having a plethora of theories that can inform their work, yet most scholars lack access to the theories of other disciplines, and this problem is only magnified across the natural–social sciences divide. Which theories should form the foundation for broad, multidisciplinary, environmental research? Most traditional theories of population–environment relationships tried to posit the simplest models to explain phenomena at a national or international level. Previously accepted theories, in some cases, have turned out to be myths rather than empirically supported theories (Lambin et al. 2001; Richerson 1977).

Population, Technology, and Central Place Theories[1]

One of the most influential theories is that of Malthus, and followers of these views are often referred to as Malthusians or neo-Malthusians (no negative connotations intended or implied). The Reverend Thomas Robert

[1] This section is based on an earlier discussion found in Chapter 2 of Moran and Ostrom (2005). Readers from the social sciences may find the discussions here gloss over a lot of

Malthus, writing at the turn of the nineteenth century, remains one of the most influential figures to have written about population (Malthus [1803]1989). He formulated a theory of population and environment that focused on the ability of the environment to produce food, and one that is applicable to any human population, from a community all the way up to all of humanity, which explains why his theory has been so useful and influential across the social sciences. His first observation was that without starvation, disease, or fertility limitation, human populations increase in geometric form. His second observation was that the productivity of agriculture, in contrast, only increases linearly over time. Malthus foresaw no limit to the potential expansion of productivity but he saw a limit to the rate of increase in productivity.

Malthus studied ways to avoid population growth's outpacing the growth of productivity and described preventative checks on population's outpacing agriculture, including social customs that governed fertility (e.g. age at marriage, proportion of women marrying, norms assigning responsibility to fathers), infanticide, and out-migration. The essential components of Malthus's argument are (1) population growth will outstrip the ability of the environment to provide, and (2) lack of sufficient resources will cause a decrease in population via famine, disease, and conflicts over land. Malthus's theory has two essential flaws. First, he did not allow for the possibility of nonlinearities in the growth of agricultural productivity, such as jumps in productivity associated with new agricultural technologies. Second, Malthus did not include agricultural innovation among the possible reactions to scarcity. In his theory, population pressure on limited resources will lead instead to population reduction. The "green revolution" showed how wrong Malthus's assumptions were – as population pressure led to rapid agricultural technological innovation.

While neo-Malthusian theories have focused largely on population as the driving force of negative environmental change (Hopfenberg 2003), an alternative theory has been used by scholars broadly following the work of Ester Boserup (1981, 1983, 1990). These scholars have focused more on how scarcities coming from population growth may stimulate changes in technology. Boserup challenged the presumption that either population or technology was the dominant engine of agricultural change and development. Rather, Boserup posited that increases in population density leading to land scarcity could be seen as a trigger that stimulates agricultural intensification.

---

important details. I wish to remind readers that this chapter is meant to introduce ecologists and natural scientists to some of the important theories that shape the thinking of social scientists, and that this familiarity could help them converse and engage social scientists more effectively – without becoming themselves social scientists. Social scientists are encouraged to read the next chapter which is meant to introduce them to some of the biological theories that shape bioecologists.

Boserup argued that farmers who faced little scarcity were not motivated to search for ways of increasing productivity. When faced with increased population density, however, farmers would be motivated to increase the amount of effort they invested in land by terracing, building irrigation systems, and carrying crop residues and forest litter to fertilize their land. Because of this focus on farmers and their immediate experience of scarcity, Boserup's work has been applied most successfully in studies at the community level. Considerable research has shown that some farming groups have devised intensive agricultural technologies that are dramatically more efficient and less harmful to the environment than extensive technologies (Netting 1968, 1993; B. Turner et al. 1993). While some scholars have viewed this theory and Malthusian theories as similarly mechanistic, more sensitive interpreters of Boserup's work point to the complexity of the processes involved. Changing technology in particular environments requires considerable experimentation and investment in new tools and techniques. Some groups may therefore be faced with such rapid changes in population and scarcity of resources that they cannot adjust fast enough. Ruttan's theory of induced innovation is a direct successor of the work of Boserup, as is the work of Simon (Binswanger and Ruttan 1978; Hayami and Ruttan 1987a, 1987b; L. Simon 1981). An intriguing effort to integrate the views of Malthus, Boserup and Ricardo has been made by Richerson and Boyd (1997/98).

One of the permanent lessons of the exploration of Boserup's theory is recognition that there is no "natural carrying capacity" for a particular environmental region; many scholars continue to use this term despite ample evidence over the last several decades that such carrying capacity is a function of available technology (cf. the work of Cohen 1995 for a thoughtful discussion of a range of carrying-capacity estimates). The level of productivity that is achievable in a particular environmental zone depends on the technology or physical capital available or invented as well as the available human and social capital. Boserup's work is also consistent with viewing actors more broadly as decision makers trying to improve their well-being by choosing among the productive options that appear to be available to them or, when necessity calls for it, inventing new options (i.e. contemporary emphasis on "agency").

Another major influence on contemporary research was the work of von Thünen (originally published in 1826, see P. G. Hall 1966). Von Thünen tried to uncover basic empirical laws that related agricultural prices, distance to markets, and land uses. The concept of central place hierarchy and contemporary spatial economics has direct links to von Thünen (Samuelson 1983; Krugman 1995). One of the core questions von Thünen asked was how location affected potential land use. By focusing only on the distance from a central place on a homogeneous plain, von Thünen and hundreds of other scholars since have examined how land value and rents are related to distance to a central place (effectively adding transportation costs to production costs in the decisions of farmers). Numerous studies have provided support for the proposition that the types of crops planted are strongly determined by transportation costs and that changes in external market value or cost of transportation are reflected relatively rapidly in the spatial allocation of agricultural activities (e.g. see Muller 1973; O'Kelly and Bryan 1996).

Related to the work of Boserup, scholars in this tradition have also studied how spatial factors affect the intensity of agricultural production using a variety of specifications for the production function, for the number of crops, and for scale economies (see particularly Webber 1973; Visser 1982). Researchers have found that, even among individual fields, farmers make substantial, differential investments so they invest less labor and capital in fields located a greater distance from a central place (de Lisle 1978). Thus, one should expect that the level of deforestation that occurs as a result of agricultural expansion will be directly related to the presence of roads and the transportation costs that farmers face for the crops that they may invest in (Moran 1976, 1981; Chomitz and Gray 1996).

Concern over a direct effect of population growth on land cover is at least implicitly based on an understanding of how population growth rates change over time. Demographers describe the typical changes in vital rates of birth, death, and growth experienced by a population over the course of development as *demographic transition theory* (see Kirk 1996 for a description and history of the theory of the demographic transition). For the majority of the long course of human history, populations were in the first stage of the demographic transition, experiencing high death and birth rates (see Figure 2.1 for a diagram illustrating the stages of demographic transition theory). These rates balanced each other and population growth was minimal. As communities, countries, and regions developed modern public health programs, and to a lesser extent modern medicine, death rates began to fall.

During the second stage of the demographic transition, death rates fall rapidly while birth rates remain high and stable, leading to increasing rates of population growth. The growth rate of the population, in the absence of migration, is the birth rate minus the death rate. As countries or regions enter the third stage of the demographic transition, death rates stabilize at a relatively low level (not quite the level achieved by today's developed countries, but quite low compared to earlier rates) and birth rates begin to fall. Population growth rates are maximized on the cusp between the second and third stages, when death rates have fallen and

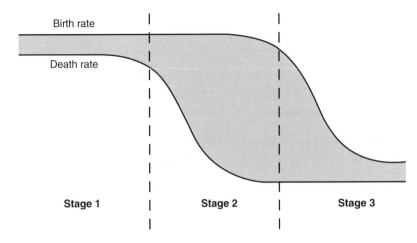

Figure 2.1 The demographic transition from high birth and death rates to low birth and death rates

birth rates are just beginning to fall. During the third stage, birth rates fall, with death rates low and stable, leading to declining growth rates. Once birth rates have fallen to the same low level as death rates, marking entry into stage 4 of the demographic transition, population growth is minimal. The distribution of countries across these stages, with many of the world's largest countries still in stage 3, creates understandable alarm among theorists positing a direct negative effect of population size or growth on the environment.

Falling death rates are driven by the discovery and adoption of public health practices (sanitary sewers, landfills, etc.), as well as by the adoption by later-developing countries of modern medical techniques (particularly vaccination) (Livi Bacci 2001). The declining death rates, and corresponding economic development, are often associated with high rates of urbanization and greater access to schooling for girls. Changes in birth rates are then driven by a variety of factors pertaining to the changing costs and benefits of children in urban areas and in nonagricultural lifestyles (Szreter 1996).

The demographic transition most accurately describes the experience of northern and western Europe, the sources of the data on which it was based. Both the ordering of declines in birth rates and mortality rates and the time elapsed between stages vary across other regions of the world, and indeed even within northern and western Europe (Coale and Watkins 1986). Early demographic transition theorists considered the mortality decline to be a

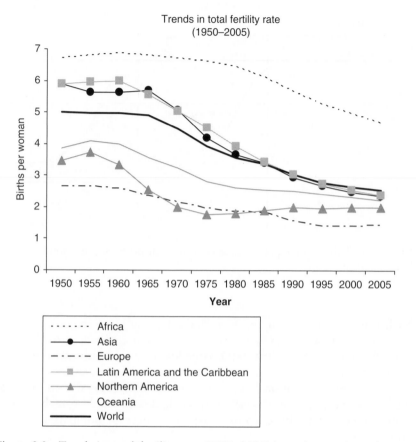

Figure 2.2   Trends in total fertility rate (1950–2000) in major continental areas. Note the general trend downwards
Source: Population Division of the Dept. of Economic and Social Affairs of the United Nations Secretariat. World Population Prospects: the 2004 Revision and World Urbanization Prospects.

necessary cause of the birth rate decline, while later research called into question this assertion (Chesnais 1992; Mason 1997). The experiences of today's developing countries, which were able to import rather than develop many of the drivers of mortality decline, point to the causal disconnect between mortality rate declines and birth rate declines. For population and environment researchers, the demographic transition theory serves as an organizing principle for thinking about geographic variation in human growth rates, and in the potential for future growth of human populations, by distinguishing between countries likely to have declining growth rates and those likely to continue to have high growth rates. Figure 2.2 illustrates the globally scaled phenomenon of declining total fertility rate across regions of the world from 1950 to 2000 and how highly variable the rates of decline can be (and the surprising uptick for North America in the most recent decade).

Population and Environment Theories

In contrast, and at a whole different scale of analysis, we find considerable value in the use of the theory of the *household life cycle*. The anthropologist Goody (1958) described households as the locus of social reproduction, and described the cycle followed by households over time. Households pass from an expansion stage (where birth rates are high and the family is growing) through a dispersion stage (where children are leaving the household) to a decay stage (when the original household head dies and is replaced by a son or daughter). The economist Chayanov ([1925]1966), writing much earlier, had described the household-farm economy of Russian peasants. According to Chayanov, the extent of agricultural cultivation by individual households depends on the demographic characteristics of the household. Available household labor is a limiting factor, but the consumption needs of the household are what ultimately determine the behavior of the household. Combining the theoretical ideas of Goody on changing household demographics over the life cycle and the work of Chayanov on how household demographics determine land-use decisions, recent population and environment researchers have modeled land use as a function of stage in the household life cycle (Walker and Homma 1996; S. McCracken et al. 1999; Moran, McCracken, and Brondizio 2001; Perz 2001).

Important advances have been taking place in the field of population and environment, recently summarized in a state-of-knowledge report from the National Academy of Sciences (NRC 2005a). The NRC Panel concluded that research to date shows the importance of demography for land-use change. Population growth, density, fertility, mortality, and age/gender composition of households influence land-use and land-cover change (NRC 2005a:9; Gutmann et al. 2005; Moran, Brondizio, and VanWey 2005; Walsh et al. 2005). Large resettlement schemes, such as those one finds in Amazonia and Indonesia, can rapidly affect the condition of land cover (Moran 1981, 1993; Geist and Lambin 2002). Recent research also shows that the condition of land cover is affected by land settlement policies, road building, market forces, and characteristics of the biophysical area. These contextual variables interact with each other and affect land use and other decisions settlers make, including their reproductive choices (Moran 1993; Bilsborrow 1994; Moran, Brondizio, and VanWey 2005; D'Antona et al. in review;

Siqueira et al. 2003, 2007). Based on these findings to date, the Panel recommended that future research should be pursued in two substantive areas: the study of frontier areas, and that of regions experiencing rapid urban development.

The size and spatial configuration of urban areas directly impacts energy and material flows such as carbon emissions and infrastructure demands, and thus has consequences on the functioning of Earth as a system. Levels of many atmospheric gases are elevated in urban areas and can affect biogeochemical processes (Pataki et al. 2003). Most recent research has focused at the subnational level and the role of migration is particularly pronounced (NRC 2005a:13). There are studies examining the role of a permanent move to a frontier (e.g. Gutmann et al. 2005; Moran, Brondizio, and VanWey 2005) or to urbanizing areas (e.g. Redman 2005; Seto 2005), and seasonal and circular migrants (Walsh et al. 2005). Recent work in the Ecuadorian Amazon has begun to examine migration within the frontier (Bilsborrow et al. 2004; Barbieri et al. 2005; Pan and Bilsborrow 2005). Migration into frontiers changes the environment by bringing people with a different pattern of land use to a new area, thereby transforming its land cover, biogeochemical cycles, and precipitation patterns.

To date site-specific studies have been common in rural areas. The focus on site- specific studies permits close attention to the decision-making processes of households and the outcomes for the land and the members of the household. The use of remote sensing along with intensive field campaigns and surveys has permitted expanding the areal extent of these areas to thousands of square kilometers (e.g. to $1,300\,km^2$, Walsh et al. 2005; $2,000\,km^2$, Liu et al. 2005; $3,800\,km^2$, Moran, Brondizio, and VanWey 2005). Site-specific studies have also allowed refinement by our team of classifications of satellite data, allowing, for example, the discrimination of age classes of secondary forests growing after deforestation of primary forests, types of pasture, and types of crops (Moran et al. 1994, 1996; Moran, Brondizio, and Mausel 1994; Moran, Brondizio, and McCracken 2002; Moran and Brondizio 2001; Brondizio et al. 1994, 2002). However, the NRC Panel and other experts in the field have increasingly argued for the need for comparative studies to address the importance of context and to bridge between household processes and political economy.

A second methodological advance called for, based on this past decade of research, is longitudinal data collection for the study of population and environment. As migration researchers have long known, decadal censuses do a poor job of tracking in- and out-migration, hiding what can be a very dynamic rate of turnover, seasonal migration, short-term migration, and circular migration. Beyond these issues of measurement error, land use, employment and migration decisions are often made jointly. Cross-sectional analyses are biased by the endogeneity of these processes. Longitudinal data allow researchers to overcome some of the problems of endogeneity. Thus, we need instruments and research designs explicitly focused on capturing causes and consequences of migration and other population dynamics. In these dynamic settings we need finer instruments than the census to capture the rapidly occurring changes through regularly scheduled waves of data collection that are spatially explicit, multilevel, and longitudinal (NRC 2005a:22).

Just as research on population and environment has come to focus on households as key units for understanding processes of environmental change (Entwisle et al. 2005; Liu et al. 2003; Mackellar et al. 1995), research on migration from rural agricultural communities considers the household the key decision-making unit (Schmink 1984; Stark and Lucas 1988; Stark 1991; Ellis 1998; Fox et al. 2003). In conceptualizing analyses of rural–urban migration, and related land use and off-farm employment decisions, one might draw on the New Economics of Labor Migration (Stark and Bloom 1985; Stark 1991). This approach treats migration as a response to the failure of various markets, primarily insurance and credit. Migration (and, similarly, off-farm employment) allows households to diversify income across sectors, protecting against shortfalls in income due to crop failure (for the household members remaining in the rural area) or unemployment (for migrants or household members working off-farm) (Stark and Levhari 1982; De Haan 1999; Wood and Porro 2002). Migration also allows rural households to access capital for the purchase of, for example, land, agricultural machinery, or home improvements in the absence of fully functioning credit markets, a condition that characterizes the rural areas of many developing countries. While credit is available in our study areas, it is not equally available to all residents and it is not available for the purchase of agricultural land by smallholders.

These theories argue that remittances are part and parcel of the migration process. Migrants send money in the event of an income shortfall if the migration is serving to overcome a failure of insurance markets while they send money more regularly up to a certain level if the migration results from a failure of credit markets. These theories can inform our understanding of the rural–urban or rural–rural migration of household members and children of households in smallholder households. As credit is unevenly available, one would expect that families without access to credit would be more likely to have children or former household members (with whom they maintain contact) living in urban areas or in rural areas with different crops (with weakly or uncorrelated prices, or sold in different locations [local, regional, or international]). One might also expect to see some migration and remittance responses to economic shocks.

These theories have been tested extensively in studying the migration decision in rural areas (Lucas and Stark 1985; Massey et al. 1993; Hoddinott 1994; VanWey 2003, 2005). Results of models of the effects of land ownership on migration are consistent with the premise that families are sending migrants to diversify income sources and to overcome credit constraints. However, some work has directly demonstrated the insurance function of migration. Lucas and Stark (1985) show that households in Botswana more susceptible to drought are more likely to send migrants, but they do not directly demonstrate the remittances in response to drought conditions. These theories of migration provide an important framework for understanding the processes of household income diversification and risk minimization through migration, land-use choices and off-farm employment.

Agency and History

In most of the theoretical approaches reviewed above, relationships among variables were presented in a mechanistic manner. Demographic "pressures" or "driving forces" affect environmental change without human agency playing more than an incidental role. In presuming that increases in demographic pressures may lead to agricultural intensification, Boserup (1981) does envision a role for human actors who face definite costs and benefits of continuing or changing their agricultural technology. Much of the research in this tradition, however, has continued to look at changes in population density as a driving force rather than as a change in the incentives facing individuals who then make choices about future actions. Similarly, von Thünen focused on farmers' maximizing decisions, but simply increased the number of variables that could be viewed as determining causes of a location or production decision. Because he saw the goal as determining the equilibrium of a system, decision makers at equilibrium had little or no strategic input (P. G. Hall 1966).

A contrasting tradition starts from models of social and environmental change that view actors (whether they are individuals, households, or larger collectives) as making real decisions after taking into account the strategies available to them in a particular setting. In this sense, actors are the ultimate drivers of change. They do act within certain constraints, commonly those identified in structural theories, but also have an independent impact on environmental change. Theories involving individual actors allow us to explain the microlevel changes that make up any macrostructural change. However, we must guard against considering individuals as simply rational actors seeking to maximize personal rewards at the expense of any other potentially desirable outcome.

One approach emphasizing human agency comes from historical ecology in its focus on the dialectic process by which people transform the environment that they use (Gragson 2005). Historical ecology offers valuable insights to scholars from all disciplines interested in global environmental change, as well as a bridge between the social sciences and the humanities. History represents the recent record of what we know as the longer record of evolution we can document from geology and paleoecology – except that the historical record tends to be more detailed, more nuanced, and closer to contemporary conditions and offers provocative insights into alternatives to our current environmental dilemma. Global models tend to be coarse in scale, and lack anything like an adequate representation of human variability and real biotic differences. One of the current and most exciting areas of research is the collaboration of paleoclimatologists, archeologists and historians in reconstructing the record of the past 300 years (under Biome 300, a PAGES program which is part of IGBP).

Recent recognition that current earth system changes are strongly associated with changes in the coupled human–environment system make the integration of human history and earth system history an important step in understanding the factors leading to global change and in developing coping and adaptation strategies for the future. A challenge to development of an integrated history of the human and earth system is the reconciliation of the various disciplinary perspectives on representing history and events. Resolving differences between quantitative and qualitative information, and between knowledge sets from different disciplines, is a necessary step in successful development of interdisciplinary studies. Development of a framework and shared conventions to interconnect these diverse views and to provide a mechanism to harmonize different perspectives will be needed to achieve the integrated history of human–environmental systems. Such an effort is being undertaken by a community of scholars. This community works toward the development of shared conventions between the biophysical and social science communities. Resolving issues related to understanding what factors or principles jointly affect coupled human–environment system dynamics is fundamental to the progress of studies. This will involve resolving scale issues of time and space (as mentioned in the previous section), conciliation of impacts and drivers between different components of the coupled system, and alternate views of the structure of the analytical framework. Human–environment systems are intimately linked in ways that we are only beginning to appreciate (van der Leeuw 1998; Redman 1999; Steffen et al. 2003; Diamond 2005; Kirch 2005). In order to fully understand the history of the earth, it is necessary to integrate the different perspectives, theories, tools, and knowledge of multiple disciplines across the full spectrum of social and natural sciences and the humanities (Hibbard et al. 2007).

Landscape history (Crumley 1994:6), seen by some as an offshoot of historical ecology, refers to the study of changing landscapes over time and in space. Human beings adapt to, and bring about, modifications in ecosystems – and have done so for thousands, if not millions, of years. Historically informed environmental analysis is a necessity if for no other reason than to correct the misperception that past environments were "pristine" and that only recently have humans begun to have an impact on the earth (Jacobsen and Firor 1992; Redman 1999; Redman et al. 2004; Diamond 2005). Hardly any spot on earth is unaffected by human action, and humans have brought about changes in all landscapes, both positive and negative. This record of human impact on environment offers a rich menu of choices we have made, and of their consequences, providing a view of alternatives much richer than a focus on the present ever would, of choices to avoid, and alternatives to be taken. Historical ecology brings together the approaches of ethnography, archeology, history, and paleoscience to address environmental issues at regional and global scale (Crumley 1994). The marriage of environmental history with historical ecology has not been consummated (Winterhalder 1994). This is the result of the former coming from the discipline of history, and therefore having reluctance to theorizing, while the latter sees itself as a research program that emphasizes agency and historical context. This is not an insurmountable problem and is one that could be resolved by more interaction, given the desire of some environmental historians to ally themselves with ecological anthropological theory (Wooster 1984). To focus together on a given historical problem or landscape is likely to be the way forward.

In a recent volume, Balée and Erickson (2006) suggest that historical ecology is a new research program, distinct from previous approaches. They suggest that their strategy is distinct from that of landscape ecology because they focus on how human beings bring about changes in landscapes. They take a very strong position that there are no pristine environments but, rather, as soon as humans enter into an environment, it is made into a human landscape and modified by human actions for human objectives. They argue that human beings do not adapt to the physical conditions of the environment by adjusting their population size and settlement size to environmental initial conditions. Rather, they propose that humans transform those constraints into negligible analytical phenomena (Balée and Erickson 2006:4) through transformation of soils, drainage, cropping practices, and so on. Further, they dismiss cultural ecology, ecosystem ecology, adaptationist approaches, and systems ecology because they "ultimately deny human agency" in positively changing the environment over time (ibid. 2006:4). While there is value in emphasizing how local populations modify an environment to achieve their goals (Balée 1998), it is an overstatement to say that all adaptationist approaches deny human agency.

Decision-theoretic Approaches

Theories that overtly examine the decision processes and outcomes of individuals and households vary among themselves in the specific models of human behavior that they use. For neoclassical economists and economic geographers, the individual actor weighs the material benefits and costs of making particular choices and makes decisions to maximize short-term returns. When this model of human behavior is used to explain behavior of actors embedded in a highly competitive environment, such as an open competitive market, predictions from the theory assuming individual, maximizing, self-interested returns have been supported by extensive field and experimental research. As Alchian (1950) long ago addressed, however, this success can be largely attributed to the strong selection pressure of the institutional environment leaving those who maximize profits as the survivors rather than to the internal decision-making calculus of the individual actor. Approaches still anchored in neoclassical economics, known as environmental economics, have come forth to meet the challenge, but ecologists together with some economists have proposed alternative ways of thinking about these relations, and call themselves ecological economists (Constanza 1991). Efforts to reconcile these two different approaches to economic valuation have been few (cf. an exception being Venkatachalam 2007).

One of the significant trends of the eighties and nineties was a shift away from ecosystem models and towards models of the individual or actor-based models. This shift went along with interests in microeconomics, evolutionary ecology, a rise in individualism and self-interest, and other approaches that privileged the individual over the community and the ecosystem (Bodenhorn 2000; Gaines and Gaines 2000). While the individual has always been the object of research and observation in human and evolutionary studies, ecosystem approaches tended to aggregate individual information because interests were in higher units of analysis and in how these units operated (NRC 2005b). Evolutionary ecology, optimal foraging theory, and microeconomics were far more interested in *why* individuals made the decisions they did. The preference was to highlight the variability of individuals in a system in order to understand the origin of particular traits or behaviors (e.g. food sharing), rather than focus on the remarkable dynamic equilibrium of whole systems. Both approaches are necessary to address the full panoply of questions of interest to human ecology and the human dimensions of global change. These are now seen as processes occurring at different levels of analysis, linked by complex articulations across scales which remain to be investigated.

The narrow model of rational behavior and a heavy emphasis on finding the equilibrium of a static situation dominated economic approaches to the study of human–environment interactions until quite recently. Resource economics and economic geography textbooks tended to presume that individual maximizers were driven to particular production and location decisions by factors in their environment. This work was therefore highly consistent with the "driving forces" literature that focused primarily at a macrolevel. Further, unless individuals had secure private property tenure, they would not take into account the long-term consequences of their use of natural resources (Demsetz 1967; Welch 1983). Consequently, the presumption was that rational decision makers would take actions that adversely affect the environment (see Dales 1968; Dasgupta and Heal 1979). Institutions designed to curb these strategic actions were viewed as necessary changes that would have to be imposed by external authorities on local resource users.

Contemporary microtheories of human action affecting natural resources are less likely to view humans as mechanically and narrowly rational – pursuing their own immediate and material ends (cf. Simon 1985, 1997; Camerer 1998, 2003). Contemporary research presumes that actors have a broader set of values that they take into account, that they have access to less than complete information, and that they have weaker calculation prowess and less information than was presumed (e.g. see E. Ostrom and Walker 2003 for multiple papers examining how and why individuals trust one another when rational actors should not extend trust). Behavioral economics shares many theoretical insights with the work of sociologists (particularly Coleman 1990), political scientists (Young 1999), and institutional economists (North 1990). For example, recent demographic work revisiting the causes of fertility decline has focused on the role of social networks in regulating the flow of information and indeed in determining the way in which information is evaluated (Mason 1997; Kohler 2000).

Collective-action theory has become a core theory across all of the social sciences used to explain the costs and difficulties involved with organizing cooperation to achieve collective ends. The theory has roots in the 1950s, when H. Gordon (1954) and Scott (1955) analyzed open-access fisheries to show that fishermen would always overharvest. In 1965, a study conceptualized individuals facing such problems as making decisions independently without an external enforcement agency to make them keep agreements (Olson 1965). In this setting, Olson predicted that unless individuals were in very small groups or had established selective incentives, they would not cooperate to achieve these joint benefits. In 1968, Hardin published "The Tragedy of the Commons," in which he envisioned individuals jointly harvesting from a commons as being inexorably trapped in overuse and destruction. Drawing on a simple view of a resource (a common pool) and of the users (the self-seeking, maximizers of short-term gains in the prevalent model of rational behavior of the time), he argued that there were only two solutions to a wide variety of environmental problems: the imposition of a government agency as regulator or the imposition of private rights.

Until recently, the possibility that the users themselves would find ways to organize themselves had not been seriously considered. Organizing to create rules that specify the rights and duties of participants creates a public good for those involved. Anyone who is included in the community of users benefits from this public good, whether they contribute or not. Evidence from both experimental and field research challenges the generalizability of the earlier accepted theory (Ostrom, Gardner and Walker 1994). While it is generally successful in predicting outcomes in settings where users are alienated from each other or cannot communicate effectively, it does not provide an explanation for settings where users are able to create and sustain agreements to avoid serious problems of overuse. Nor does it predict well when government ownership will perform well or how privatization will improve outcomes. Scholars familiar with the results of field research substantially agree on a set of variables that enhance the likelihood of users organizing themselves to avoid the social losses associated with open-access, common-pool resources (Schlager 1990; McKean 1992; Tang 1992; Ostrom 1992; Wade 1994; Baland and Platteau 1996; NRC 2002a). Consensus is growing that key attributes of a resource, of the users, and of higher levels of government provide a strong context within which individuals may or may not self-organize to protect resources (Libecap 1995; Dietz, Ostrom and Stern 2003). The resource attributes have to do with its size, its predictability, the presence of reliable indicators, and the existence of damage to the resource that can be repaired. The attributes of users have to do with their dependency on the resource, their time horizons, the trust they have developed, their autonomy, their organizational experience, and the distribution of interests within a community (Ostrom 1999).

Environmental psychology and human psychology bring substantively to human–environment research particular strengths in understanding behavior at the individual level (Stern 2000). They bring not only insight, but also sophisticated methods and experimentation that clarify cause and effect at this level. Studies in this field help us understand better how people use information about the environment, and thus understand important questions in human–environment studies such as how people respond to climate forecasts and ecological risk assessments (Stern et al. 1995; NRC 1999c). Individuals play key roles in making choices about alternative technologies, about pollution, about use of cars and energy, all of which translate when aggregated to very large environmental outcomes. However, individual choice is constrained by structural processes, by other members of the household and the community, and by cultural traditions. This is particularly true when referring to consumption, as is the case for the emerging middle class of many developing countries. To ask them not to consume is likely to be rejected; however, they could be offered more or less environmentally friendly forms of transportation, refrigeration, and other consumption items by society. Psychological research points out, for example, that providing efficiency is more palatable than expecting curtailment of consumption (Gardner and Stern 1996).

Psychological theories help us understand some of the more difficult conundrums in human–environment research. For example, we see countries which have high levels of environmental concern but where the population behaves in a very polluting way. Research shows that behaviors that harm the environment do not flow from anti-environmental values and attitudes, and that pro-environmental values do not guarantee environmental protection. Rather, a range of theories propose that cognitive dissonance (Katzev and Johnson 1983, 1987), norm activation (Black, Stern and Elworth 1985; Stern, Dietz and Black 1986; Widegren 1998), and theories of reasoned action and planned behavior (Jones 1990; Bamberg and Schmidt 1999) better account for these unexpected outcomes. In short, psychological theories point out that environmentally relevant behavior lies at the end of a long causal chain of factors, and that the most notable key to behavioral change is the immediate context of behavior, and not deeply held values (P. Stern 2000:525). The role of environmental values has been reviewed by Dietz, Fitzgerald and Shwom (2005). Norm activation and trust have been shown to be particularly important in understanding risk perception (Slovic 1999; Earle, Siegrist and Gutscher 2007; Siegrist, Earle, and Gutscher 2007).

Research in the field of *psychology* has yielded also some valuable observations on how a self-organizing system develops and functions. If stored information and past routines are simple and small in number, simple groping can be effective in decision making. In groping, the organism goes through its repertoire of activities until the proper response is elicited (Mackay 1968:363). Although groping is used by people and is, at times, a major source of new and inventive solutions to problems, it is largely an ineffective system. This is particularly true if the situation is complex or the social or physical environment changes rapidly and unpredictably. If one can establish any regularity (that is, redundancy) in the statistical structure of a situation, then one can use such redundancy to save time by the use of "imitative organizers" or control sequences based on the statistical characteristics of redundant phenomena (Mackay 1968:363). These allow the organism to induce the correct adaptive response without major investments in groping. Groping and control sequences assume that one knows in advance the range of options available and constraints present, but this is not often realistic. Human systems are self-organizing – that is, they are able to receive inputs of new information and to develop characteristic organizing sequences as a result of new and old information.

The human informational system probably works at various levels, depending on the level of difficulty in making choices. Decisions can be made in a climate of certainty, uncertainty, or risk. Certainty exists when one can predict what will happen in the period relevant to the decision. Uncertainty describes a situation wherein one cannot specify the probability of outcomes. Risk refers to situations where one can specify the probability distribution of several possible outcomes (Levin and Kirkpatrick 1975:106). Under conditions of certainty about a situation (for example, at breakfast I have a choice between cereal and eggs, with coffee in either case), a set of simple rules or pathways may be followed in arriving at a decision. As certainty decreases and there is a greater possibility of inappropriate or maladaptive choices, increasingly complex logic and structure must be used to help sift the information and allow for decision making under conditions of risk and uncertainty. Solutions may be elicited from the use of simulation, probability, and "judgment heuristics" (that is, nonprobabilistic methods that make use of consensus between knowledgeable people). Effective research tools for dealing with conditions of risk have not achieved the sophistication of those dealing with uncertainty. Both areas offer fallow ground for new contributions, given the paucity of analytical tools available and the importance of this aspect of human systems (Levin and Kirkpatrick 1975:529–30). Theories of risk management are increasingly applied to issues in environmental social science, such as how pastoral groups manage risk in a hazardous physical environment (e.g. McCabe 2004; Bollig 2006).

Methods developed in microeconomics and in the field of *management and decision theory* can be usefully applied to the problem of choosing from different possible courses of action (Rapport and Turner 1977). If one has too many choices in a given set of circumstances, one may be immobilized by indecision. Thus, one of the typical responses of information flow systems is to have complex rules to simplify the number of options. Over time, social scientists have presented a variety of theories that seek to give primacy to one factor or another. Perhaps dominant for many years has been the assumption behind the behavior of economic man (that is, maximization of expected utility). Much of the behavior has been simplified so that economists can focus on those aspects of behavior that are aimed at advancing the interests of business, households, and so forth. However, both theorists and field-workers have seriously attacked those assumptions. The key assumption, that the decision maker's objective is maximization of expected utility, is useful for analysis, but does not represent the actual behavior of actors.

Critics have shown that economic men sometimes seek to maximize "noneconomic" things, such as prestige (Cancian 1972; Schneider 1974), or that they simply try to minimize risk and uncertainty (Johnson 1971). Leibenstein, in his book *Beyond Economic Man* (1976), called for an overhaul of economic theory that would take into account "selective rationality" – that is, choice making that reflects a compromise between what one might do in the absence of constraints and what one does when they are present. One's preference reflects social, cultural, and psychological standards of behavior that may be in direct conflict with the calculus of maximization. Similar theories have been proposed by business psychologists (March and Simon 1958; Cyert and March 1963; Lindblom 1964) and geographers (Heijnen and Kates 1974; Slovic, Kunreuther and White 1974). The emphasis of these studies is on how decision makers do not necessarily maximize utility, but aim instead at *satisfactory* solutions to problems – often invoking simplified "programs" that lack the complete knowledge often assumed in economic analysis (see also Ostrom 1998; Gigerenzer, Czerlinski and Martignon 2002). Linking economic theory and rational choice to selective rationality is proving of growing interest across the social sciences (Boudon 2003; Miller 2005; Ostrom 2005). A particularly intriguing new area is one that examines how contracts are made. Legal enforcement, alone, cannot ensure that contracts work in cooperative ventures. Even the intervention of the state in legal enforcement has but a limited role to play. More effective results come about when parties negotiate incomplete contracts that, from the start, emphasize renegotiation and rely upon enforcement through informal mechanisms, such as reputation, repeated dealing between parties, and norms of reciprocity (Scott 2006). This view of law as not individualist but, rather, as socially engaged helps us understand not only the behavior of traditional populations, but also effective contemporary legal contracts through the use of "smart heuristics" (Schwartz 2000; Gigerenzer, Czerslinski and Martignon 2002; Udehn 2002).

To integrate relevant information flows into matter/energy models, we must be able to assign logic to human acts. This logic is derived from the sorts of decision models we have just described. A new generation of models, intelligent agent-based models (Grimm et al. 2006), offer exciting opportunities to "grow" social systems through rule-based iterative approaches that take advantage of artificial intelligence (Epstein and Axtell 1996; Xu and Li 2002).

Political Economy and Political Ecology

World system theory lays the blame for land-use/land-cover change not on population per se, but rather on the organization of the world political economy (Ehrhardt-Martinez 1998; Ehrhardt-Martinez, Crenshaw and Jenkins 2002). This theory has been termed *dependency theory* by development economists (e.g. see Frank 1967) and world systems theory by sociologists (e.g. see Wallerstein 1974; Chase-Dunn 1998). We focus here on the sociological variant. The nations of the world are organized into a "world system" based on capitalism and market connections (Wallerstein 1974; Chase-Dunn 1998). This system was set in place in the sixteenth century as Europe expanded into the rest of the world through the expansion of mercantilism. Nations are unequally advantaged in this system, with the "core" nations having the most power in the market and in the political organization of the world. Core nations use their power to maintain their privileged position through the exploitation of "peripheral" and "semi-peripheral" countries. Core countries are more developed (economically), contain the headquarters of most transnational corporations, and wield considerable political influence over peripheral and semi-peripheral countries. As core countries export capitalism, peripheral and semi-peripheral countries are drawn into world economic markets. This unequal organization and the diffusion of capitalism affect a whole host of economic outcomes. When considering land-use change, it is particularly important to consider the role of world food markets. Less developed countries enact programs of export agriculture for these markets and consequently develop unsustainable agricultural practices in order to produce enough cash crops to allow them to purchase other goods on the world market.

The entry of peripheral and semi-peripheral countries into world markets leads to poverty and population growth, and to unsustainable land-use change (Rudel 1989). The decline of traditional subsistence agriculture and its entry into world economic markets from a disadvantaged position lead to poverty among the populations of developing countries. This poverty leads to population growth as children represent a net (economic) benefit to families in the absence of mandatory education and child labor laws. The entry into world economic markets simultaneously causes conversion of land from forest and traditional agriculture to commercial agriculture by increasing the value of land for agriculture and introducing capital-intensive methods of cultivation. The transition from traditional to commercial agriculture in early developing regions of a country leads also to the dislocation of farmers from traditional employment and modes of living (Sassen 1988; Massey et al. 1993). This population of dislocated farmers is highly mobile and in turn contributes to environmental change in frontier areas and other migration destinations. Thus, any relationship observed between population growth and environmental degradation is spurious. Population growth and land-use change both result from the penetration of capitalism into less developed countries and the unequal nature of the world system, according to these theories.

A different body of theory focuses on economic factors as they affect land use and levels of deforestation. These theories are consistent with the type of *general equilibrium models* posited by leading economists such as Deacon (1994, 1995). General equilibrium models explore the cumulative effects of decisions by actors in an economy under diverse taxes and inducements. If there are no government policies related to land-use changes from forested land to agriculture or pasture uses, general equilibrium models posit that an inefficient equilibrium will exist, since standing forests – and the ecosystem services produced by them – are not given any value in such a setting. Further, when ownership rights to property are insecure, deforestation rates have been shown to be higher (Bohn and Deacon 2000).

Once taxes and inducements are introduced, the results can be either better or worse, depending on the particular pattern of taxation and subsidy undertaken by a government. Some developing countries adopt policies that have the effect of reducing the overall return to agricultural production (see Repetto 1989), but in other developing countries the "net force of government policy runs in the opposite direction and subsidizes agricultural production. The leading example is the system of tax credits, tax exemptions, and loan subsidies provided by the Brazilian government for cattle ranching in the Amazon" (Deacon 1995:11).

One current and popular theoretical approach used by environmentally oriented anthropologists and geographers is that of *political ecology*. A few years ago the section on cultural ecology of the Association of American Geographers, for example, was renamed the section on cultural and political ecology (cf. Jarosz 2004). Human ecologists have become increasingly aware that power relations affect human uses of the environment. We are now aware of the role of environmental movements in exerting pressure on political bodies, corporations, and institutions. There is a renewed awareness of the potential value of human ecology in influencing policy and understanding the future of how humans impact the environment (Greenberg and Park 1994; Brosius 1999).

Studies with a political ecological bent are reinterpreting our understanding of hunter/gatherers (Wilmsen 1989), pastoralists (McCay and Acheson 1987; Bromley 1992), agriculturalists (Sheridan 1988), and urban-industrial populations (Heynen, Kaika, and Swyngedouw 2006). We now recognize the long interaction of foragers with larger systems and their complex adaptations and accommodation to this unequal relationship. In some cases, foragers have chosen to artfully pose as "primitives," while in others they have abandoned their mode of production in favor of agriculture. Some agricultural populations, when faced with potential enslavement by more powerful neighbors, have deculturated into small bands of foragers capable of staying one step ahead of slavers (Gomes 1988; Balée 1994).

Few if any places in the world today are untouched by global forces such as climate change, capitalism, media, and the reach of the United Nations (Braudel 1973; Wolf 1982, 1999; Blaikie and Brookfield 1987; Rappaport 1993). We cannot ignore in environmental analysis the ways these relationships of local to global systems lead to particular outcomes (Moran 1982b).

Political ecology bears great affinity with political economy, as both explore the role of power relations in affecting human uses of the environment, particularly the impact of capitalism on developing societies (Harvey 1973; Brosius 1997, 1999; Gezon 1999; Kottak 1999). Unlike political economy (with its central interest on class relations), political ecology is centered on the ravages that capitalism brings upon the environment and on human/habitat relations (Lansing 1991; Rappaport 1993; Peet and Watts 1994; Johnson 1995). It has been noted that political ecology has a tendency to privilege the local scale as more desirable than other scales, often viewing larger scales as oppressive of the local, and that this "local trap" can lead to major analytical errors (Brown and Purcell 2005). As a relatively new approach, political ecology still lacks a robust theory or a settled paradigm (Biersack 1999). The above-noted scale preference is just one of several philosophical and theoretical traps that remain to be solved. It could develop closer to the concerns of the environmental social sciences (Crumley 1994; Bates and Lees 1996) or to so-called "critical theory" and cultural studies (Peet and Watts 1996; Biersack 1999).

At present, the bulk of political ecological analysis has stayed well within the concerns of the social sciences and distant from the physical and biological sciences in its data collection and methods of research. It has been more concerned with cultural and political critique, and has only rarely presented a substantive body of environmental data as part of the analysis of political ecology. In short, it has been stimulating on the politics side, but less substantive on the environmental side. Vayda and Walters (1999) take considerable issue with what they consider to be the dominant role claimed for political and political-economic influences in advance of the research (Bryant and Bailey 1997) instead of empirically examining a broader set of factors in which the outcome of what is most important is not known in advance. Gezon (1997, 1999), among others espousing political ecology, focuses on examining how people engage politically in contesting access to resources, but only rarely presents environmental data on the resources being contested. Vayda and Walters (1999:170) argue that ignoring the biological data can lead to unwarranted conclusions about the primacy of political influences. This may be a sign of political ecology's relative newness as a field, and of the felt need of these scholars to address the valid concerns of environmentalism and other political causes. But if its results cannot be integrated with the enormous efforts at understanding human dimensions of global change, conservation biology, environmental NGOs, and other local and regional agencies engaged in environmental protection, it may grow marginal to the very policy world it wishes to influence. The best course is for political ecologists to join biophysical scientists in examining together the complex forces at play. As any other complex adaptive system, human ecosystem outcomes are nonlinear, have emergent properties, and can be remarkably counterintuitive.

Political ecology and other theories used by environmental social scientists need to seek ever new ways to integrate knowledge and advance understanding of the complexities inherent in ecological systems. To be most effective, they will need to integrate the above theories with those coming from the natural sciences, as we will see in the next chapter.

Cultural Ecology

Before going to the next chapter, there is one theory that has proven to be useful over the years in anthropology, archeology and geography, and whose framework has influenced many who work in human–environment research – *cultural ecology* (Steward 1955; Sauer 1958; Netting 1981, 1993; Moran 1981, 2007). The cultural ecological approach proposed by Julian Steward involves both a problem and a method. The problem is to test whether the adjustments of human societies to their environments require specific types of behavior or whether there is considerable latitude in human responses (Steward 1955:36). The method consists of three procedures: (1) to analyze the relationship between subsistence system and environment; (2) to analyze the behavior patterns associated with a given subsistence technology; and (3) to ascertain the extent to which the behavior pattern entailed in a given subsistence system affects other aspects of culture (Steward 1955:40–1). In short, the cultural ecological approach postulates a relationship between environmental resources, subsistence technology, and the behavior required to bring technology to bear upon resources.

The crucial element in Steward's approach is neither nature nor culture but, rather, the process of resource utilization. The reasons for the priority he gave to subsistence are clear: obtaining food and shelter are immediate and urgent problems in all societies, and patterns of work at a given level of technology are limited in their ability to exploit resources. The approach is best illustrated by his study of the Western Shoshoni.

The Shoshoni inhabited the Great Basin of North America, a semiarid land with widely dispersed resources. The Shoshoni were hunter/gatherers with simple tools and relied heavily on the collection of grass seeds, roots, and berries. Steward showed how almost every resource could best be exploited by individuals – except rabbits and antelope, which required seasonal group hunting. Each fall the Shoshoni gathered pine nuts that were stored for the long, cold winter. Although in winter they formed larger population concentrations, they did not form stable social units because pine nuts were not available in the same places each year, and groups therefore had to remain fluid to adequately exploit the Basin. Thus, the requirements of subsistence produced fluid and fragmentary social units that were lacking in distinct patterns of leadership.

To Steward, the Shoshoni presented an extreme case of the limitations placed by environment on the workable options available to a culture. Steward hypothesized that the immediate impact of environment upon behavior decreased as technological complexity improved the human capacity to modify the environment. He suggested that in complex societies, social factors may be more important in explaining change than subsistence technology or environment (Steward 1938:262).

The research strategy proposed by Steward is all the more striking if one considers its historical backdrop. Until Steward's time, human–environment theories either dealt in broad generalities lacking a firm grounding in empirical research or emphasized lists of cultural traits. Cultural ecology put the emphasis on careful analysis of social interaction, recording of movement, timing of work activity, and so forth. Through such research, it was possible to more effectively delimit the field of study and arrive at cause-and-effect relationships.

In an earlier study (1936), Steward compared hunter-gatherers in extremely varied environments. The groups chosen lived in territorially based bands and were characterized by patrilocal residence, patrilineal descent, and *exogamous* marriage. The environmental determinist approach had long been baffled by the social similarities between groups as different as the Kalahari Bushmen, the Australian aborigines, and the rain forest pygmies. Steward showed that the ecological parallels between these groups were low population density, reliance on foot transportation, and the hunting of scattered nonmigratory animals. The requirements of knowing the resources of a territory anchored each population to it. Their limited means of transportation reduced the range that could be effectively exploited and favored the maintenance of low densities. Although not totally correct in his conclusion, Steward motivated others to study the interactions of hunter/gatherers with their habitats.

Steward has been criticized by some scholars because his approach assigns primacy to subsistence behaviors. The focus on subsistence is essential to the cultural ecological approach. There are cases when other factors may have far greater control over a social system, and over the years Steward expanded the scope of cultural ecology to include political, religious, military, and aesthetic features of culture (1955:93). Geertz (1963) concluded in his study of Indonesian agriculture that historical and political factors are part of the total environment to which populations adapt and must not be dismissed as secondary.

While revolutionary in his emphasis on human–environment interactions, Steward seemed to have slighted several environmental phenomena that could well affect the cultural development of human groups. For instance, he had little to say regarding the influences of demographic makeup, epidemiology, competition with other groups in a given area, or human physiological adaptations (Vayda and Rappaport 1976). More serious is the charge that the comparative approach cannot yield cause-and-effect relationships. Vayda and Rappaport question whether correlations between adaptations and cultural traits can be translated into causes and effects (Vayda and Rappaport 1976:14). Steward never followed a clear statistical sample, and his correlations left out the number of cases in which the correlation did not hold. Steward usually succeeded in demonstrating functional relationships, but not in establishing causality.

The contribution of Steward was to delimit, more than anyone before him, the field of human–environment interaction. He did so by emphasizing behavior, subsistence, and technology. The weaknesses of such an approach became apparent within a decade and spawned other research strategies. Dissatisfaction with the research approach of cultural ecology led some scholars to search for new theories, new data collecting techniques, and new analytical tools. The major influence on this new research approach came from general, or biological, ecology. The ecosystem concept provided a conceptual framework more satisfactory to some scientists than the behavior/social structure equation stressed by Steward. Little and Morren succinctly expressed the strategy: "We are concerned with those cultural and biological responses, factors, processes and cycles that affect or are directly connected with the survival, reproduction, development, longevity or spatial positions of people. This set of questions rather than the traditional division of scientific labor defines the subject matter" (1976:5). We develop in the next chapter this fundamental theoretical approach (i.e. the ecosystem) from ecology that has served many research teams well in connecting human and environmental research – and several other foundational theories from the biological sciences.

3

Theories and Concepts from the Biological Sciences[1]

When biologists think about individual and species responses to global environmental change they have several guiding theories that are fundamental and which underlie their views – theories social scientists need at least a basic understanding of to effectively work with biologists. That is one of the goals of this chapter. Obviously, it is impossible in a brief chapter to cover all the relevant theories from the biological sciences, and thus I trust readers from the natural sciences will be forgiving if some important theories and concepts are omitted here. The goal is to introduce social scientists to those guiding theories that seem most relevant to current issues of cross-disciplinary human–environment interaction research, particularly to work on global environmental change.

Biological ecology, rather than human ecology, is very much the focus here. It is rooted at one end on population genetics and the process of natural selection, and it extends all the way at the other end to studies of the structure of whole ecosystems (Richerson 1977). A chain of theory links natural selection at the individual level to the behavior of populations, and deduces testable theories of ecosystemic and community properties from the interaction of populations (ibid.). Among these fundamental theories and concepts are: (1) evolution by natural selection; (2) that species respond individualistically, not as communities; (3) that interactions with other species help determine if a particular species will persist in a particular place; (4) whether top-down vs. bottom-up control of the community is operative in a given situation; (5) the role of succession in creating plant associations; (6) the implications of island biogeography to understand fragmentation

[1] I am grateful for the many suggestions made for this chapter by Emily V. Moran (Duke University) and Johanna Schmitt (Brown University). Any errors, however, are entirely my responsibility.

and change; (7) the importance of biodiversity and ecosystem processes/ services; and (8) ecosystem structure and function.

Evolution by Natural Selection

At the foundation of biological thought, one must consider evolution by natural selection, i.e. genetic variation within populations which helps determine the potential for persistence via adaptive evolution to a rapidly changing environment. The theory of evolution drastically changed our perception of the world and of our place in it. Charles Darwin (and Richard Wallace) put forth a coherent theory of evolution and amassed a great body of evidence in support of this theory. Before Darwin, most scientists believed that each organism and each adaptation was the work of the creator. Linnaeus, remembered for his system of biological classification that we still use today, subscribed to such a view that saw similarities and differences as a consequence of omnipotent design.

In contrast, Darwin's theory of evolution posed an alternative explanation: that organisms changed over time, that many organisms that once lived were now extinct, that the world is constantly changing, and that the fossil record provided evidence for evolution. This record shows populations branching out as a result of external forces such as changing environment and competition for niches. He viewed change as slow, taking place over long time periods – a fact supported by the fossil record. More recent views of "punctuated equilibrium," in which powerful external shocks can bring about sudden extinctions and speciation, is an alternative view that explains some cases in the fossil record (Gould and Eldredge 1977; see also Eldredge and Gould 1972; Gould 2007).

For Darwin, the mechanism of evolutionary change was natural selection. Natural selection is a process that occurs over successive generations. In each generation, individuals seek to reproduce; they differ in this ability and compete for resources, and over generations those more able to produce offspring will persist and pass on their traits resulting in selection of the more fit individuals. In short, there must be heritable variation in some traits, such as beak size, color, or wing spread, and there must be differential survival and reproduction associated with the possession of that given trait. The randomness of evolution by natural selection is based on the way variation occurs in genetics, wherein variants do not come about because they are needed but result from random processes governed by genetics, though once they appear they can confer advantages, or disadvantages, to individuals in the struggle to survive and reproduce. This random element in evolution by natural selection is one of the most significant elements and has huge implications for efforts to manage populations, communities, and ecosystems.

Species Respond Individualistically, Not as Communities

The original idea came from Gleason (1926) in his "the individualistic concept of the plant association" in opposition to earlier characterizations of a plant community being like an organism, with a particular pattern of development and moving towards a defined "climax" (e.g. Clements 1916). Clements formulated the concept of a climax as a major unit of vegetation, constituted of associated species, that is the basis for the classification of plant commuties. The concept of the climax assumes the stabilizing role of a slowly changing climate over given regions and thus the stable presence of major climaxes such as tundra, boreal and deciduous forest, and prairie. Its focus was not on all individual species but rather on a few dominant species that were seen as characteristic of the climax formation.

Gleason argued that, instead of there being fixed vegetation types as suggested by notions of climax, the presence of a species was determined by (a) whether a species could get there, and (b) if it did, whether it could grow under current conditions. He questions very convincingly the earlier notions of fixed or natural plant associations. Rather, he finds that there is no inherent reason for any two areas of the earth's surface to bear precisely the same vegetation. The fortuitous immigration of plants through seed dispersal, and the unique conditions it finds in an ever fluctuating and variable environment, creates unique conditions for survival in each generation. Even the same location is likely to have had different plant associations in the past, and will surely have different associations in the future. The similarity of plant communities within a given region is a result of the fact that a general region has a large flora within which migrating seeds are available, and thus has material from species for distribution, as well as similar environmental conditions – and so, for a given period of time, these similar conditions result in similar combinations of plant species. Given that climatic change has been slower than the generation time of plants, one is likely to see similar plant associations in a given region. This results in the gradual clines one sees across space, as from one end of the Mississippi to the other.

This is now a very well accepted idea among biologists and it is important to keep it in mind since it ties closely to views of evolution where, again, the basic unit is the individual rather than the community. It is also a very "modern" concept as this quote from Gleason makes clear:

> A species disappears from areas where the environment is no longer endurable. It grows in company with any other species of similar environmental requirements, irrespective of their normal associational affiliations ... plant associations, the most conspicuous illustration of the space relation of plants,

depend solely on the coincidence of environmental selection and migration over an area of recognizable extent and usually for a time of considerable duration. (Gleason 1926:26)

The above quote from Gleason is a formulation remarkable in its newness, and in its concern with rapid environmental change, given when it was written, and is very relevant to our contemporary concerns (see also Davis 1969). One might note that paleoecologists speak of "non-analog" plant communities in the past (i.e. some associations that have never been seen today) and predict there will be non-analog future communities as well.

Interactions with Other Species: Niche and Neutral Theories

A closely related concept to the above is that of the *fundamental niche* (i.e. the n-dimensional space representing environmental conditions under which a species *could* live) vis-à-vis the *realized niche* (the conditions under which it *does* live). Hutchinson (1957) formulated this key distinction in which the realized niche is generally smaller, due to competition or dispersal limitations. Hutchinson found that the large number of species we observe is

> at least partly because complex trophic organization of a community is more stable than a simple one, but that limits are set by the tendency of food chains to shorten or become blurred, by unfavorable physical factors, by space, by the fineness of possible subdivision of niches, and by those characters of the environmental mosaic which permit a greater diversity of small than of large allied species. (Hutchinson 1959)

The key premise here is the role of competition and the persistence of a particular species in a space. The classic experiment demonstrating this concept was carried out by Connell (1961) using barnacles, which showed that the distribution of a species was constrained by a combination of physical factors (dessication), competition (presence of other barnacle species), and predation (sea stars).

Hubbell (1979) challenged the above niche view with his proposal for a "Neutral Theory," which proposes that patterns of diversity can be explained by treating similar species (for example, all tree species) as being demographically the same – e.g. that the only driver of population dynamics is random variation in births, deaths, and dispersal. These stochastic demographic processes, and random extinction, dominate in shaping the diversity of the community – which tends to decline over time unless speciation rates balance extinctions. This theory overemphasizes species similarities, rather than differences, as explaining the high diversity of many natural communities. It builds on the assumption that species are identical in their fitness and in their effects on one another. Much of ecology is built on the assumption that species differ in niches (Adler, HilleRisLambers and Levine 2007:95) but few studies have quantified the importance of niches for maintaining the diversity we observe in natural communities (Silvertown 2004). In fact, niche and neutral theories focus on complementary processes that control community dynamics, and each theory complements the other. Neutral theory "can help refine the niche paradigm by focusing our attention on fitness equivalence and emphasizing that in many natural communities niche differences may be more subtle than traditionally expected yet still generate stable coexistence" (Adler, HilleRisLambers and Levine 2007:103).

Top-down vs. Bottom-up Control in Ecosystems

Ecosystems are structured by flows of energy and by how much of the primary productivity cascades across the trophic chains. The key debate here is whether ecosystems are controlled by predators keeping herbivore populations low, allowing plants to flourish, or whether plant productivity itself and chemical defenses limited herbivore abundance (Terborgh et al. 2001). Of course, it turns out that it is a little of both (McQueen et al. 1989). In intact communities, predators are really important – which we know because they are the first to be lost after almost any perturbation (Peterson 1999) but especially where fragmentation occurs (e.g. Terborgh 2001; Feeley and Terborgh 2008 based on his Lago Guri studies), and their loss has been observed to trigger a wave of other ecosystem changes. The loss of large seed dispersers to fragmentation of forest and the impact of hunting can also significantly impact plant regeneration in tropical forests (Terborgh et al. 2008).

This is a critical debate, and one in which social scientists and biological conservationists tend to fall in opposite camps. The debate goes back to a paper by Redford (1992) in which he warned of likely changes that would take place in an "empty forest" wherein animals had been removed by hunters (particularly in areas where bushmeat is an important source of income). "Animals pollinate flowers, disperse seeds, consume seeds, and eat the foliage of seedlings and established plants ... recent research has demonstrated that tropical forests depleted of large vertebrates experience reduced dispersal, altered patterns of tree recruitment, shifts in the relative abundance of species, and various types of functional compensation" (Terborgh et al. 2008:1757). The key insight here is that even a few hunters per square kilometer can decimate a population of large-bodied vertebrates (Peres and Dolman 2000) and thus bring about major changes in vegetation. This pits conservation ecologists against those social scientists who view hunting as a fundamental subsistence strategy of forest peoples. Social scientists need to understand these findings and engage with conservation ecologists in thinking through how to balance the needs of the human populations with those of maintaining the structure and function of the ecosystem.

Herbivore populations explode in the absence of predators, but this is but a transient phenomenon. In due time, the species composition of the vegetation adjusts and imposes regulation from the bottom up (Terborgh et al. 2001:1925). Adding predators, as when predatory fish are introduced to a lake, can also have dramatic effects (Carpenter et al. 1985), having cascading trophic interactions and impacting lake productivity. More importantly, once top predators are gone herbivores may be controlled only by lack of food – changing the direction of control of ecosystem composition. The spatial distribution of hunters in a forest ecosystem, for example, is not even but very patchy, as they seek to maximize returns for their hunting effort. Thus, hunting impact may be severe in one place for a brief time, but be widely dispersed, permitting the fauna to recover and to return to places where they were "hunted out." This may depend on whether we are speaking of small nomadic hunting bands, or of settled hunters who follow logging roads to supply the construction workers with bushmeat. The impact of hunting on the forest fauna will be quite different in each of these two situations. Is the forest really empty, or is this an artifact of sampling? Sampling larger vertebrates is a particularly difficult activity, given that so many are either nocturnal or arboreal in tropical forests, and hard to count.

Succession

The idea that some organisms are good colonizers, that they are later replaced by other species that are good competitors (e.g. can grow in their own shade, or are more efficient at gathering nutrients), and that in a given place this follows a fairly predictable pattern is the fundamental idea of succession. Odum (1969) in his "strategy of ecosystem development," and Vitousek and Reiners (1975) in their "ecosystem succession and nutrient retention" explored these ideas that build on the classic work by Clements (1916), who provided a historical description of succession research.

Succession refers to the tendency of plant communities to change through time in a somewhat predictable pattern (Luken 1990). Plant communities everywhere change as they age. This involves replacement of individuals and species, shifts in population structure, and changes in light and soil nutrients. Beyond that, there are many views of how succession proceeds, as can be noted in Figure 3.1 (based on Luken 1990:4). The view of Clements starts with a patch of bare soil which is then colonized by seeds inherent or

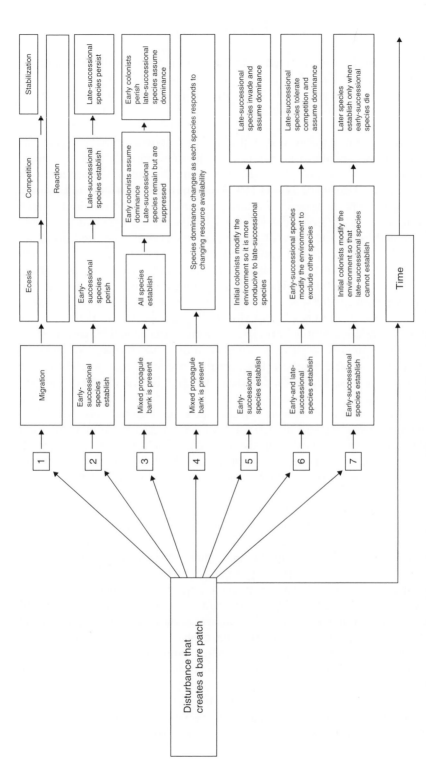

Figure 3.1 Theories proposed to account for successional dynamics, following disturbance
Source: Luken 1990:4

migrating to the patch, which establish themselves, or not, depending on available nutrients and light; as they grow these plants engage in competition with other plants with some becoming winners and others being removed, and eventually stabilizing to some degree over time as dominant species monopolize the space. Such "relay floristics" is now viewed as a poor description of the process. Egler (1954) proposed "initial floristics" as an alternative, emphasizing the role of the presence or absence of propagules (seeds or sprouts) of a given species in the patch at the beginning of the sequence. Drury and Nisbet (1973) emphasized the sorting out process along a gradient of resources because each individual species has a unique optimum for growth or reproduction. Pickett (1976, 1982) added the role of competition to the views of Drury and Nisbet and supported his views with a 20-year record of succession established in permanent plots. Connell and Slatyer proposed three distinct models of succession (1977): facilitation, tolerance, and inhibition. The facilitation model seems to work mostly in cases where one plant species greatly improves the nutrient status of a soil, as when nitrogen-fixing plants colonize nutrient poor glacial till or river sand. The tolerance model proposes that late successional species must be able to tolerate low resource availability in order to emerge as dominants. Pickett, Collins, and Armesto (1987) further developed a comprehensive list of causes, processes, and modifying factors implicated in succession (see Figure 3.2).

In disturbed and fragmented areas, early successional species tend to dominate at the expense of later successional species. Since they are good colonizers, early successional species may also be better able to keep up with climate change via migration – and facilitate the migration and adaptation of late successional species. How this plays out in a rapidly changing environment remains to be seen and is hard to predict, given the individualistic species argument presented earlier.

During the past ten millennia or so, people have cut and burned vegetation, have cultivated the soil, and put livestock on it favoring grassy vegetation. In so doing, they have managed plant communities in order to benefit from these activities, while continuing to exploit forests and other later successional communities. This anthropogenic impact on the successional pathways further adds complexity to the natural successional processes discussed above. Human impacts, too, ebb and flow as they more or less intensively manage the land, intensively cultivating it for sometimes hundreds of years, only to abandon areas due to soil impoverishment, war, migration, and any number of other drivers that change human priorities over given patches of land.

Thinking more broadly, this has implied some degree of forest transition over time. Secondary successional forest regrowth and planted forests can account for significant amounts of carbon sequestration that offset at least

General causes	Contributing processes	Modifying factors
Site availability	Disturbance	Size, severity, time, dispersion
Species availability	Dispersal	Landscape configuration, dispersal agents
	Propagules	Land use, Time since last disturbance
	Resources	Soil, topography, site history
Species performance	Ecophysiology	Germination requirements, Assimilation rates, Growth rates, Genetic differentiation
	Life history	Allocation, Reproductive timing and mode
	Stress	Climate, site history, Prior occupants
	Competition	Competition, herbivory, resource availability
	Allelopathy	Soil chemistry, microbes, Neighboring species
	Herbivory	Climate, predators, Plant defenses and vigor, Community patchiness

Figure 3.2 General causes of succession and contributing processes and modifying factors
Source: Pickett, Collins, and Armesto 1987 as found in Luken 1990:6

part of the emissions from clear cutting and selective logging of forests (Nilsson and Schopfhauser 1995). The conditions under which a region transitions from a phase of deforestation to one of reforestation is largely an untapped research frontier. One exception has been the formulation in recent years of Forest Transition Theory (Rudel 1998; Rudel et al. 2005). Scientific discourse and policy analysis are impacted by the unwarranted assumption that the dynamics of deforestation and restoration are the same. It is reasonable to hypothesize that as deforestation slows down and is replaced by an increased rate of forest restoration, there are shifts in civil society and government regulations that facilitate the transition from deforestation to restoration. Such a behavioral change is a process affected by both local-level actors and state and federal agents of change.

In a number of recent publications, Rudel et al. (e.g. 2005:23–31) have alluded to the experiences of many countries that seem to undergo a

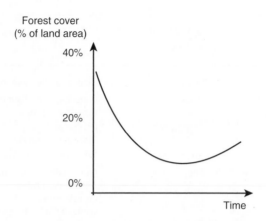

Figure 3.3   Diagram illustrating Forest Transition Theory, in which forest area is steadily reduced over time, and at some point along the time trajectory reforestation begins to increase above the rate of deforestation, resulting in a restoration of forest cover

forest transition from a period of high deforestation to a period of declining rates, and some eventually to reforestation. This transition occurs in many cases, but the turnaround from deforestation to restoration takes place at very different temporal and spatial scales – and in some notable cases not at all. It took place in northern Europe between 1850 and 1980, but it does not appear to have happened in southern Europe. Further research is needed to understand the dynamics of social and environmental systems to have a better sense of what social and environmental feedbacks may come into play at different stages of this potential transition. In some places this dynamic seems to be associated with the creation of nonfarm employment that pulls farmers off the land (Polanyi 1944; Mather 1992), thereby inducing spontaneous recovery of forests on old and abandoned fields. In other places, scarcity of forest products has prompted restoration efforts by both government and private owners (Foster and Rosenzweig 2003).

Figure 3.3 illustrates a schematic model of the forest transition (dark line). The curve can diverge along various courses at the trough (forest going toward zero, staying flat, or increasing) as well as along the reforestation route (with declining rates in reforestation, flattening out at some percentage of forest cover, or increasing steadily). This transition occurs at various scales from individual property to counties, states, and nations. Rudel et al. (2005) examined these processes at national scale using data from the Food and Agricultural Organization (FAO) of the United Nations, and it is at this level that forest transition theory has been mostly proposed and tested.

While national and global datasets offer the benefit of broader spatial scale, they are often marred by inconsistencies in the quality of data reported and different definitions of what constitutes forest. To better understand the dynamics of land-cover change, it may be useful to focus on states within countries for which there is high-quality data and that permit more detailed examination of both social and environmental processes. The transition is not trivial in its environmental consequences (i.e. carbon sequestration, biodiversity; Foley et al. 2005). During the 1990s, 38% of the world's countries experienced increases in forest cover, but the turnaround has come at very different points in their deforestation trajectory. Some countries have started a reforestation phase at 40% of the original forest cover, while others began only when forest cover was nearly 0%. The difference of when the transition takes place has huge implications for the biodiversity of forests that grow back. Rudel et al. (2005:27) note there are very different dynamics characterizing northern European transition in the twentieth century and what has been happening in Asia in the past 15 years. The role of government in parts of Asia, in response to scarcity of forest products and increased floods, is much greater and has resulted in aggressive reforestation campaigns. In China, this effort was centrally organized (Zhang et al. 2000; Fang and Wang 2001), while in India it seems that village committees increased the forest cover in decentralized fashion (Singh 2002; Foster and Rosenzweig 2003).

Island Biogeography

Island biogeography is one of the most influential theories in biology and has been the focus of considerable theoretical and experimental efforts (MacArthur and Wilson 1967; Simberloff and Wilson 1969). The basic concept is that the number of species an island has is a function of its size (a proxy for resources) and its distance from a mainland source of immigrants. It seems to apply well to islands on the ocean separated by good distances from other islands, and from continents, but there are serious questions about how well it applies when it is used conceptually to treat habitat "islands" within large land masses (e.g. Ferraz et al. 2007) since the required isolation is not as great as imagined by those who attempted to apply it to the study of, for example, Amazonian forest fragments.

Edge effects can have crucial consequences on forest dynamics (Laurance et al. 2006) by reducing significantly the size of the patch which is non-edge, and by the difficulty of maintaining isolation between patches in a continental land mass due to the rapidly changing vegetation composition, successional dynamics, and competition that result in connectivity and corridors between patches. Bailey (2007) addresses the issue of fragmentation vs. total habitat loss and the impact of corridors in maintaining biodiversity. The author proposes that the goal should not be biodiversity per se but rather the sustainability of the woodland community, and that, in doing so, the biodiversity objective takes care of itself, but not the other way around.

Although landscapes are affected by human decisions at many levels of society, the physical processes that produce landscape change (e.g. clear-cutting, grazing, home construction) most often involve communities and individuals. The decisions of individuals acting either individually or collectively are impacted by local ecology, but they also determine the local ecology. Human actors have the ability to choose among patterns of land use that have similar social and economic characteristics, but which may have very different ecological impacts.

From the landscape perspective, a major result of community and individual land-use decisions is that natural or seminatural habitats no longer exist in large patches, but now are reduced to fragments. The decreasing size of natural patches creates a situation in which the ratio of area on the edge of the patch (and consequently exposed to areas with different characteristics) to the area in the center of the patch is substantially higher than prior to human impact. As a result, greater area is at increased risk of invasion by nearby livestock, hunters and gatherers who would find it difficult or inconvenient to travel to the center of a larger patch, and so on. Because of increased disturbance at the edges, small patches lose more species than their small size alone would suggest. Edge areas also are at increased risk of accidental fire, are at increased risk of invasion by nonnative plant species, are more accessible to predators from surrounding habitat patches, and experience more damage from wind than interior areas. Changes in temperature, humidity, and light along patch edges can further change the characteristics of a small patch and alter the plant communities and animals that depend on them (Schelhas and Greenberg 1996; Laurance and Bierregaard 1997; Bierregaard et al. 2001).

Connectivity, the capacity of a landscape to support movement by any given species across the landscape, is of increasing concern for conservation biologists (Meffe and Carroll 1997). As the connectivity of a landscape increases from the human perspective (generally through increases in road networks), connectivity decreases for many other species (With and King 1999). Although we may see many species of animals moving across human landscapes (e.g. deer, wolves, and turtles crossing roads or wandering through our backyards), landscapes substantially altered for human use act as barriers to movement of both animal and plant species. In some cases these barriers are incomplete – many turtles die on roads, but some make it across. In other cases, passage is essentially impossible – cities along landscape corridors such as river valleys can effectively eliminate genetic exchange between previously connected plant and animal populations;

dams can permanently halt spawning of fish by blocking travel to their breeding grounds. Thus, edge effects and lack of connectivity can decrease the conservation value of remaining habitat below what its mapped area might suggest, increasing the impact of fragmentation (Debinski and Holt 2000).

Equilibrium and Nonequilibrium Theories

The use of the ecosystem concept was criticized in the 1980s for what appeared to be an overemphasis on equilibrium. From this period has emerged a new paradigm that, as Zimmerer has said, is characterized by its emphasis on disequilibria, instability, and even chaotic fluctuations (1994). This is an important shift in thinking that has been challenging for social scientists to incorporate, as they may have limited interactions with ecologists who have embraced this more dynamic approach to system complexity, competition, coexistence, and community composition. Holling (1973) was among the first to suggest that natural systems are continually in a transient state and that attention had to be focused on how they persisted (and, later, on characteristics such as resilience that contributed to persistence). Later, Wiens (1977) found that notions of equilibrium did not seem to fit the empirical realities in arid and semiarid environments, particularly the responses of avian communities to environmental variation (cf. Wiens 1984). He proposed that natural communities existed along a continuum – from equilibrium to nonequilibrium states. The former would be found where there was low to moderate variation, whereas the latter would be found where conditions were harsher and more unpredictable (Wiens 1977). Ellis and Swift (1988; Ellis, Caughenour, and Swift 1993) went on to identify a number of rangelands which could best be characterized as nonequilibrial but persistent systems, particularly in areas where the coefficient of variance for rainfall exceeded 30 percent.

Recent studies have gone further and questioned where equilibrium may exist at all (Berkes, Colding and Folke 2003; McCabe 2004). They suggest that thinking of coupled social–ecological systems better fits with what we find in resource and environmental management where uncertainty, unpredictability, and scalar issues dominate – further complexified by considerations of politics, economics, and so on. This is not to say that equilibria do not exist, and some suggest that systems may organize around a number of equilibria or stable states (Berkes, Colding, and Folke 2003; Gunderson and Holling 2002). This is a more complex view of the early proposals of Holling, wherein systems are dynamic, adaptive, and responsive to changing conditions, but may shift in states to maintain resilience.

Biodiversity and Ecosystem Processes/Services

This issue can drive a wedge between conservation ecologists and social scientists over their different emphasis on environment or people. Biodiversity as a priority of biologists can be controversial. It is generally thought that higher biodiversity equals higher productivity and greater ecosystem stability at least at local scales (Loreau et al. 2001). This alone gives it a hallowed place in biologists' priorities. Much more work is needed to establish how true this may be, or not, at larger scales. "There is consensus that at least some minimum number of species is essential for ecosystem functioning under constant conditions and that a larger number of species is probably essential for maintaining the stability of ecosystems processes in changing environments" (Loreau et al. 2001). However, it is still an open question whether it is diversity per se, or the presence of particular species performing particular functions, that brings this about.

What social scientists working with conservation ecologists and biologists need to understand is that there are many reasons, among them aesthetic, cultural, and economic (and not just biological), for why we may wish to conserve biodiversity. From a functional perspective, species matter insofar as their individual traits and interactions contribute to maintain the functions and stability of ecosystems and the biogeochemical cycles that sustain them. Yet, we are still only in the earliest stages of understanding the role of particular species in an ecosystem, and to be able to predict ecosystem responses to the removal or absence of a given species. Some biologists have proposed the concept of "keystone species" – a species that has a disproportionate effect on the structure of its community – as a way of addressing this need, but there is a paucity of empirical evidence definitely defining what is a keystone species, and what is not (cf. Paine 1969 first defined the concept of keystone species). Often, the "keystone" qualities of a species only become clear after it is removed from the ecosystem – for instance, the near-extinction of sea otters led to destabilization of the Pacific kelp forests. Thus, it is virtually impossible to know what a keystone species is until the system has been stressed by, say, removal of a major predator.

Less controversial, but still a source of some misunderstandings, is the value given by biologists to ecosystem goods and services. There are numerous efforts to quantify the value of ecosystem goods and services, perhaps most importantly in terms of clean air and clean water, and its role in carbon sequestration (Daly and Cobb 1994). Economists seem to have less of a problem, in part because ecologists adopted an economic terminology of goods and services for what are fundamentally natural resources in an effort to have value assigned to them, rather than being viewed as free goods and thus subject to the "tragedy of the commons." However, cultural anthropologists and others with a more humanistic perspective sometimes balk at the idea that air, water, and carbon can or should be quantified in monetary terms. This is not a very serious problem, and in modeling ecosystems today, it is fundamental to seek to assign value to every component and to revisit these values as our scientific understanding gives us a better way to calibrate these values. It is also important to note, and to remind conservation ecologists and biologists, that surprising findings in recent years from the human–environment interactions community suggest that people tend to conserve forests on private properties motivated more by aesthetic and moral values than by economic ones (Koontz 1997; Moran and Ostrom 2005; Moran et al. in preparation) –and that most government programs are not effective in making individuals conserve forests.

The Ecosystem Concept in Biology and the Social Sciences[2]

The ecological system, or *ecosystem*, has been one of the most enduring approaches coming from the biological sciences but one with which many social scientists have not grown up. This fundamental unit is a heuristic tool used to describe the interaction between living and nonliving components of a given habitat. It has been noted that both terrestrial and aquatic ecosystems show remarkable similarities in how they respond to stress: reduced biodiversity, altered primary and secondary productivity, increased disease prevalence, reduced efficiency of nutrient cycling, increased dominance of exotic species, and increased presence of smaller, shorter-lived opportunistic species (Rapport and Whitford 1999).

Although references to the interdependence of biological organisms can be found throughout most of the nineteenth century, the ecosystem concept was not actually articulated until 1935 when A. G. Tansley proposed it in an effort to emphasize the dynamic aspects of populations and communities. An ecosystem includes "all the organisms in a given area, interacting with the physical environment, so that a flow of energy leads to a clearly defined trophic structure, biotic diversity and material cycles" (Odum 1971:8; see also the detailed examination by Golley 1984 of the concept as used in biology).

Ecosystems are said to be self-maintained and self-regulating, an assumption that has affected ecosystem studies and that has also been questioned by both biologists and anthropologists. The concept of homeostasis, which in the past has been defined as the tendency for biological systems to resist change and to remain in a state of equilibrium (Odum 1971:34), led to an overemphasis on static considerations and to an evaluation of man's role as basically disruptive.

---

[2]   This section is based on earlier discussions found in Moran 2007.

More recent ecosystem studies have emphasized, instead, the emergent properties of complex systems as characteristic of ecosystems (Levin 1998).

The cybernetic quality of ecosystems leads naturally to the use of systems analysis. Systems analysis has become a useful approach since it begins with a holistic model of the components and interrelations of an ecosystem. However, it then proceeds to simplify these complex interactions so that it can quantitatively study the behavior of both the whole and particular parts of an ecological system (Odum 1971:276–92). Systems theory provides a broad framework for analyzing empirical reality and for cutting across disciplinary boundaries. By way of limitation, system approaches still have to rely on other theories and have to develop measurements based on criteria other than those suggested by the system itself. Essentially, systems theory is a perspective that bears a great deal of similarity to holism: a system is an integral whole and no part can be understood apart from the entire system. At first, studies focused on closed systems, understood through the negative feedbacks that maintained functional equilibrium. Later system analyses dealt with open systems reflecting positive feedback, nonlinear oscillating phenomena, and the purposive behavior of human actors. Such purposiveness is unevenly and differentially distributed, leading to conflict over goals and to system behavior reflecting the internal distribution of power. Stochastic approaches are now more common using dynamic modeling approaches such as STELLA (Constanza et al. 1993) and intelligent agent-based models such as SWARM and SUGARSCAPE (Epstein and Axtell 1996; Grimm et al. 2006; Walker Perez-Barberia, and Marion 2006; Parker et al. 2003). The former is an ecosystem-type model, whereas the latter is of a new class of models that simulate "intelligent agent's behavior" based upon principles of artificial intelligence (cf. Deadman 1999 and Deadman et al. 2004; LeBars et al. 2005; Macy and Willer 2002; Parker et al. 2008). The study of complex adaptive systems recognizes the nonlinear nature of systems and assumes that the complexity associated with a system is simply an emergent phenomenon of the local interactions of the parts of the system (DeAngelis and Gross 1992; Openshaw 1994, 1995; Epstein and Axtell 1996; Langton 1997).

The ecosystem concept presented a conceptual framework more satisfactory to some scientists than many previous theories in that it provided a single setting within which both natural and social processes took place. Unlike cultural ecology (Steward 1955), it did not put culture first and ecology in second place, nor did it give primacy to the social organization for utilizing resources as the necessary most central research task. Ecosystems are said to be scaled to the needs of the researcher and can, thus, be defined as anything from a tiny pond to the entire biosphere.

The use of the ecosystem concept in the social sciences is associated with the work of Andrew Vayda and Roy Rappaport (1976) who gave the strongest impetus to an ecosystem approach in the field of anthropology and to its use under the International Biological Program's Human Adaptability research agenda (Moran 1979). The assumption made was that, given that humans are but one species in nature, subject to the same laws as other species, use of the principles, methods, and analytical tools of the ecological sciences would greatly add to our understanding of our own species. Vayda and Rappaport believed that anthropologists should not hesitate to adopt biological units (such as population, community, and ecosystem) as units of study since this allows a more comprehensive approach to ecological studies. Even the topics of research can be couched in terms that make sense across both disciplines. Vayda and Rappaport pointed out that ecologists have shared various areas of interest with anthropology: ways of defining territorial rights, ways of establishing group identity, and mechanisms for establishing buffer zones. All these can be viewed "ecologically" as regulating behavior or serving a homeostatic function. This view has been roundly criticized because it sounds like a group selection argument. To test ecological hypotheses properly, a wealth of information is required, and no single researcher can expect to succeed in gathering it all – and it is no surprise that their own experience of fieldwork in Papua New Guinea as part of a large interdisciplinary team studying war in that region led them to see the value of the ecosystem as an integrator of work across ecology, geography, and anthropology (Vayda and Rappaport 1976:23).

Vayda's study of how warfare in New Guinea was related to population fluctuations, changes in man/resource ratios, and the competition of different highland clans for gardens and pigs is a notable example of the ecosystem approach (Vayda 1974, 1976). Rappaport, working in the same region, was more concerned with how ritual serves to regulate: (l) the size of the pig herd; (2) the frequency of warfare; (3) the availability of horticultural land within reasonable walking distance of the village; (4) the length of the fallow cycle; and (5) the military strength and alliances of a tribe and the likelihood that it will hold onto its territory. Rappaport is not really concerned with the individual decisions of the Tsembaga Maring as they see their pig herd increase to the point that they become a threat to the human ecological system. Rather, he finds that the system "senses" the increased burden of having too many pigs. When a system threshold is reached, the elders call for a ritual pig slaughter. The ritual reduces the number of pigs and facilitates the creation of alliances between neighboring groups. Warfare follows, and its occurrence serves to distribute the population over the landscape and to return the system to "initial conditions" or a state of equilibrium.

Bennett criticized Rappaport's approach for its use of biological analogies, but concedes that Rappaport's study is important "as a concrete demonstration of the fact that the behavior of men toward each other, as well as toward Nature, is part of ecosystems" (1976:182). The major difference between Rappaport and Bennett lies in the former's emphasis on the fact that the systemic nature of the feedback loops can be found in culturally patterned behavior, such as the ritual warfare complex. Bennett agrees that such patterned behavior may indeed be pervasive in technologically simple cultures. However, he argues that if this fact is always taken as a "given," the role of individual decision making can be overlooked. Such decision making, he feels, plays a greater role in the technologically complex cultures of our day. There are populations that are more "teleconnected" to the global economy than others, and thus influenced by distant events in their decision making. While there are hardly any populations in the world who are decoupled from the global economy, there are rural populations who still respond directly to the environmental signals around them, and adjust their behavior accordingly – whereas there are others who take no action without consulting the prices in commodity markets. Today human decisions about the use of the environment are predicated increasingly on institutional and technological considerations.

Bennett found the distinction between cultural ecology and the ecosystem approach artificial. The choice of one approach over the other depended for him on the size and complexity of the group under study. Among small tribes with primitive technologies, the ecosystem approach can be employed since much of the human/environment interactions in such tribes are embedded in cultural traditions (Rappaport 1968). On the other hand, in larger, complex, and technologically advanced cultures, institutions and technology have created a distance between the population and its environment. Studies of modern societies must investigate these institutions and the processes of decisions that affect nature and humans. In these contexts, Bennett argues, the ecosystem approach does not work well because it cannot research the dynamic processes of institutions and the conscious processes of choice among alternatives due to the complexity of the systems. A similar problem also affected cultural ecology (see Chapter 2) which applied well to studies of populations like hunter-gatherers who organized in distinct ways to exploit the behavioral characteristic of game and plants growing in their environment in the wild – but was not applicable to the political economy of sugar in the Caribbean – one of the earliest examples of a global industry driven by commodity price fluctuations. This was one of the leading reasons for the move away from an ecosystem approach in the 1980s when actor-based approaches became dominant. However, the development in the late 1990s and early 2000s of agent-based modeling now permits the analysis of complex systems and the behavior of individual agents in spatially explicit landscapes (Deadman 1999; Evans and Kelley 2004, 2008; Parker et al. 2003; Deadman et al. 2004; among others), without having to abandon the concept of the ecosystem.

An important issue raised by Rappaport's study (1968) is the utility of the concept of homeostasis. As used by Rappaport, the concept was equivalent to equilibrium. In equilibrium models, attention is paid to how cultural practices help maintain human populations in a stable relationship with their environment. This view is the prototype of neofunctionalism and it has its drawbacks. It views the current state of the system as the norm and over-emphasizes the functions of negative feedback to the neglect of the dynamics of change accelerated by positive feedback. This viewpoint tends to preclude the possibility that behaviors might be maladaptive – which they surely are in certain situations (Alland 1975; Eder 1987).

Adaptation to environment is, however, not a simple matter of negative feedback. System correction through negative feedback operates most effec-tively at lower levels in a system. Higher levels operate at a more general level wherein ambiguity and vagueness permit constant reinterpretation and restructuring of system properties as responses to perturbations. Homeostasis and dynamic equilibrium do not imply changelessness. On the contrary, they require constant adjustment of system parts and even some change in struc-ture (in response to perturbations) (Rappaport 1977:69). In other words, while systems have lower order mechanisms geared to the maintenance of stabil-ity, they also have higher level, less specialized responses that can reorder the system to assure its survival. Although group selection was largely rejected under the logic of kin selection and reciprocal altruism, there has been a resurgence in studies of biological evolution in theories that consider and find a place for group selection (Wilson 1980, 1983; Sober and Wilson 1998).

A number of problems must be recognized in how the ecosystem concept was used: a tendency to reify the ecosystem and to give it properties of a biological organism; an overemphasis on energetic flows and measurement of calories; a tendency for models to ignore time and structural change (and to overemphasize homeostasis); a tendency to neglect the role of the indi-vidual; a lack of clear criteria for defining boundaries of systems; and level shifting between field study and analysis of data (see review in Moran 1990 of these problems). Problems of reification have been addressed by an emphasis on how individuals modify the environment and not simply adapt to a reified nature (Boster 1983; Crumley 1994; Balée 1998). Today, few scholars would suggest that measurement of energy flow ought to be a cen-tral concern of ecosystem studies. Concerns have shifted to nutrient cycling, decision making, complexity in systems, and loss of biodiversity (Jordan 1987; National Science Board 1989; Levin 1998; NRC 1999a; Lansing 2003). The role of individuals and households has also blossomed (Lees and Bates 1990; Wilk 1990; Rindfuss et al. 2003; Chowdhury and Turner 2006). How to bound one's research is one of the most persistent challenges to researchers, but more sophisticated approaches have been proposed, such as historically variant "graded boundaries" (Ellen 1990; Allen 1988).

No one should expect the ecosystem perspective to resolve the challenge posed by linking the natural and the social dimensions of environmental change. Close cooperation will be required between biological and behavioral scientists to generate an integrated study of people in ecosystems (cf. Moran and Ostrom 2005). In the future, studies are likely to be most fruitful when they integrate the general systems approach, such as the ecosystem approach, with the study of how actors develop their own individual strategies. There is no reason why both perspectives cannot be used, and there is evidence that researchers have already begun to balance a concern for the individual with a concern for the population. One way to overcome the tendency towards static equilibrium models might be to study how populations adapt to certain kinds of stress. By studying the response of individuals to hazards, we can answer such questions as: Who responds? Does stress lead to changes in the structuring of the population? Are cultural patterns changed? How do people perceive the severity of the stress to which they are responding? How does the human population adjust to termination of the stress? These questions are more likely to be productive in outlining systemic interrelations in populations experiencing changing situations than in those with stable situations (cf. Lees and Bates 1990; and Vayda 1983; for an analysis using a nonhomeostatic perspective see McCabe 2004).

Related to the ecosystem concept are more recent views that highlight "landscape ecology", i.e. the study of patterns of land cover, their causes, and their implications (M. Turner et al. 2001). Land cover may refer to vegetation communities and other natural features, such as sand dunes, or to human communities and other human constructions, or, most usefully, to all of these. By considering the processes underlying these patterns, landscape ecology points to the importance of context in the study of human–environment relations. Whereas humans once existed in islands of homes, pastures, and fields set within forests and grasslands, the reverse is now often true. Forests and uncultivated grasslands exist as islands within urban, suburban, and agricultural landscapes. Yet these patterns do not occur universally, even within zones of largely similar biophysical endowments. The focus on the different processes that lead to different outcomes within similarly endowed areas, or that lead to similar outcomes in differently endowed areas, points our attention to the interactions between variables leading to land-cover change.

Initially, landscape ecologists tended to treat human communities and their roads, cattle, and other accessories as exogenous disturbances, and focused their efforts on understanding how biophysical processes shaped landscape patterns – for example, how underlying patterns in soil or topography affect the distribution of vegetation types. As social sciences have been incorporated into landscape ecology (NRC 1998a), human actions and processes have joined the list of factors that produce landscape patterns. In the development of the field of global change, the interacting impacts of human and biophysical processes on landscape patterns are at last being fully explored and modeled. It is critical that theories from the natural and biological sciences, and from the social sciences, be brought together to effect a more complete understanding of these complex systems. One way to bring them together is through use of spatially explicit methods that can fully utilize the empirical data and the theories from all the sciences, as we discuss in the next chapter.

4

Spatially Explicit Approaches

This chapter focuses on the growing recognition of the importance of making social sciences' and natural sciences' research spatially explicit if it is to be relevant to the understanding of our environmental conundrums. The use of geographic information systems (GIS), global positioning system (GPS), and remotely sensed data is covered with an emphasis on how to make space and place relevant parts of the analysis, its implications for sampling, and for explanation. While geography clearly leads in this area, there is growing use of these methods in anthropology, political science, and ecology.

Perhaps nothing has revolutionized the study of human–environment interactions more than the development of spatially explicit methods for collecting and analyzing data. Just a few decades ago, most natural and social scientists collected their data without precise spatial referents. References were made to watersheds, to communities, to villages, to cities, to proximity to rivers, and so on. In some cases (in anthropology mostly), there was even the custom of changing the name of the community and even its location, "to protect the informants." While confidentiality remains an important concern when working with human subjects, the extreme to which this was done was largely unjustified. Everyone knew more or less where these studied communities were, and any one interested could have found out. Be that as it may, there was very little interest, except in geography, to precisely locate a study area on a map with coordinates. Geography persisted (e.g. Haggett, Cliff, and Frey 1977), and finally convinced the rest of us, that *place* was fundamentally important to understand human–environment dynamics.

Other fields began to see relevant applications. Dow (1994) noted that geographical information could illuminate many features of culture that cannot be seen otherwise – something that archeologists had discovered earlier, particularly in dry environments where features stood out more clearly.

Figure 4.1 Researcher taking a GPS reading in the field, Brazilian Amazonia, and checking the location against a printed satellite image in hand
Source: ACT collection of photos from fieldwork

Conklin (1980) much earlier had used aerial photography to map the complex irrigation terraces in Ifugao at a level of detail that still is unsurpassed. The danger then, as now, is that the technology of GIS will take on a life of its own and distract from fieldwork and from the fundamental questions that should be asked. This danger is even present in geography, where it was necessary to distinguish between GIS and GIScience to emphasize in the latter case that the goals are scientific propositions and not just map-making.

What do we mean by spatially explicit research? (For extended discussions see Goodchild et al. 2000; Goodchild, Fu, and Rich 2007.) The most common usage is to have all the collected data georeferenced, that is, a precise location on a lat/long (latitude/longitude) or Universal Transverse Mercator (UTM) coordinate system is provided so that the information collected is place-based precisely. That means that if one conducts a household interview, the location of the interview, be it house or field, is located using a GPS (see Figure 4.1). If a soil or vegetation sample is taken, it is precisely located using a GPS. If observations of human behavior, urban forms, vegetation types, and what have you are made, they are registered in a spatially explicit way in the database. The advantages of doing this are many. It is later possible to return to the exact same location, without regard to how it might have changed, permitting very precise observation and measurement of how the place and the people have changed. Most researchers who have returned to a study area many times know how difficult it is to be sure of whether it was here, or way over there, where one observed something 15 years before. Most likely all the vegetation, or urban forms, would have changed. So, for the study of environmental change, whether local or global, it is essential that the data be recorded in a spatially explicit fashion.

GIS is an enabling technology that permits the integration of satellite remote sensing and other kinds of information. However, data on the human population and its socioeconomic characteristics have lagged behind physical data. The analysis of population, and the use of modeling, promises to resolve some of these problems, including residential patterns, industrial location requirements, and the connectedness between socioeconomic variables and physical features (Martin and Bracken 1993).

Economists, too, if in smaller numbers, are increasingly adopting spatial analytical and spatial econometric techniques to study questions such as the geographical targeting of policies, regional clustering, technology diffusion, and the causes and consequences of land-cover change (Muller 2005). It is now possible to import geographic data into Stata (a widely used statistical software), in order to draw systematic spatial samples and then export data and estimates in a form usable by standard GIS software.

Geographic information systems (GIS) appeared in the 1980s and brought the prospect of simplified management and analysis of spatial data and of its use as a scientific tool (Goodchild 1994). Spatial analysis can be defined as a set of methods whose results are not invariant under changes in the locations of the objects of analysis. The map of a cholera outbreak in London in the mid-nineteenth century provides the classic example of the power of the spatial perspective (see Koch and Denike 2004 for a discussion of the now famous Snow map, and Figure 4.2 here) and other cases of mapping disease. Despite the obvious abilities of the human eye to detect pattern, spatial intuition can be misleading, and false inference is all too common. Moreover the connections between behavioral processes and spatial pattern may be both tenuous and sensitive to boundary conditions.

Contemporary GIScience provides a more rigorous framework. The field and object views are distinguished, and their relative importance is evaluated in modeling spatial processes. The object view underlies much of human spatial cognition and is the focus of contemporary research on user interfaces

Figure 4.2   Classic map from Snow, illustrating the spatial location of cholera cases in London, one of the first published examples of the value of spatially explicit data used to identify the source of the polluted water pump accounting for most cholera cases
Source: Goodchild and Janelle 2004:7

for GIS, while the field view has value in coping with problems of statistical aggregation and modifiable areal units. Both are necessary and important, but contemporary software designs tend to support one to the exclusion of the other. Much of the attraction of GIS lies in its visual content, which many users see as replacing more rigorous mathematical and statistical analysis. This would be most unfortunate and remains a tension in the user and scientific community. GIS-based analysis can be much more rigorous and objective than the techniques of cartographic and a-spatial analysis that it replaces (Goodchild 1994).

Remote Sensing and GIS

It is hard to imagine being able to address many of the questions of the contemporary human dimensions of global environmental change without taking advantage of the availability of earth-orbiting satellites capable of providing time-series data on earth features such as soils, vegetation, moisture, urban sprawl, and water covered areas (Campbell 1987; Lillesand and Kiefer 1994; NRC 1998a, 2005a; Jensen 2005, 2007; McCoy 2005), and studying impacts of climatic variability on populations (Gutmann 2000; Galvin et al. 2001; Moran et al. 2006). There are, of course, some research questions for which these methods might not be appropriate. Since the launch in 1972 of Landsat 1, complemented later with improved sensors and spatial resolution (the latest being Landsat 7 launched successfully in 1999), of the French SPOT satellites with still better resolution, and most recently with a new generation of commercial satellites such as IKONOS with 1–5 meter resolution, the opportunities have grown steadily more useful for human–environment scientists.

The use of GIS to overlay data layers in spatially explicit ways added to this powerful set of techniques (Campbell and Sayer 2003; Goodchild 2003; Goodchild and Janelle 2004; Aronoff 2005; Okabe 2006; Steinberg and Steinberg 2006). GIS is now one of the fundamental and necessary tools in the environmental analysis toolkit, and is also widely used by environmental NGOs, urban planners, and scientists in the natural and social sciences (Evans, Munroe, and Parker 2005; Greene and Pick 2006; Hesse-Biber and Leavy 2006).

Remote sensing techniques have been of some interest among social scientists. For example, Conklin (1980) used aerial photography in his *Ethnographic Atlas of Ifugao*. He integrated ethnographic and ecological data to show land-use zones from the perspective of the local population (cf. review of aerial photo usage in anthropology in Lyons, Inglis, and Hitchcock 1972 and Vogt 1974). Attempts at using satellite remote sensing in anthropology started in the 1970s, with Reining (1973) using Landsat's MSS images to locate individual Mali villages on West Africa and Conant (1978) examining Pokot population distribution. However, it is only after the advancement in spatial resolution brought about in 1984 with the Landsat TM sensor that more researchers have turned to this tool (see Conant 1990 for an overview).

Analysis of land-use intensification is one of the most promising topics addressed by social scientists using remote sensing and GIS tools (Behrens 1990). In Nigeria, Guyer and Lambin (1993) used remote sensing combined with ethnographic research to study agricultural intensification, demonstrating the potential of remote sensing to address site-specific ethnographic issues within a larger land-use perspective. A special issue of *Human Ecology*, September 1994, was dedicated to the topic of regional analysis and land use in anthropology. There was substantial agreement among the articles about the importance of local-level research to inform land-use analysis at regional scale. This conclusion was reinforced in an issue of *Cultural Survival Quarterly* (1995) dedicated to showing the fruitful connection between local-level knowledge and remote sensing, GIS, and mapping tools. The growing interest and competence using remote sensing within the social sciences is found in *People and Pixels: Linking Remote Sensing and Social Science* (NRC 1998a).

A number of challenges are presented by the use of spatial data in analysis. Scale persists as a problem, even at the basic level of terminology (Green, Schweik, and Randolph 2005). In cartography the term "large scale" refers to detailed resolution, while for most other disciplines "large scale" refers to a large study area. Another basic problem is the interplay between absolute and relative scales which, consequently, results in confusion in modeling ecological processes. This challenge is being addressed by landscape ecology. It has become very attractive to scholars to use landscape ecological methods to better understand land-use dynamics. More importance has been given to refining spectral analysis to work at local level with more detailed requirements. In order for social scientists to continue to make distinct contributions to solving some of these challenges posed by multi-scalar research on global change, it is important to develop research methods that are explicitly multi-scale and capable of nesting data and sampling strategy in such a way that scaling up or down is feasible and integral to the research strategy (see part 3 in Moran and Ostrom 2005:127–214, for a discussion of methods linking remote sensing, GIS, and social science; also NRC 1998a).

To make use of these techniques requires considerable training and familiarity with the technical requirements of different sensors, sources of variability, and whether comparison is of one area across time, or of several areas at one point of time. The representation of space and time in a GIS is also nontrivial in its complexity. Evans, VanWey, and Moran (2005) provide a detailed and user-friendly introduction to the handling of spatially explicit data. One of the key decisions in spatially explicit analysis is whether to use raster or vector data (Bolstad 2002 and Lo and Yeung 2002, cited in Evans, VanWey, and Moran 2005). Raster data are more suitable to certain kinds of modeling such as cellular automata and agent-based modeling because raster data structures simplify the process of integrating and overlaying datasets.

Orford, Harris, and Dorling (1999) review scientific visualization in the social sciences and discusses the extent to which four key visualization technologies – the World Wide Web, multimedia, virtual reality, and computer graphics – are prevalent in the different social sciences. The review includes examples taken from political science, psychology, social statistics, economics, and geography. It concludes that visualization research in the social sciences is relatively uncoordinated with no central core. It tends to be dominated by those subjects with the closest links to the natural sciences, with a clear pattern of diffusion from scientific to social scientific research. It is precisely for this reason that Goodchild and others created a Center for Spatially Integrated Social Science at the University of California at Santa Barbara (CSISS) and synthesized some of the work of the center in a single volume (Goodchild and Janelle 2004).

There are several reasons why space matters and why we stand to gain insights and solve problems if we pay close attention to spatial processes. Spatial analysis examines data in cross-section, at given time intervals, rather than continuously over time. When cross-sectional data are put in tables, there is a loss of information about spatial context. When the same data are represented in a map, the spatial relationships become evident and lead to sudden insights, such as one immediately notices in the classic map made by Dr. John Snow displaying the incidence of cholera in London in 1854 (see Figure 4.2). The contaminated water pump jumps out when the data are spatially displayed. Spatial analysis is an excellent exploratory technique and one that can result in provocative and testable hypotheses.

GIS has considerable value for historians and others in the humanities and social sciences. In one interesting application of these techniques, an environmental historian used GIS in a case study of the Kickapoo Valley in Wisconsin to examine social and ecological processes of rural transformation during the twentieth century, and how these processes have shaped modern property rights debates (Heasley 2003). Spatial analysis provided an important picture of landscape dynamics and land ownership in the valley since the 1930s. Together with historical methods, GIS mapping helped explore the ways in which residents had constructed their own stories about property and the environment. These cultural narratives included the economic inevitability of land concentration and fragmentation, ethnic differences in land use, the struggle of local places vs. the federal government, and of local communities vs. newer outsiders. Results illustrated that change on the ground over many decades – rather than any inherent ideological resistance to federal policies – better explained contemporary debates over private and public property (Heasley 2003).

The incorporation of landscape ecological and fragmentation analyses within remote sensing and GIScience has expanded the inferential capabilities of such research (Nagendra, Munroe, and Southworth 2004). Researchers have sought to link spatial pattern to land-use process by integrating GIS, socioeconomic, and remote sensing techniques with landscape ecological approaches. A diversity of methods is necessary to evaluate the complex linkages between pattern and process in landscapes across the world – particularly around the interface of agricultural and urban land, agriculture and forestry, and other pertinent topics dealing with environmental policy and management.

An example of just such an approach is a paper exploring how well the application of Amazonian forest change models applies to the Guinea savanna environment of western Africa (Nyerges and Green 2000). In particular, the authors examine recent research documenting the growth of peri-village forest islands in the area of Kissidougou, Guinea, which purports to challenge the pervasive view of Guinea savanna deforestation brought about by human activity. As a more systematic approach to the analysis of human–environmental interactions, Nyerges and Green (2000) propose an "ethnography of landscape," in which the findings of detailed, local ethnographic and ecological case studies are combined with remotely sensed information on what the wider region looks like as it changes over time. In pursuing this research, we employ aerial photography and GIS techniques to examine the study area of Kilimi in northwestern Sierra Leone. They show that a Kissidougou-type model of peri-village forest island growth is not applicable to this region, where other environmental change processes are underway.

The forest composition we witness today anywhere on the planet is a product of temporal anthropogenic and nonanthropogenic transformations (Schweik 2000). Scholars from geography, anthropology, and other disciplines have long been aware of the value of paying attention to spatial relationships: human actions in the past leave imprints in today's landscape. Traditional empirical studies of forest conditions typically ignored this type of information and relied, instead, on aggregated forest-level indicators developed from a-spatial plot-level analyses. Schweik (2000) conducted a spatial analysis of one important forest product species, *Shorea robusta,* in a foraging setting in southern Nepal. Forest plots were located using Differential Global Positioning Systems (DGPS) and were processed using a GIS. Three rival hypotheses of the geographic distribution of *Shorea robusta* were evaluated: (1) a pattern of no human disturbance; (2) a pattern of open access and optimal foraging; and (3) a pattern of optimal foraging altered by the geographic configuration of enforced institutions. Multivariate regression models and optimal foraging patterns were used. Statistical tests lent support to the third hypothesis. The author finds the use of spatial analytical approaches, together with statistical methods, as particularly useful to better understand the geographic implications of institutional design on human behavior and the environmental outcomes that result (Schweik 2000).

A Case Study Using GIS/Remote Sensing to Study Amazonian Deforestation

The Amazon region experienced deforestation prior to 1975, but on a small scale. The population collapse of indigenous communities through war and disease following European discovery resulted in a pattern of small communities practicing shifting cultivation and moving their settlements frequently (Meggers 1971; Roosevelt 1989; Beckerman 1991). Assessments using Landsat MSS found that less than one percent of the Amazon Basin evidenced deforestation in 1975 (though the resolution of MSS probably hid many areas that were in secondary succession). Initiated in 1970, Brazil's Program of National Integration, associated with a major initiative to build roads across the Amazon and to settle land along these roads with colonists, began to change the rates of deforestation. The east–west Transamazon Highway, constructed in less than four years, cut a path from the northeast of Brazil to the frontier with Peru. The north–south Cuiabá-Santarém highway and the Belem–Brasília highway linked, respectively, the central and eastern parts of the Amazon to the central part of Brazil (Moran 1981).

These roads were catalysts of land-cover and land-use change in the Amazon. Human settlements, promoted by a series of settlement schemes providing incentives and virtually free land, attracted people who quickly began cutting forest in order to ensure their claims to land (Moran 1976, 1981; Smith 1982; Fearnside 1986). For the period up to 1988, Skole and Tucker (1993) were able to document that up to 15 percent of the Brazilian Amazon had been deforested and seriously fragmented – a rate close to 0.5 percent per year. This rate actually hides the real local rates of deforestation. In settlement areas the rates of deforestation were commonly in excess of one percent per year, while vast areas remained out of reach of human occupation by Brazilian society. Percentages, too, tend to hide the scope and magnitude of deforestation in the Amazon: one percent of the Brazilian Amazon is equivalent to 50,000 km^2 or an area the size of Belgium. Thus, while the percentage of deforestation is higher in Ecuador and Mexico's tropical forests, the area being deforested in Brazil is several orders of magnitude larger. Updates by European Union scientists provide a needed reassessment (Achard et al. 2002) and one finds that the "hot spots" of deforestation change over time, and very quickly, making it difficult to respond effectively to the spatial location of major deforestation events.

Rates of deforestation in the Brazilian Amazon reached an initial peak near 1987–8, followed by a notable decline (see Figure 4.3). The drop was not a result, as some thought, of more effective conservation or of a more effective set of policies, and turned out to be temporary. It was, rather, the result of hyperinflation and a serious credit deficit in Brazil. After the introduction of the new currency, and effective control over inflation and exchange rates in 1994, the rate of deforestation surpassed (nearly doubled) the first peak of 1987–8, generating serious concern for policy makers. This second spike in the rate of deforestation can probably be explained by the suppressed rates of deforestation from 1988 to 1993, and the opportunities that economic stabilization offered. Within two years, deforestation rates settled down to the more common rates of about 0.5 percent for the Basin,

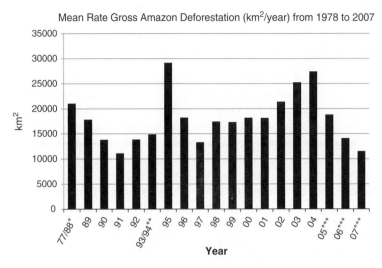

Mean Rate Gross Amazon Deforestation (km²/year) from 1978 to 2007

(*) Average between 1977 and 1988

(**) Average between 1993 and 1994

(***) Consolidated Annual Rates

Figure 4.3 Deforestation in the Brazilian Amazon, 1978 to 2007. Modified from INPE data
Source: www.inpe.br

although in settlement areas the rates remained considerably higher, i.e. above 1 percent annually (Wood and Skole 1998; Brondizio et al. 2002; Moran, Brondizio, and McCracken 2002).

Land change begins with the clearing of forest through slash-and-burn techniques, commonly followed by the planting of annual crops or the creation of pastures. In some cases, fields are kept in cultivation continuously, but this is rare. Only in areas with alfisols of relatively high fertility with favorable texture are there examples of continuous cultivation for over 25 years with some crop rotations in place (Moran, Brondizio, and McCracken 2002). In most places the low nutrient conditions of oxisols and ultisols, dominant in over 75 percent of the Amazon Basin, present constraints to continuous cultivation without major fertilizer inputs – which remain prohibitively expensive throughout most of the Amazon Basin. Without fertilizers, farmers have tended to plant pastures and graze cattle at very low densities as a preferred strategy. Cattle ranching has a long tradition in Latin America and receives favorable treatment by policy makers as a repository of value and a hedge against inflation and uncertain economic cycles. It is the traditional tool for occupying large areas of the vast frontiers of Latin

America with few people and labor scarcity (Walker, Moran, and Anselin 2000). Thus, Rondonia (predicted in the 1970s to become a center for cocoa production) and the Altamira region of Brazil, both of which have patches of high-quality soils, are dominated by pasture land (Moran 1988). Less than ten percent of the land area is in crops, with less than four percent in annual or staple crops (e.g. rice, corn, beans, manioc), and the rest in some form of plantation or tree crop (e.g. cocoa, rubber, sugar cane, coffee) (Brondizio et al. 2002). Nevertheless, the typical nature of change is one from undisturbed forest to a landscape cleared for management for cultivation or ranching, with a significant component of secondary regrowth on abandoned land.

Farmers experiment with a variety of strategies. They tend to clear more land than they can manage at the outset, and rates of six percent per year are not unusual when first arriving (McCracken et al. 2002). This rate quickly drops as farmers realize the high cost of managing regrowth through secondary successional dynamics (Moran et al. 1994, 1996, 2000; Moran, Brondizio, and Mausel 1994; Moran, Brondizio, and McCracken 2002; Steininger 1996; Tucker, Brondizio, and Moran 1998; Laurence et al. 2001; Mesquita et al. 2001; Zarin et al. 2001, 2002). Those with more favorable biophysical initial conditions and some capital move towards plantations and pasture formation; those with less favorable conditions continue to combine annual crops with modest increments in pastures on lands with exhausted fertility as a way of combating the return of woody species by succession. Over time, those with favorable conditions tend to evolve a balance of crops and pasture, while those with unfavorable soil conditions, and poor labor and capital resources, tend to concentrate most of their land in pastures.

Research on causes and driving forces of tropical deforestation reveals that neither single-factor causation (e.g. poverty, population growth) nor irreducible complexity adequately explain the dynamics of tropical deforestation (Geist and Lambin 2001). Deforestation is driven by regional causes, of which the most prominent are economic, institutional, and policy factors which seem to drive agricultural expansion, logging, and infrastructure development (Angelson and Kaimowitz 1999; Lambin et al. 2001). Logging appears to be a more important driver at the outset of forest clearing in Africa and Asia than in Amazonia, where farming and ranching seem to precede logging activities. In Middle America, selective logging (not clear cutting) has provided road networks ultimately followed by farmers (e.g. Turner, Gardner, and O'Neill 2001). The vastness of the Amazon and the precariousness of infrastructure have probably mitigated the impact of logging in the Amazon as a primary driver of land change. Work by Cochrane (2000, 2001), Cochrane and Laurance (2002), and Nepstad et al. (1999, 2000) suggests that loggers are beginning to lead the way in places where some primary road infrastructure has been created.

Important insights have been gained in recent studies that couple demographic study of household composition in the Brazilian Amazon, using survey research, with analysis of land-cover change using satellite data. To do this, researchers overlaid the property boundaries on a time-series of satellite data, which permitted querying changes in land cover at both the individual property and the landscape (3,800 properties or 3,800 square kilometers); see Plate 1 for this overlay. Moreover, it was possible to assign each property membership in a given cohort of arriving settlers, thereby permitting the stratified sampling to take into consideration cohort membership (see Plate 2) and to distinguish between cohort and period effects (McCracken et al. 1999; Moran, Brondizio, and VanWey 2005). This research has shown that the gender and age structure of households plays a key role in the deforestation trajectories of households. As young house-holds arrive in the frontier they deforest large areas of forest (as a percent of the property) in the first five years as they seek to establish their farms. This is followed by a steady reduction in annual rates of deforestation and with a shift from the annual crops planted upon arrival to provide sustenance to more permanent crops such as plantation crops (cocoa, sugar cane) and pasture. As time passes, and they progress in their life cycle, they undertake a brief increase in deforestation to consolidate their farm and to prepare the way for the system of production that will characterize their later years as an aging household. The deforestation of mature forest declines over this life cycle from 6 percent per year in the early years to steadily declining lev-els that terminate some 20–25 years later (Brondizio et al. 2002; Evans and Moran 2002; McCracken et al. 2002; Moran et al. 2000; Moran, Brondizio, and McCracken 2002). This trajectory, moreover, is profoundly affected by the biophysical conditions on the property (see Figure 4.4). Farmers with fertile soils develop a more diverse portfolio of crops than those with infer-tile soils who appear to be forced into a mostly planted pasture strategy, given the infertility of soils, and do not appear able to develop their farm with permanent crops such as cocoa, sugar cane and others which require more fertile conditions (Moran, Brondizio, and McCracken 2002).

The study of life cycles in an environmental context is but one example of a whole family of examples of what merging remotely sensed data with social survey research, econometric analysis and ethnographic approaches can do to advance current understanding of the consequences of land-use change (Walker 2003). This is an area particularly amenable to integration of social science methods and GIS/remote sensing. Another likely examina-tion is that of cycles of commodity prices in the world market with cycles of land use as farmers shift their cropping pattern in response to shifts in com-modity prices. A sudden drop in, say, soybean prices can result in significant areas not being planted the following year if the future's market suggests that prices will remain low.

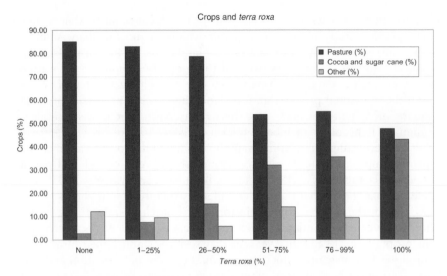

Figure 4.4 Crop choice is affected by soil quality. In this case as the proportion of *terra roxa estruturada eutrofica* (a fertile and well-drained alfisol) increases, it is possible to diversify the crop portfolio away from mostly pasture to other crops such as cocoa and sugar cane
Source: ACT data; see publications in www.indiana.edu/~act

A number of recent books provide a superb set of case studies on how to link social research with GIS and remote sensing. Fox et al. (2003) bring together a substantial number of cases from Mexico, Brazil, Ecuador, Thailand, Kenya, Vietnam, China, and other places with a focus on linking properties and households in spatially explicit ways using GIS tools. A volume more oriented towards policy applications is that of Walsh and Crews-Meyer (2002). Plate 3 illustrates an example from our own work that shows the way to use remote sensing and GIS in studying households. In this example, we have three properties that exist side by side, and thus where differences in biophysical features may not be great, though they could exist. We see one property where the owner has cleared far more forest and developed it as a farm more than the other two. This kind of "remote" observation raises useful questions to take to the field, and to develop useful inferences: what characterizes that household differently from the other two? More initial capital? More labor? Factors such as distance to market (cf. vonThunen discussion in Chapter 2) are not relevant here. What else might be behind this radical difference in farm development? The household developmental cycle? The two less developed ones being either very young or much older household heads? And what sort of development is undertaken? Pasture? Crops? Agroforestry? These choices, evident in the classification, lead to reasonable inferences about the household's situation, and decision making.

Urban–Rural Spatial Dynamics

Most researchers studying land-use and land-cover change have ignored the role of urban areas in driving land-cover conversion and bringing about environmental change – and even Marx connected urban development to rural environmental degradation (Foster 1999). The data from orbital satellites are well suited for providing information to analyze a number of important environmental changes. However, there is very little agreed upon with regard to the methods for systematically characterizing urban land cover and examining land use in an urban context. Part of the challenge is defining the difference between urban and rural so that change can be adequately assessed (e.g. the expansion of urban areas into peri-urban and rural landscapes over time accompanying population growth and development). Land cover is the most important source of anthropogenic change on the planet (Turner, Meyer, and Skole 1994; Lambin et al. 1999). The conversion of forest and grasslands to agropastoral uses has received the most attention by scientists because of its link to deforestation, biodiversity loss, and carbon emissions (Walker and Steffen 1997). This has resulted in a relative neglect of urban studies focusing on land-cover change, which is now being corrected.

Much of the research conducted by the remote sensing community in the urban context has either been concerned with management and planning or with the general problem of urban expansion (Jensen 1983; Jensen et al. 1994). This focus on urban and suburban expansion (and sprawl in the North American context), though implicitly connected to larger concerns about the environment and the consumption and exploitation of material resources and energy, has not been explicitly linked to regional land-use and land-cover conversion processes occurring on the periphery of urban centers or their surrounding regions, particularly in the developing world. There are a few cases where urban expansion and influences upon the urban fringe have been analyzed. However, these analyses have focused on North American (Canadian), European, and Chinese locations (examples include, respectively, Treitz, Howard, and Gong 1992; Wu 1998; Antrop 2000) that have a long history of dense urbanization. These studies' focus is on to the general measure of urban expansion, rather than on regional land use and conversion. This is a serious oversight, albeit partly produced as a consequence of technological limitations. All around the globe, including areas like the Amazon region, a process of rapid urbanization is underway. Urban areas are the loci of human activities, and urban interests increasingly drive rural land-cover change (Browder and Godfrey 1997). Urbanization concentrates populations and results in significant impacts on land, water, materials, and energy. Thus, to understand land-cover change, one must study the process of urbanization itself.

Currently there is no standardized description of urban land cover; nor is there a generally accepted definition of a city (Davis 1969; Whyte 1985; Foresman, Pickett, and Zipperer 1997; Lambin et al. 1999). In Peru, urban areas are defined as "populated centers with 100 or more dwellings," while in Japan urban is defined as places having 50,000 or more inhabitants (UN 1994). There is a mismatch between administrative boundaries and actual built-up land, and the human population is therefore over- or underrepresented depending on city boundaries (UN 1994). This problem is a result of administrative boundaries routinely lagging behind urban growth and areal expansion. Despite the lack of a globally recognized definition of a city, it is possible to determine urban characteristics of land cover and land use using remotely sensed imagery gathered from satellites and airplanes. Land-cover classification approaches that rely on Landsat MSS and TM imagery (79-meter and 30-meter resolutions, respectively), also often fail to capture urban land cover because the resolution is too coarse for adequately capturing the complexity of the urban landscape (see Plate 4 contrasting TM with Quickbird views of the same urban area). This is also due in part to the use of image classification techniques that rely primarily on the spectral information in the image without adequately incorporating texture or spatial structure. The primary limitation in the developing world, however, is access to adequate financial resources and technology to acquire and make use of detailed remotely sensed imagery.

High spatial resolution imagery in the form of aerial photographs has been available for close to a century in some parts of the world but is costly to acquire and process. In the past forty years, with the advent of remotely sensed satellite imagery, it has become possible to classify and analyze much larger portions of the earth's surface. Concurrently, a greater range of classification and accuracy has become possible as a result of technological improvements that have increased the range of observations of physical properties of the objects/surfaces being imaged. These advantages result from the use of a wider range of the electromagnetic spectrum – beyond normal human vision – and the use of radar and laser systems (see for instance textbooks on remote sensing and image analysis by Jensen 2005 and 2007). At the same time that advancements have been made using a variety of methods to determine the physical properties of the earth's surface and the objects on it, there have also been improvements in the resolution or grain at which those properties can be observed. Cowen and Jensen (1998) suggest that in order to capture better than a USGS Level 1 urban classification, it is necessary to use imagery with a ground resolution of better than 20 meters and for many urban applications better than half a meter. These are now available in a variety of satellites such as IKONOS, Quickbird, and others (see Plate 4 for an example of these submeter images, contrasting them to a Landsat TM image for the same area). For information on appropriate spatial and temporal scales, see Cowen and Jensen (1998). They also state that remote sensing can only provide a suggestion of the details of human activity.

To capture the complexity of the urban landscape, it would be useful to create an urban–rural gradient or transect of the transitions from one condition to the other (including urban areas that may end up over time abandoned and reclaimed for other uses). One can begin such an approach by defining the elements that characterize urbanization (McDonnell and Pickett 1990) and standardizing them across world regions (Whyte 1985). In doing this, there are considerable advantages to using remote sensing. However, the use of remote sensing in capturing urban elements is challenging, particularly in representing accurately the complex mosaic of human modifications and built structures (Zipperer et al. 2000). Urban areas vary in terms of density of dwellings, the three-dimensional structure of buildings, the types of construction materials used, and the amount and type of vegetation present, among other factors. It is important to recall that from the outset, the Chicago School of Human Ecology thought in spatially explicit terms, and incorporated a notion of succession in their propositions. Unfortunately, this emphasis was abandoned and sociologists explicitly moved away from it (Hawley 1986).

The first requirement of developing standardized methods is to represent the range of physical, biological, and socioeconomic variations present (Moran 1995). In urban areas this means coming up with a gradient of cities that combines population size, spatial settlement patterns, and differences in settlement history. Population size and differences in settlement history can be obtained largely from census and archival research and help in defining the number of urban area types that might be desirable to characterize. The spatial settlement pattern, particularly as it relates to the type and distribution of land covers, can probably best be done by combining Landsat TM with aerial videography. Aerial videography captured in digital image format can be made into a mosaic, visually analyzed, and then classified using automated methods to compare with TM imagery (Hess et al. 2002). This can be further improved with the use of either Quickbird or IKONOS imagery (the former with 61 cm spatial resolution in panchromatic and 2.4 m in multispectral, and the latter with 1 m panchromatic and 4 m multispectral) should funds be available for this detailed imagery. The drawbacks of using aerial videography and the high spatial resolution IKONOS and Quickbird imagery are the cost, storage, and processing requirements.

However the clarity of observations is an enormous advantage, as is clear from Plate 4 and from casual use of Google Earth.

Aerial videography can help to identify precisely the components of urban land cover. The better-than-one-meter resolution of aerial videography permits a refined observation of components of the landscape, such as types of roofs, number of trees in backyards, quality of roads, size of buildings, types of infrastructure, and water bodies. These observations can be used to build a library of reflectance spectra for urban materials. It is then possible to derive Vegetation-Impervious Surface-Soil (VIS) fractions (Ridd 1995) for each TM pixel using spectral mixture analysis, eventually resulting in the development of maps of land-cover change based on the VIS components (Madhavan et al. 2001; Powell, Roberts, and Hess 2001). This approach seeks to address the problem of spatial resolution associated with that Landsat TM. Its 30 m pixels capture multiple urban surface materials, hence each pixel is made up of heterogeneous urban structures that hide the distinct urban components (Roberts et al. 1998). Selecting end members for spectral mixture analysis is particularly problematic in urban areas because of the great variety of materials used in the construction of buildings, roads, and other urban surfaces. Simple spectral mixture analysis will not model successfully the components of the urban landscape.

A variation of spectral mixture analysis that allows each pixel to be modeled as different end-member combinations (known as multiple end-member spectral mixture analysis) seems to overcome this problem (Roberts et al. 1998). Urban materials can then be grouped minimally into three classes: vegetation, impervious surfaces, and soils. These quantities can be compared regardless of local environment or construction materials (Ridd 1995). This approach eventually permits the comparison of urban land-cover change with the socioeconomic structure of cities over time and space. If a sufficiently detailed time series is constructed (Powell, Roberts, and Hess 2001), it is then possible to develop inferences about the behavior of households in and around their buildings and other structures of land cover. This approach is advantageous in that it provides a gradient of change that can be used to determine transition from urban to rural, although this is also dependent on the land cover of the surrounding region.

One approach to linking urban households to the satellite imagery at a cluster-of-households-level is to infer the behavior of households by generating historical maps of change in the urban–rural gradient. This can provide valuable information about the transformations experienced by households in urban areas over time. For example, if one takes a small urban area in the Amazon frontier, one will see thatch roofs dominating cover of houses, with only a few tile roofs indicative of the elite families from the period before growth and development that began in the 1970s across that region (Moran 1993; Wood and Perz 1996). After that, one sees replacement of many thatch roofs with corrugated fiberglass, and the thatch roofs moving to the outskirts in what may be called shanty towns. Over time one will see these shanty towns improve in quality and this can be measured by the shift in materials used in houses and roofs, by the paving of roads, by the dispersion of warehouses from the riverside towards the roadsides, and by the planting of trees on promenades and in large patios surrounding the houses of the elite. These too will be more numerous and move towards peri-urban areas and away from the river towards the road to indicate the shift in economic infrastructure that marks the importance of road transportation and the decline of river transport. As the urban area grows, and the number of warehouses increases, indicating the growth of commerce, one can see shifts in land cover in the rural areas. This may be measured by the shift from smaller to larger properties, and from subsistence cultivation plots to larger pasture-dominated ranches – a preferred form of land use by absentee owners living in the city. The measurement of these shifts is possible using the techniques mentioned above, and inferences about economic development, population change, and social stratification can be derived with reasonable accuracy.

Analysis of land use and land cover in urban areas, along the urban fringe and urban periphery, and analyses that incorporate holistic objectives seeking to characterize and model processes of urbanization in relation to the surrounding landscape, would include methods that incorporate a larger variety of land-use/cover classes (LUCC) classes and buffering techniques that take into account the shape and the population density of urban centers. Frequently, in spatial analyses that use buffers, the buffers are arbitrary or they are derived using linear distances from a given point, line, or polygon. Other buffer methods are possible that use shapes that take into account human or biophysical processes, including ellipses that incorporate directional processes, and region boundaries that are produced using raster rule-based boundaries that incorporate topography (or a cost distance) and natural barriers (rivers, water bodies, cliffs, etc.) (for examples, see Evans 1998).

Alternative methods for quantifying LUCC for the regional landscape would also include alternative spatial sampling procedures, such as hexagonal, triangular, or rectangular (square) grids of predetermined size, providing a strategy that compares many like-size regions rather than the unequal areal extents that are frequently produced by using uniform buffers. Alternatives also include the use of different classification techniques that produce change-based LUUC classes, rather than hard single-time-period classes or classifications that are based on fuzzy or gradient classes (continuous rather than discrete). Methods should also be borrowed from landscape ecology that derive landscape fragmentation metrics for landscapes, individual classes, and patches. Methods for deriving landscape fragmentation metrics have found great utility in landscape ecology (Turner 1989; Baker and Cai 1992) and should also be considered for use in the analysis of urban–rural landscape processes.

A final methodological component for the improvement of, and incorporation into, such analyses is the use of texture or spatial structure. Much LUCC research uses remotely sensed imagery that is classified by methods that rely on spectral differences but that do not take into account very well the texture or overall spatial structure of the data. Two ways to address this are to (1) incorporate image (spatial) texture derived from neighborhood-based (kernel) calculations; and, (2) include geostatistical metrics derived from spatial variation in the data via the use of the semivariogram. Incorporation of texture is important in urban regions because of the spectral heterogeneity that is often encountered in such regions, but it has also recently found application in forest analyses. The semivariogram is used most frequently for modeling continuous (and often sparse) data: however, there has been recent application of its use for modeling differences between urban and nonurban regions from remotely sensed imagery (Brivio and Zilioli 2001). These methods when incorporated with methods already developed that use image-derived data and spatial data, such as census tract or block group population and household structure (e.g. Cowen and Jensen 1998), provide many opportunities for improving the description and modeling of urban, urban–rural, and environmental change.

Modeling and GIS

In contemporary modeling one large divide we see is between those who model in a spatially explicit fashion, and those who do not. A model is spatially explicit when it differentiates behaviors and predictions according to spatial location (Goodchild and Janelle 2004), and where the data are geolocated as part of the analysis. This is important because it allows the modeler to include the impact of heterogeneous space in the outcome of the model; and because the spatial properties of the outcomes are important in assessing the success of the model in predicting outcomes.

Models present an appealing means to explore what social and biophysical dynamics may have been present. The land-use/land-cover change community has used various techniques for modeling complex social-ecological systems. Examples include spatial interaction models, cellular automata (Clarke and Gaydos 1998; Messina and Walsh 2001), and dynamic systems models (Evans et al. 2001). Agent-based modeling approaches have been used to explore the decision-making processes of land managers in the context of spatial and social interactions. Reviews of applications of agent-based models (ABMs) to land-cover change scenarios have demonstrated the utility of a local-level representation of land-use decision making (Berger and Parker 2002; Parker et al. 2003). Early ABMs were comparatively abstract representations that explored fundamental aspects of spatially explicit systems but were not necessarily related to specific real-world applications (e.g. Epstein and Axtell 1996). Recent applications of ABMs have produced comparatively complex representations of social-ecological systems (Berger and Ringler 2002; Hoffmann, Kelley, and Evans 2002; An et al. 2005; Brown et al. 2005). Berger and Parker (2002) characterize these models in terms of whether environmental and agent model components are empirically grounded or designed but not substantiated.

A fundamental reason why agent-based approaches are an effective tool for exploring the complexities of land-cover change processes is the spatial pattern and heterogeneous nature of actors and topography found in many geographic locations. Land-cover patterns are highly correlated with topographic distribution in many cases. However, in addition to these land-suitability heterogeneities is the variety of landowner characteristics, histories, and experiences that contribute to the overall complexity in land-use/land-cover change dynamics. Koontz (2001) found that while the majority of landowners in a 1997 household-level survey noted nonmonetary reasons in their land-use decision making, the relative importance of nonmonetary factors varied by the size of the parcel owned by the landowner, household income, and educational attainment.

A particular challenge with modeling historical land-cover change is to develop an understanding of how path dependence and initial conditions determine specific future land-cover change trajectories. Previous research has explored the roles of initial conditions and path dependence in land-use modeling (Atkinson and Oleson 1996; Wilson 2000; Balmann 2001; Brown et al. 2005). In ABMs there are particular sensitivities in the initial conditions for land-use scenarios (Brown et al. 2005). Sensitivity analysis has proven a valuable tool to explore the impact of these historical uncertainties in the development of agent-based and other spatially explicit models of land-cover change.

In agent-based modeling, a major challenge is the development of explicit datasets to validate the agent interactions and heterogeneities in models (Manson 2002). Several disciplines have strong traditions of laboratory- and field-based experimental methods that have proven helpful in the design and development of behavioral models. In particular, psychology and economics have considerable literatures drawing on controlled experimental scenarios to explore key aspects of decision-making processes such as risk, cognition, bargaining, and trust. To a lesser extent, experimental approaches have been applied in anthropology (Henrich et al. 2001; Bernard 2002), political science (e.g. Ostrom, Gardner, and Walker 1994), and sociology (Kanazawa 1999). There has clearly been some reluctance to the adoption of experimental methods in disciplines such as anthropology (e.g. Chibnik

2005), but in each of these disciplines there is tacit acceptance of experimental methodologies within subdisciplinary fields. Two classic experimental designs are the Prisoner's Dilemma (e.g. Ostrom, Gardner, and Walker 1994; Wedekind and Milinski 1996; Milinski and Wedekind 1998) and the Ultimatum Game (e.g. Henrich et al. 2001; Oosterbeek, Sloof, and Van De Kuilen 2004), both of which have been conducted and replicated with varying subject populations and have resulted in numerous derivative experiments.

There are limited examples of spatial representation in experimental research. Spatial cognition research has employed the use of human subjects for experiments integrating principles from psychology and geography, and there is considerable research in this particular area (e.g. Golledge 1999; Klatzky et al. 2002). However, the objective has focused on aspects of cognition and perception rather than the dynamics of economic contexts. One of the most widely cited examples of spatially explicit experimental research is Schelling's segregation model (1971, 1978). Despite the prevalence of spatial methods such as GIS, cellular automata, and agent-based modeling in land-use/land-cover change research, and the contributions of economics to land-use theory, there are relatively few examples of experimental applications to land-use management in recent literature (the work of Bousquet et al. (2002), Wilke, Hutchinson, and Todd (2004), and Goldstone and Janssen (2005) are exceptions).

Another challenge in agent-based modeling (ABM) of land-cover change is the difficulty in balancing the complexity within the social and biophysical components of a model. Previous ABMs of land-cover change have incorporated relatively basic forest dynamics (e.g. Evans and Kelley 2004). The ABM community has made considerable progress in designing complex decision-making dynamics in agent-based models of land-cover change, and there is now an opportunity to couple these dynamics with more sophisticated representations of forest regrowth processes. Models of recovering forest dynamics require an understanding of the drivers of resource heterogeneity that determine the structure and composition of forest communities through time. Typically, two distinct forms of heterogeneity are defined; exogenous heterogeneity describes differences in the physical environment, including topography, climate, and soil characteristics, while endogenous heterogeneity describes those aspects of resource heterogeneity induced by the spatial dynamics of the forest community. Processes such as tree establishment and mortality are the primary cause of endogenous heterogeneity that can have a substantial effect on the trajectory of recovering forest dynamics. For example, an analysis of a forest recovery chronosequence in Venezuela indicated that the forest biomass was still increasing almost 200 years after abandonment of slash-and-burn agriculture (Saldarriaga et al. 1988). Subsequent analysis demonstrated that the slow rate of forest recovery was almost entirely caused by the presence of height-structured competition, successional diversity, and the demography of age- and size-structured populations (Moorcroft, Hurtt, and Pacala 2001). The important role that endogenous heterogeneity plays in forest dynamics has been recognized and addressed through the early and continued development of "gap models" (Botkin, Janak, and Wallis 1972; Shugart and West 1977; Smith and Urban 1988; Pacala et al. 1996). These models simulate the stochastic nature of the birth, growth, and mortality of individual trees within a small, forested area.

The application of gap models over large spatial extents has historically been limited by the computational difficulty of simulating individual-based demographic processes that occur in single gaps (15 m × 15 m) within landscapes that cover 100–1000 km^2. However, a number of recent strategies have been developed to accommodate the disparity between these fine-scale processes that determine forest dynamics and the need for broader-scale descriptions of vegetation dynamics within recovering landscapes. These include the development of Markov transition models based on underlying individual dynamics (cf. Acevedo, Urban, and Ablan 1995), and the derivation of partial differential equations that describe the underlying "statistical mechanics" of the individual-based models (Hurtt et al. 1998).

Europe's rural areas are expected to witness massive and rapid changes in land use due to changes in demography, global trade, technology, and enlargement of the European Union (Verburg, Eickhout, and Van Meijl 2008). Changes in demand for agricultural products and agrarian production structure are likely to have a large impact on landscape quality and the value of natural areas. Most studies address these changes either from a macroeconomic perspective (focusing on changes in the agricultural sector) or from a local perspective (by analyzing recent changes in landscapes for small case studies).

Verburg, Eickhout, and Van Meijl (2008) describe a methodology in which a series of models has been used to link global level developments influencing land use to local-level impacts. They argue that such an approach more properly addresses the processes at different scales that give rise to the patterns of land-use dynamics in Europe. An extended version of the global economic model (GTAP) and an integrated assessment model (IMAGE) are used to calculate changes in demand for agricultural areas at the country level while a spatially explicit land-use change model (CLUE-s) was used to translate these demands to land-use patterns at one square kilometer resolution. GTAP ensures an appropriate treatment of macroeconomic, demographic, and technology developments and changes in agricultural and trade policies influencing the demand and supply for land-use related products – while IMAGE accounts for changes in productivity as result of climate change and global land allocation. The land-use change simulations at a high spatial resolution make use of country-specific driving factors that influence the spatial patterns of land use, accounting for the spatial variation in the biophysical and socioeconomic environment. Results indicate the large impact abandonment of agricultural land and urbanization may have on future European landscapes. Such results have the potential to support discussions on the future of the rural area and identify hot spots of landscape change that need specific consideration. The high spatial and thematic resolution of the results allows the assessment of impacts of these changes on different environmental indicators, such as carbon sequestration and biodiversity. The global assessment allows, at the same time, to account for the tradeoffs between impacts in Europe and effects outside Europe.

This sort of complex coupling of models at different scales of resolution would be inconceivable without a spatially explicit approach, and a database supporting such models (CLUE model, widely used in Europe, cf. Veldkamp et al. 2002 where they discuss applications of the CLUE framework).The CLUE model simulates land-use and land-cover change using time steps of one year. It consists of a demand and allocation module. The demand module estimates the demanded physical output from agricultural land-use systems at the highest aggregation level considered. The allocation module calculates spatially explicit land-use and land-cover change at the level of individual cells (for different resolutions) considering changes in national demands as well as site-specific values of biophysical and socioeconomic variables. The next chapter explores the challenges and approaches to multi-scale and multi-temporal research implicit in these models.

5

Multi-scale and Multi-temporal Analysis

Scale issues in the study of ecological phenomena are of fundamental importance. The natural sciences have long understood the importance of scale (though not always adequately dealt with its implications). Research regarding scale in the social sciences, in contrast, has been less explicit and less precise (Gibson, Ostrom, and Ahn 2000). Research on human–environment interactions demands that one address interdisciplinary work on scaling across the natural/social science divide. Very recently, provocative notions have been proposed that rethink the scale issue (Manson 2008). According to Manson, scale pervades interdisciplinary research on human–environment systems, yet, he asks, "Does scale exist?" More precisely, can one definition of scale meet the multiple needs of research on human–environment systems? The challenge comes from the multidisciplinary nature of human–environment research, with each discipline bringing different and often conflicting scale concepts (cf. Marston 2000 on the growing body of scholars who view scale as "socially constructed").

The geographic literature is particularly rich in the social sciences in discussing the importance of scale (Marceau 1999; Sheppard and McMaster 2004). Scale is recognized as a fundamental concept in describing the hierarchical organization of the world – particularly with regard to spatial scale. Note that scale can refer to the size of the unit of analysis, and to spatial scale, with different size "grid cells" embedded in one another to represent different spatial scales. In turn, these two uses of the term do not "map onto" institutions and other social phenomena easily. Environmental problems such as the impact of climate change on ecosystems require an understanding of how processes operate at different scales and how they might be related across scales. While disciplinary differences persist, there has been steady progress, and convergence, towards ways to deal with the scale issue across the social sciences and in human–environment research (for an excellent overview of the concept of scale across the social sciences and ecology, see Gibson, Ostrom, and Ahn 1998, 2000).

At the heart of the challenge posed by multi-scale analysis lies the difference between microscopic analysis (i.e. focusing on the individual, small group, intra-community interactions, the local) and macroscopic analysis, which tends to focus more on structural conditions such as institutions, social organization, ecosystems, and biomes (Alexander et al. 1987). We find this distinction across the natural and the social sciences (e.g. microeconomics vs. macroeconomics; plot analysis in biology vs. ecosystem analysis and global biology and so on). It has been easier in analysis to let these two scales be treated as largely distinct from one another – and to ignore the connectivity between local level processes and larger, more inclusive scales. A scale is separable from other scales as an analytical convenience, yet its separableness is not a reflection of reality, nor of the interconnectivity of events in time and space.

Particularly in the area of common-pool resources, for several decades the focus was on community-based resource management case studies that were used to develop and advance theory. This made it easier to observe the processes of self-governance, given the relative simplicity of local scale dynamics. However, it also immediately raised issues of scale: to what extent do the findings of small-scale, community-based interactions scale up to regional or global commons? While one might scale up, some investigators concluded, there are likely to be new and different principles operative at higher scales (Berkes 2006).

This separation between local and global analyses has begun to change as a growing number of scholars began to focus on human–environment interactions at a variety of scales, and on cross-scale interactions. Whether one examines institutions or cross-scale interactions between stakeholders, air pollution, or carbon emissions, one is soon faced with the implications of these interactions: higher level government regulators, for example, can access and mobilize information and resources that strengthen their power and thereby weaken trust and cooperation by lower level stakeholders whose role is diminished. Thus, how higher level institutions use their power in relation to lower level institutions can determine the effectiveness of these cross-scale interactions and their success in managing some environmental resource (Adger, Brown, and Tompkins 2005). There is, to date, no accepted typology for cross-scale linking of institutions. The term co-management is used to capture these multiple arrangements but Berkes (2002) finds that this term hides the complexity of the cross-scale dynamics of institutional change. Preferable, it is argued, may be an approach that is better described as "adaptive management." The development of adaptive management focuses on how local groups self-organize, learn, and actively adapt to and shape change with social networks that connect institutions and organizations across levels and scales, and that facilitate information flows (Olsson, Folke, and Berkes 2004).

This challenge of cross-scale and multi-scale analysis is made clear by an examination of air pollutants, such as mercury, ozone, and persistent organics. Such pollutants can be transported over scales from about one hundred to several thousands of kilometers, and thereby across state, national, and even continental boundaries. Regulating and managing these pollutants requires dealing with local, state, national, and international political, economic, and cultural differences across geographic scales (Bergin et al. 2005). A central challenge of understanding cross-scale interactions is the inherent complexity of ecological systems and human systems (Liu et al. 2007a, 2007b). The origin of this complexity arises from the very diversity of organisms in such systems and from the nonequilibrium, nonlinear, historically contingent, self-organizing behaviors that they exhibit (Cadotte, Drake, and Fukami 2005). Capturing the behavior of these human–environment systems is difficult even when we can collect large amounts of data because of the diversity of conditions, many of which are difficult to replicate. To address this challenge we need to combine laboratory approaches, computer-based simulations and modeling, historical and field studies by teams of scientists from many disciplines to overcome the persistent trap of thinking that this study at this scale represents the human–environment interactions across scales.

In a number of disciplines, where attention to the local reigns supreme, such as anthropology, and among many well-intentioned social and biological scientists, there exists what has been called "the local trap" in which it is assumed that organization, policies, and action at local scale, are inherently more likely to have the desired social and ecological results than activities organized at higher scales. However, there is nothing inherent about any scale, and even local scale is profoundly influenced and dependent on higher scales. It is necessary to view each scale, even local ones, as interacting with other scales, and it is in the cross-scale process that desirable or undesirable outcomes are produced (Brown and Purcell 2005). One way to move forward that has been proposed is "distributed assessment systems," characterized by multi-scale assessments that engage local, regional, and national stakeholders in the co-production of assessments thereby addressing this necessary sensitivity of the multi-level nature of environmental problems (Cash 2000). The convergence of scholarship addressing "knowledge co-production, mediation, translation, and negotiation across scale-related boundaries may facilitate solutions to complex problems that decision makers have historically been unable to solve" (Cash et al. 2006). Among the challenges faced by stakeholders and decision makers in the process of cross-scale assessments, one can note in particular that of matching scales of biogeophysical systems with scales of management systems, avoiding scale discordance (i.e. matching the scale of the assessment with the scale of management), and accounting for cross-scale dynamics (Cash and Moser 2000).

This view from the social sciences is matched by analysis from the natural sciences. Constanza et al. (2001) note that large scale ecosystems are not simply larger versions of smaller systems, and micro-scale ecosystems are not merely microcosms of large scale systems, but that they operate at different levels and exhibit distinct patterns. Therefore, traditional management practices that do well at the local level should not be expected to do equally well in handling activities organized at the continental or global scale. Likewise, efforts to apply a national or global logic to local systems are likely to result in local ecosystem destruction. "The challenge is to match ecosystems and governance systems in ways that maximize the compatibility of these systems" (Constanza et al. 2001). They argue for the use of a combination of a broad global database, a large pool of local case studies, and the use of simulation modeling to test hypotheses, discover emergent properties of differently scaled systems, and to find matches between governance systems and ecosystems at a variety of scales.

One solution to this challenge was offered by full-scale integrated assessment models (IAMs) that allow many components of the global climate change problem to be examined in one framework. The main advantage of IAMs over less complete modeling frameworks is that the socioeconomic and environmental consequences of policy choices can be evaluated in their totality. However, the highly aggregated functional forms that IAMs currently use lack sufficient regional and local detail to be totally credible. Easterling (1997) argues that one needs regional studies in order to arrive at credible IAMs, and a cross-scale exercise that involves both regional and global integrative modeling. This is a position that a sizable portion of the environmental social science community has come to, and they have successfully pushed both the natural and social sciences towards regional modeling, as a meso-level that allows for consideration of both local and global phenomena.

Geist and Lambin (2002) used a different approach, but one that shows the complexity of matching scales. They analyzed the proximate causes and underlying driving forces of deforestation, including their interactions, as reported in 152 subnational case studies. They show that tropical deforestation is driven by identifiable regional patterns and that prior studies had given too much emphasis to population growth and shifting cultivation as primary causes of deforestation. Analysis of these 152 studies shows that tropical forest decline is determined by different combinations of various proximate causes and underlying driving forces depending on both geographic and cultural contexts. Some of these combinations are robust across regions of the globe (such as the role of market economies and the expansion of permanently cropped land), whereas most of them are region-specific. Their findings challenge single-factor explanations that put most of the blame of deforestation upon shifting cultivators and population growth. Rather, the analysis reveals that, at the underlying level, public and individual decisions largely respond to national- to global-scale economic policies, and that, at the proximate level, regionally distinct modes of agricultural expansion, wood extraction, and infrastructure expansion (especially road building) prevail as causes of deforestation. The study shows just how proximate causes and underlying driving forces affect forest-cover changes in a given location and how policy instruments need to be sensitive to this complexity if they are to achieve the goal of forest conservation in any given area. Notable also is the use of qualitative comparative analysis (QCA [Ragin 1987]) by Rudel (2005) as a way of extending the generalizability of his study of forests. QCA is an analytic technique that uses Boolean algebra to implement principles of comparison used by scholars engaged in the qualitative study of macro-social phenomena. Typically, qualitatively oriented scholars examine only a few cases at a time, but their analyses are both intensive – addressing many aspects of cases – and integrative – examining how the different parts of a case fit together, both contextually and historically. By formalizing the logic of qualitative analysis, QCA makes it possible to bring the logic and empirical intensity of qualitative approaches to studies that embrace more than a handful of cases – research situations that normally call for the use of variable-oriented, quantitative methods.

An Approach to Multidisciplinary, Multi-scale Research

The approach proposed here is not presented as an ultimate solution for the challenges posed by multi-scale research. Rather, it is presented as a realistic approach that has been used successfully by a sizable research group across a large number of sites, in different countries, and in different continents that allows for multi-scale comparative analysis across the natural and social sciences. This work was facilitated by center-level funding by the National Science Foundation from 1996 to 2006, and by Indiana University, and was based at the Center for the Study of Institutions, Population and Environmental Change (CIPEC, cf. Moran and Ostrom 2005 for a synthesis, or check the website of the Center, www.indiana.edu/~cipec). Moreover, the approach was taught for seven of those years at an intensive Summer Institute that shared these approaches with 132 faculty members and advanced graduate students from 34 countries that have since then proceeded to apply these approaches in their work. Obviously, they have adapted the overall approach to meet their particular goals but there is a consistency of approach that has proven robust. While the approach focused on forest ecosystems and on land-use and land-cover change, it has broader applicability.

Contemporary attention in the research community and in policy circles to the "human dimensions of global environmental change" offers a rare opportunity for integrative studies. Policy makers and the physical sciences' community acknowledge the central place of humans in environmental modification (Vitousek et al. 1997; Peck 1990) and thus implicitly accept what the social sciences might have to say about it. Solutions to contemporary environmental problems require the integration of experimental and theoretical approaches at a variety of levels of analysis, from local to global (Levin 1998).

Contemporary environmental social science builds on the past experience of scholars working on human–environment interactions, but must perforce go beyond those approaches. Generally agreed upon ways of selecting sample communities or sites and what data is to be collected across highly variable sites must be undertaken despite significant differences in environment, culture, economy, and history (Moran and Brondizio 2001). Approaches of the past emphasizing equilibrium and predictability that were necessary to test null hypotheses do not serve this research agenda well, as they hide the dynamic processes of ecosystems – and patches within ecosystems. Dynamic, stochastic ecosystem models are necessary to address the questions of global environmental change (Xu and Li 2002; Walker, Perez-Barberia, and Marion 2006). Environmental social scientists need to use such approaches to engage issues, for example, of ecosystem restoration (Pietsch and Hasenauer 2002; Mitsch and Day 2004), biodiversity (Tilman 1999; Nagendra 2001; Wätzold et al. 2006), agroecology (Vandermeer 2003; Wojtkowski 2004), and deforestation (Skole and Tucker 1993; Kaimowitz and Angelson 1998; Moran and Ostrom 2005; Lambin and Geist 2006).

One of the first steps in developing an approach across the natural and social science disciplines to facilitate multidisciplinary multi-scale research is to have a lingua franca, a set of tools that facilitate communication and that are inherently multi-scale or permit aggregation and disaggregation without serious loss of information. Such a set of tools is provided by geographic information systems (GIS) and the techniques of satellite remote sensing (see Chapter 4 for a full discussion). Remote sensing from satellite platforms such as the National Oceanographic and Atmospheric Administration (NOAA)'s AVHRR sensor, the National Aeronautics and Space Administration (NASA)'s Landsat Thematic Mapper (TM), and the French SPOT satellite provide information of considerable environmental richness for local, regional, and global analysis (Conant 1978, 1990; Liverman et al. 1998; Moran and Brondizio 1998; Brondizio 2008). For analysis of global processes of large continental areas such as the entire

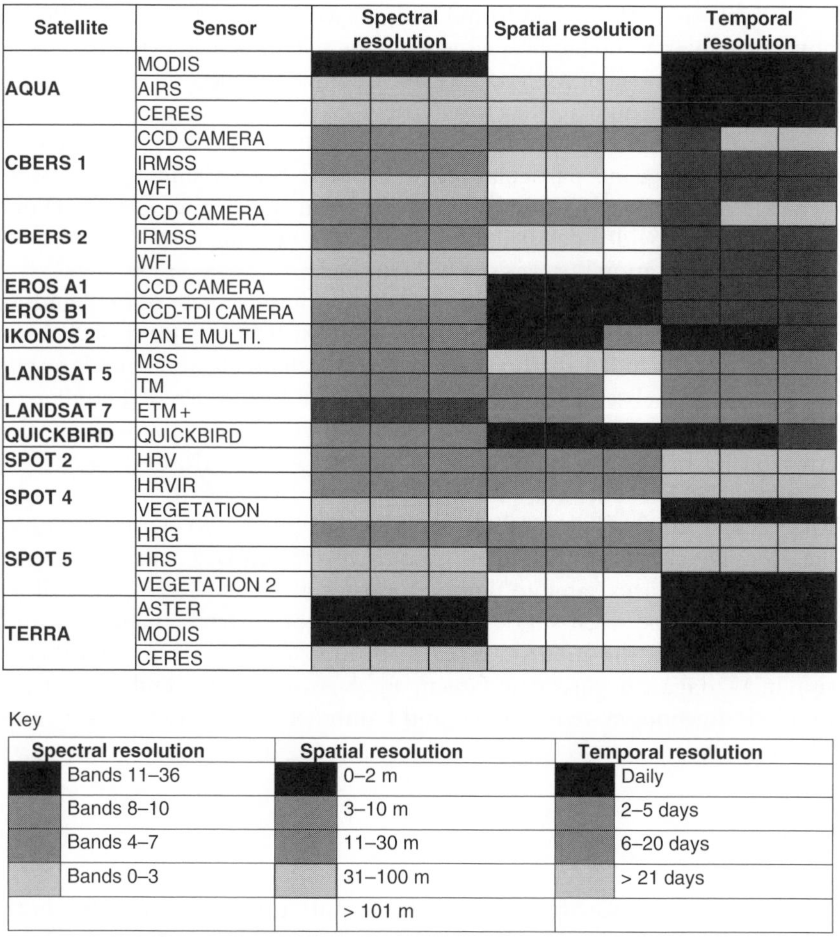

Satellite	Sensor	Spectral resolution	Spatial resolution	Temporal resolution
AQUA	MODIS			
AQUA	AIRS			
AQUA	CERES			
CBERS 1	CCD CAMERA			
CBERS 1	IRMSS			
CBERS 1	WFI			
CBERS 2	CCD CAMERA			
CBERS 2	IRMSS			
CBERS 2	WFI			
EROS A1	CCD CAMERA			
EROS B1	CCD-TDI CAMERA			
IKONOS 2	PAN E MULTI.			
LANDSAT 5	MSS			
LANDSAT 5	TM			
LANDSAT 7	ETM+			
QUICKBIRD	QUICKBIRD			
SPOT 2	HRV			
SPOT 4	HRVIR			
SPOT 4	VEGETATION			
SPOT 5	HRG			
SPOT 5	HRS			
SPOT 5	VEGETATION 2			
TERRA	ASTER			
TERRA	MODIS			
TERRA	CERES			

Key

Spectral resolution		Spatial resolution		Temporal resolution	
	Bands 11–36		0–2 m		Daily
	Bands 8–10		3–10 m		2–5 days
	Bands 4–7		11–30 m		6–20 days
	Bands 0–3		31–100 m		> 21 days
			> 101 m		

Figure 5.1 Comparison of the spatial, spectral, and temporal resolution of the main remote sensing platforms available
Source: Batistella and Moran 2008:31

Amazon Basin, NOAA's AVHRR is the most appropriate satellite sensor because of its daily coverage, despite its coarser resolution. More recently, MODIS, a mid-range resolution satellite with 250 m spatial resolution that provides daily coverage, has been used and connected to finer resolution satellites. Although designed primarily for meteorological monitoring, it has been profitably used to monitor vegetation patterns over very large areas. Figure 5.1 provides a summary of some of the many available satellites relevant to the study of land-use and land-cover change, and the different resolutions that they provide.

Available since 1972, data from Landsat's Multispectral Scanner (MSS) is now virtually free and has been used by many scientists who desire a 30-plus year time series. Use of MSS data is still valuable for the study of relatively dichotomous phenomena, such as forest vis-à-vis nonforest land cover; grassland vis-à-vis bare ground, and to establish a historical account of land-cover change in a particular region for these coarser land-cover classes. Before 1972, remotely sensed data came from aerial photographs (Vogt 1974) which provided detailed information at a very high cost of personnel time in interpretation but was spatially limited.

A significant advance took place in 1984 with the launch of the Landsat TM sensor that improved the spatial resolution from the 80 m of MSS to 30 m. It also included three visible spectrum channels and four infrared spectrum channels. This satellite has already allowed detailed studies of land-cover changes in some of the most difficult landscapes known: the Amazon Basin and the Ituri Forest of Central Africa (Moran et al. 1994; Moran, McCracken, and Brondizio 2001, Moran, Brondizio, and McCracken 2002; Wilkie 1994; Brondizio 1996, 2008). Discrimination between age classes of secondary growth vegetation was achieved for the first time using this satellite data (Moran et al. 1994, 1996), as well as discrimination between subtle palm-based agroforestry management and flooded forest in the Amazon estuary (Brondizio et al. 1994, 1996), erosion in Madagascar (Sussman, Green, and Sussman 1994), and intensification in indigenous systems (Guyer and Lambin 1993; Behrens, Baksh, and Mothes 1994).

Scale

These recent advances required careful attention to issues of scale, both temporal and spatial. Research questions and methods often are scale-specific. Appreciation for issues of scaling has increased as the challenge of integrating data and models from different disciplines and different temporal and spatial scales becomes necessary with the growth of global environmental change studies (Wessman 1992:175; Walsh et al.1999). Bioecological data, in particular, coming as it often does from study of individual organisms, must be ultimately connected to regional and global scales. This procedure is, unfortunately, not a simple task. Complex spatial variations and nonlinearities across landscapes occur which present a challenge to facile extrapolations from local scale to more inclusive scales (Green et al. 2005a). The points of articulation between different scales of analysis challenge our narrow disciplinary approaches, and require new strategies for acquiring and interpreting data (Walsh et al. 1999; Wessman 1992:175).

The preciseness of regional analysis depends on the quality of the sampling at local level. Detailed local-level sampling is far from common in traditional remote sensing. Much of what goes for "ground truthing" is visual observation of classes such as dense forest or cropland, without detailed examination of land-use history, vegetation structure, and composition. The long-standing anthropological bias for understanding local-level processes, when combined with the use of analytical tools capable of scaling up and down, makes an important contribution to the advancement of land-use/land-cover change research and to issues of articulation between differently scaled processes. Ecosystem research has historically presented challenges to multi-scalar analyses because ecosystems can be conceptualized at any number of scales.

Integrative human–environment research is capable of contributing to these multiply scaled analyses, with its forte remaining at the local to regional scale. Wessman (1992:180) has called for studies that link ground observations to regional and global scales if we are to take full advantage of the detailed data available at different scales. A number of these research efforts are currently continuing, but many have paid scant attention to the human dimensions of these processes. Extrapolation of ecosystem research to regional and global scale has been hindered in the past by difficulties in observing large-scale spatial heterogeneity. Remote sensing linked to ground-based studies provides the most promising tools for understanding ecosystem structure, function, and change. The capacity to detect long-term change in ecosystems can be enhanced by analysis of image texture, combined with spatial statistics that permit analysis of stand structure from satellite data (Wessman 1992:189). A summary of research in the social sciences on issues of scale can be found in Gibson, Ostrom, and Ahn (1998, 2000).

Multilevel research can start at any scale of analysis; hence, sampling at one level needs the ability to be aggregated to a higher level, or disaggregated, when necessary, to lower levels. To do so, it is important to pay attention to levels of analysis without subordinating scales. Land-use/land-cover analysis provides us with a setting for the study of levels of analysis that connects human behavior to economic forces and management strategies with ecological aspects of land cover. Readers will wish to consult the recently created journal of *Land Use Science* (see www.informaworld.com).

We can conceptualize multilevel analysis of land-use/land-cover change as built upon a structure of four integrated levels of research: Landscape/regional level; vegetation class level; farm/household level; and soil level. The conceptual model relies upon a nested sampling procedure that produces data that can be scaled upwards and downwards independently or in an integrated fashion. The integration of multi-temporal, high-resolution satellite data with local data on economy, management, land-use history, and site-specific vegetation/soil inventories aims to make it possible to

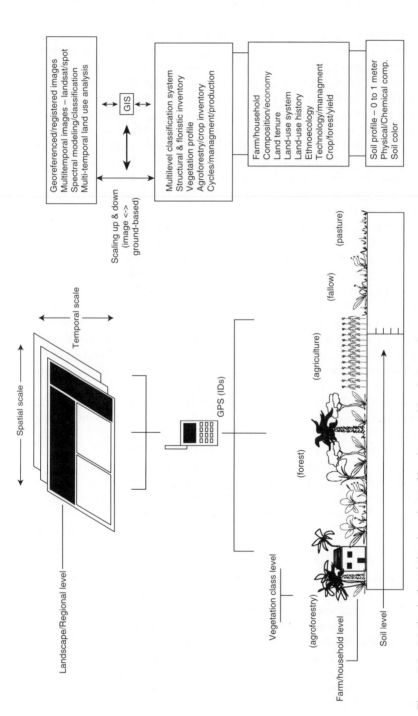

Figure 5.2 Method of multilevel analysis of land-use and land-cover change
Source: ACT, courtesy of Eduardo Brondízio

understand ecological and social dimensions of land use at local scale, and link them to regional and global scales of land use. Figure 5.2 illustrates this nested multi-scaled and multi-temporal approach used by our research group.

Local Level of Analysis

Data collection at farm/household level can include a variety of internal and external aspects of this unit of analysis (Moran 1995; Netting, Stone, and Stone 1995). It is important to collect local data so that these can be aggregated with those of larger populations within which households are nested. For instance, demographic data on household composition (including sex and age) can be aggregated to the population level to construct a demographic profile of this population, but this can occur only if the data are collected in such a way that standard intervals of five years are used, which is the way demographic data tend to be reported at more aggregated levels (Moran 1995). Another important set of data that is collected at this level and can be aggregated at higher levels is related to subsistence economy. At this level, it is important to cover the basic dimensions of social organization, such as settlement pattern, labor distribution, resource use, and kinship (cf. Netting, Stone, and Stone 1995 for a three-level approach to collecting social organization data relevant to land use).

One of the most difficult tasks in land-use analysis is to understand the decisions one must make about the boundaries of a population. In general, geographic boundaries are associated with a variety of factors, such as land tenure, landscape features, ethnic history, administrative boundaries, and inheritance. An analysis based on local information and maps/images/aerial photographs can provide more reliable information than either one alone. These boundaries, moreover, change over time in sometimes dramatic fashion that can affect the behavior of populations (Ellen 1990).

A concern with global change leads to data collection at the local level capable of aggregation to higher levels of analysis, both in geographical and database formats. Georeferencing the household, farm boundaries, and agriculture and fallow fields may be achieved through the use of global positioning system (GPS) devices. These are now small units that permit precise location of any point on the planet to within a few meters. The level of precision will vary depending on a number of factors, such as the quality of the GPS receiver, the unobstructed view of the overhead satellites, or whether the readings are taken inside forest cover. Current accuracies achieved with a GPS are, in general, acceptable for most types of land-use analysis and submeter accuracies are rarely necessary. Data collected at this level can inform the next research phase. For instance, information on the distribution of activities throughout the year, the agricultural calendar, and production can highlight the best time for future fieldwork.

Mapping of vegetation has implications for understanding the impact of land-use practices on land cover. Basic vegetation parameters need to be included so they can inform mapping at the landscape level. In general, vegetation structure, including height, ground cover, basal area, density of individuals, DBH (Diameter at Breast Height), and floristic composition, are important data to be collected. These data inform the interpretation of satellite digital data, provide clues to the characteristics of vegetation following specific types of disturbance, and take into account the spatial arrangement of vegetation cover. Remote sensing has considerable potential in vegetation analysis because it enables wide-area, nondestructive, real-time data acquisition (Inoue 2003; Loris and Damiano 2006). The applications are also important in estimating above-ground carbon stocks, relevant to effective reports on Kyoto protocol requirements (Patenaude, Milne, and Dawson 2005) to reduce human-induced emissions of carbon dioxide by at least 5 percent below 1990 levels by 2012. To do so, countries must estimate carbon stocks in 1990 and any changes since that date, whether through afforestation, reforestation, or deforestation (ibid). The applications to monitoring and predicting severe drought also have grown in sophistication (Boken, Cracknell, and Heathcoate 2005).

From the point of view of satellite data interpretation, the definition of structural parameters to differentiate vegetation types and environmental characteristics, such as temperature and humidity, are particularly important. Structural differences provide information that can be linked to the image's spectral data. Floristic composition, although important, is less directly useful in interpreting spectral responses, but it may have to be considered depending on research questions. Environmental factors, such as soil humidity, soil color, and topographic characteristics, also are associated with spectral responses of vegetation cover. For example, at the farm level, vegetation structure is the main parameter used to evaluate the impact of human management practices. Some plant species are excellent indicators of soil type which is, in turn, associated with given management practices. Farmers commonly use the presence of given species to choose a site for a given crop. For instance, the presence of *Imperata brasiliensis* may be a sign of low soil pH in parts of the Amazon estuary (Brondizio et al. 1994). This kind of ethnoecological knowledge is very much site specific, and such local knowledge does not extrapolate well to landscape, regional, or global analysis.

To determine representative sampling sites of a study area's land cover, one needs to aggregate four types of information: vegetation classification, ethnoecological information of resource use, composite satellite images, and classified image/land-use/land-cover maps of the area. Based on the analysis of these data, one can decide how sampling can best be distributed in the area to inform both the image classification (land-use/land-cover map) and the structural/floristic variability of vegetation classes. In selecting a site to be a representative sample of a vegetation type or class, one needs to consider the size of the area and its spatial location on the image. One needs to consider, too, the spatial distribution of the vegetation class to avoid clustering of the samples and biased information about the vegetation structure and floristic composition. With the use of a GPS device, geographical coordinates of the sampled area are obtained as part of the inventory. If possible, the area should be located on a hard copy of the georeferenced image while still at the site, to avoid confusion and ensure precision of the GPS information. However, it is in the laboratory, using more precise methods of georeferencing, that the site will be definitively incorporated into the image file. A nested dataset on land-use history and vegetation inventory can be related through GPS-derived coordinates to a multi-temporal image, allowing complex analysis of land-use trajectories and regrowth history at site, local, and landscape levels.

Information on land-use history is important not only in defining sampling areas of anthropogenic vegetation (e.g. fallow and managed forest), but also in verifying that natural vegetation has not been affected or used in the past. For instance, it is important to know whether a savanna has been burned, and if so, with what frequency; or if a particular forest plot has been logged, which species were taken or cleared and when the clearing event took place. Land-use and management history are more detailed in areas directly subjected to management (e.g. agroforestry), since management and technology determine the structure and composition of the site. In these areas, estimates and actual measurements of production are critical in order to analyze the importance of the activity in a broader land-use and economic context. More importance should be given to the spatial arrangements of planted species and their life cycles as part of the inventory. This has been a neglected area in past environmental anthropology research and needs to be urgently addressed by working closely with spatially-oriented scientists such as environmental geographers and ecologists.

Vegetation regrowth and agricultural production analyses are limited in their usefulness without information about soil characteristics. Soil analysis should always be associated with vegetation cover analysis; soils should be collected at inventoried vegetation, agroforestry, and crop sites of known land-use history and management and georeferenced to the image through a GPS device (Moran, Brondizio, and McCracken 2002). Ethnoecological interviews can elucidate many soil characteristics. Taxonomic classification of soil types based on color, granulometry, and fertility, in general, help identify the major soil types and their distribution with relative reliability. Folk classification can then be cross-checked and compared with systematic soil analyses. Soil analyses should include both chemical (pH, P, K, Ca, etc.)

and textural (sand, clay, silt) analyses and permit the aggregation of data to regional levels (Nicholaides and Moran 1995).

Regional Level of Analysis

The landscape/regional level provides a more aggregated picture of management practices and driving forces shaping a particular land use/cover. At this level, long-term environmental problems can be more easily identified and predicted than at farm or household scales (e.g. Booth 1989; Skole and Tucker 1993). This level integrates information from vegetation class, soil, and farm/household levels (Adams and Gillespie 2006). However, landscape level data also inform important characteristics of local-level phenomena that are not measurable at the site-specific scale. For instance, information about the heterogeneity and patchiness of the vegetation is an important parameter to include in site-specific analysis, but it can only be observed at the landscape level.

One can identify four major steps in landscape level research: (1) understand the ecological and socioeconomic nature of the features of interest in land-use/land-cover analysis; (2) identify the extent and frequency of features of interest that can inform the appropriate spatial and temporal scales of analysis; (3) increase sampling progressively, depending on the emergence of important variables, a process that landscape ecologists call using an "adaptive approach" (Turner et al. 1989) and that bears some resemblance to what Vayda calls "progressive contextualization" (1983); and (4) consider the empirical methods needed for checking map accuracy, change detection, and projections/predictions, especially when associated with land-use planning.

Satellite data are today the most important data sources for analysis at the landscape/regional level. However, it is always associated with other sources, such as radar images, aerial photography, and thematic and topographic maps. Social scientists in the past left this kind of work to others, but today a growing number of them are developing these skills and making useful contributions to the analysis of satellite images (Behrens, 1990, 1994; Brondizio 2008; Brondizio et al. 1994, 1996; Moran et al. 1994; Moran, McCracken, and Brondizio 2001; Moran, Brondizio, and McCracken 2002; Nyerges and Green 2000; Tucker et al. 2005; Tucker and Southworth 2005). Political scientists, geographers, economists, and ecologists have also become avid users of satellite data to increase the spatial coverage of observations and analyses.

The digital analysis of satellite images may be divided into four parts: pre-processing, spectral analysis, classification, and post-processing. During pre-processing one needs to define an image subset, georeference it to available maps and coordinate systems, and register it to other images available if multi-temporal analysis is desired. The georeferencing accuracy depends on the quality of the maps, availability of georeferenced coordinates collected during fieldwork, and the statistical procedure used during georeferencing (Jensen 2005). A georeferenced image is an image with a grid of geographical coordinates and is crucial for relating landscape data to site-specific data. When multi-temporal analysis is desired, images from different dates need to be registered pixel-to-pixel, creating a composite image that provides a temporal change dimension at the pixel level, thus allowing the analysis of spectral trajectories related to change in land use. For instance, in a two-date image (e.g. two images that are five years apart), one can quantify the change during regrowth of secondary vegetation or a shift in crops grown in that five-year period with considerable accuracy, including statistics for the change in area for each vegetation type or class.

Digital analysis provides one with the flexibility to use a variety of scales to analyze parameters and to define sampling procedures, depending on the land-use/land-cover pattern and extent of the study area. In general, one can work at the landscape or regional scale (e.g. the whole Landsat or SPOT image, i.e. 185 by 185 km areas for Landsat images) while staying in close association with local-scale processes (e.g. image subsets of a watershed) to help the selection of sampling areas that will inform the image about specific spectral and spatial characteristics of land-use/land-cover classes. See Plate 4 for an illustration of property level (local) analysis embedded within a regional or landscape analysis.

By taking a hybrid approach during image classification and processing, one can integrate unsupervised and supervised classification procedures. A hybrid approach allows one to develop an analysis of spectral patterns present in the image, in conjunction with ground information, and to arrive at spectral signature patterns which account for detailed differentiation of land-use/land-cover features. In this fashion, a conceptual spectral model can be developed in which the features of interest can be incorporated. The model considers the reflection and absorption characteristics of the physical components that comprise each feature. For instance, in a Landsat TM image, the model attempts to account for chlorophyll absorption in the visible bands of the spectrum, for mesophyll reflectance in the near-infrared band, and for both plant and soil water absorption in the mid-infrared bands (Mausel et al. 1993; Brondizio et al. 1996). The integration of those spectral features with field data on vegetation height, basal area, density, and dominance of species can be used to differentiate stages of secondary regrowth (Moran et al. 1994). The analysis of spectral statistics derived from unsupervised clustering and from areas of known features and land-use history allows the development of representative statistics for supervised classification of land use/cover (cf. the many publications of

Lu et al., downloadable from www.indiana.edu/~act, that discuss methodological approaches to supervised classification using hybrid approaches.)

Classification accuracy analysis requires a large amount of fieldwork. Accuracy may decrease as spatial variability increases. Thus, ground-truth sampling needs to increase in the same proportion. In this case, the use of a GPS device is necessary to provide reliable ground-truth information, whereas in areas with low spatial heterogeneity, visual spot-checking may be enough. Checking for accuracy of a time series of satellite images for an area requires the analysis of vegetation characteristics and interviews about the history of a specific site with local people, so it is possible to accurately relate past events with present aspects of land cover (Mausel et al. 1993; Brondizio 2005, 2008).

Integration of data at these scales is an interactive process during laboratory analysis of images and field data, and during fieldwork (Meyer and Turner 1994; Moran and Brondizio 1998). Advanced data integration and analysis is achieved using GIS procedures that integrate layers of spatial information with georeferenced databases of socioeconomic and ecological information. Georeferencing of the database to maps and images must be a consideration from the very beginning of the research so that appropriate integration and site-specific identification are compatible. Data on household/farm and vegetation/soil inventory need to be associated with specific identification numbers that georeference it to images and maps so that integrated associations can be derived. For instance, the boundaries of a farm property may compose a land tenure layer that overlaps with a land-use/land-cover map. These two layers may be overlapped with another layer that contains the spatial distribution of households. Each household has a specific identification that relates it to a database with socioeconomic, demographic, and other information. In another layer, all the sites used for vegetation and soil inventory can be associated with a database containing information on floristic composition, structural characteristics, and soil fertility, which will also relate to land-use history.

Global Level of Analysis

The 1990s saw the very rapid development of approaches variously called "integrated assessment modeling," GCMs (global circulation models), and other approaches at a biosphere level of analysis. Some of these have even managed to focus on the human impacts on the earth system (cf. Weyant et al. 1996). GCMs in particular were developed first, and lacked much of a human dimension at all. They were largely concerned with climate and atmospheric processes, using a very aggregated scale of analysis that made even large scale units, such as national boundaries, not always relevant to understanding differences, say, in rates of energy consumption. However, a new generation of models has emerged in the last few years that began to have relevance for environmental social scientists. These are a vast improvement from the pioneering work of the Club of Rome models that appeared in the early 1970s in *Limits to Growth* (Meadows et al. 1972). Despite the many problems with this early-generation effort, it did introduce important concepts like "feedback," "overshoot," and "resource limits" to everyday discourse and scientific debate. The next brave attempt came from the International Institute of Applied Systems Analysis (IIASA) in Austria, with its Finite World model examining global energy flows (Häfele 1980). Criticism of this attempt was very broad in the scientific community and not much happened until the first Intergovernmental Panel on Climate Change (IPCC) published its first assessment in 1990.

New generation models benefited from the progress made by GCMs, from growing evidence of the global nature of environmental problems, and the democratization of computer technology through its wide availability (Alcamo, Leemans, and Kreilerman 1998:262). The next step was clear: both social and physical aspects of the world system had to be coupled in so called "integrated assessment models." Most global modeling groups today acknowledge that to make progress on the accuracy and predictability of modeling efforts at this scale, there must be a simultaneous effort to link them to regionally scaled models that can improve the quality of the spatial resolution and the role of human drivers in global change.

One of the more sophisticated models to date is known as IMAGE 2 (Alcamo, Leemans, and Kreilerman 1998). IMAGE 2 was the first global integrated model with geographic resolution – an important feature that permits improved representation of global dynamic processes including feedbacks, and rapid and efficient ease of testing against new data. It is composed of three fully linked systems of models: the energy-industry system, the terrestrial environment system, and the atmosphere-ocean system. The energy-industry model computes emissions of greenhouse gases and other important emissions in 13 world regions. The terrestrial environmental model simulates changes in global land cover on a grid-scale based on climatic and economic factors. The atmosphere–ocean model computes the build up of greenhouse gases and aerosols and the resulting impact on average temperatures and precipitation. Factors such as population change, economic change, and technical change are particularly important in the terrestrial model – and the ones most in need of good quality regional data to inform the grid-based model. To date, few environmental social scientists have engaged this community of global modelers' efforts, forcing the modelers to make estimates based on very coarse national scale statistics rather than derived from more refined regional studies. This is an important new direction for environmental social scientists and ecologists, given the importance of global simulation models on policies such as carbon trading, setting emission ceilings for carbon dioxide by the beginning of the twenty-first century, and debt-for-nature swaps. The main participants in these exercises have been economists who have relied on the use of optimizing utility functions, rather than the less than optimal, more realistic satisficing behavior of human populations whether in the First or Third World.

The relevance of regionally informed approaches to global models becomes clearly evident when we begin to design a classification system of vegetation types and of land-use classes as a first step toward a good classification of land use/cover. Readers will want to check the recent journal *Global Change Biology* which was created to promote understanding of the interface between all aspects of current environmental change and biological systems, including rising tropospheric O_3 and CO_2 concentrations, climate change, loss of biodiversity, and eutrophication. Advances can be achieved through association of bibliography and databases of the study area, analysis of satellite images, fieldwork observation, and ethnoecological interviews with local inhabitants. Different levels of organization are required to define a vegetation cover of a region. In general, levels are organized to fit a specific scale of analysis into the phytogeographical arrangement and into the land-use types present in the area. In other words, one starts with a more aggregated level of major dominant classes (first) adequate to a regional scale and proceeds with increased detail at the next sublevel (second) to inform more detailed scales. For instance, the first level may include major vegetation covers such as forest, secondary succession, and savanna. In the second, more detailed level, forest is subdivided into open forest and closed forest, secondary succession into old secondary succession and young secondary succession, and savanna into grassland savanna and woodland savanna. At the third level of this classification system, still more detailed information needs to be included to account for the variability of vegetation required at this local scale. So, a new subdivision of the forest class may include a third structural variation of the former two and/or a floristic variation of them, such as a forest with a dominant tree species. The importance of developing a detailed classification key is crucial to inform the land-use/land-cover analysis at the landscape level, as well as the sampling distribution at the site-specific level.

Future Directions

The multi-scale analysis of human–environment interactions constitutes today one of the foci of theoretical and methodological attention by the research community, as solving the challenges of cross-scale analysis is one way to ensure that our work is realistic and useful. During the past decade we have grown accustomed to giving attention to scale issues – particularly temporal and spatial scales – in understanding human–environment interactions. While considerable advances have been made (e.g. Gibson, Ostrom, and Ahn 1998, 2000) a lot remains to be done. We still do not clearly understand, for example, why a process which explains most of the variance at one scale largely disappears as an explanatory factor at another scale (Moran and Brondizio 1998). Is it because that variable is not important at the other scale, or is it a result that data for that variable is not as available at another scale? Do we have a difference in explanation, or a difference in data quality or availability?

The problem of scale is particularly challenging in the social sciences since, as noted above, the quality of the observations decreases as one moves from local to national to global scales. The patchiness of human–environment interactions presents considerable challenges to issues of scale. People tend to be concentrated in settlements, yet their impact, or footprint, can be felt very far away. How do we quantify the impact of a human population in a Japanese city on a forest in the Philippines or Brazil, from which the Japanese population derives considerable wood products? The tradition of place-based research in both ecology and the social sciences, particularly in local places, has given us valuable insights into the interactions between species and of species with their immediate environment – and the feedback processes that help explain their adaptive behavior to the opportunities and constraints they face. Yet, this very tradition is challenged by the ever growing recognition that many species, including the human one, keep an eye out for resources not only in their local environment, but also in environments very far away. It is generally understood that negative feedback is the primary way in which we adjust to normal changes. In cases where our resources are drawn from faraway places, rather than our immediate environment, are the feedback mechanisms different, or absent due to the disconnect of consumption with places that we can't do much about? Is this a case of spatial mismatch between dependent and independent variables? How do the characteristics of those feedbacks affect decisions made in the next year or decade for using those resources? What are the lag times in feedback processes at different spatial distances between people and the resources they use?

Continued attention to how we can keep spatial and temporal scales in mind and resolve the uncertainties we currently experience in understanding processes at different scales of analysis will continue to shape science in the years ahead. This is as it should be since this challenge affects all the sciences, and our ability to make decisions that are scale-informed, rather than misinformed and destructive of those ecosystems.

6

Biocomplexity in Ecological Systems

Upon entering the twenty-first century, we face significant scientific and engineering challenges and opportunities resulting from accelerating environmental changes ... New scientific and engineering research and innovation are needed to understand the changes and impact of multiple stresses on environmental systems as well as to inform responses to natural hazards. Now more than ever, scientists and engineers must address combinations of factors, such as the interactions between human activities and natural cycles at different spatial and temporal scales.

Pfirman and NACFERA Education (2005)

Introduction

The term biocomplexity was introduced into widespread use by Rita Coldwell as she came into the directorship of the National Science Foundation. At the time, few people were sure of what she meant, but over the years this term has become emblematic of the study of the complexity of ecological systems, and is now a regularly funded program in a variety of NSF directorates, including the Social and Behavioral Sciences Directorate – where it is known as the Coupled Natural Human Systems Program.

Understanding biocomplexity requires a holistic approach, and this can be achieved by developing the capacity to identify, retrieve, and synthesize diverse data from an array of sources, across disciplines, and across scales. One such effort is known as "Knowledge Network for Biocomplexity" and it is being used by the National Center for Ecological Analysis and Synthesis, at the University of California at Santa Barbara to train new investigators in approaches that emphasize multi-scale integration and synthesis (Andelman et al. 2004).

Cadenasso, Pickett, and Grove (2006) have proposed a definition of biocomplexity that incorporates spatially explicit heterogeneity, organizational connectivity, and history as essential elements in understanding how coupled natural human systems operate. The advantages offered by this approach are many. Its emphasis on spatially explicit *heterogeneity* allows for multi-scale analysis from a vegetation patch to large-scale ecosystems. *Connectivity* addresses organizational complexity, and integrates classic approaches from ecology such as the study of fluxes of energy, matter, and information (H. Odum 1971), with a new emphasis on the coupling of the system. *History* introduces a novel element to ecology, and one that facilitates interaction with the human components of these complex systems – system structures, interactions, and outcomes are a product of historically contingent events and are subject to surprises, nonlinear behaviors, and legacies, and require attention to the specificities of time and place (Cadenasso, Pickett, and Grove 2006).

Biocomplexity and complexity theory have received considerable attention over the past decade and a half from a wide variety of disciplines. It has become shorthand for describing the rich patterns of interaction and behavior in coupled human and natural systems. Some scholars seem to suggest that this approach will lead to a unified understanding of complex systems, while others view it as a continuation with past synthesis efforts, such as hierarchy theory (Allen and Starr 1982), holism (Moran 2000), and systems analysis at the start of the cybernetic age (Buckley 1968). It is indeed possible to trace the origins and continuity of biocomplexity to these earlier efforts at systems thinking and systems analysis (Bolte et al. 2006). One big change is that biocomplexity represents a biologically centered framing (as compared with a cybernetic, social science, or engineering framing as was the case with those earlier systems' efforts) which is most appropriate in what some have called the "century of biology" (Lubchenco 1998; Wilson 1998). At present, some of its unique value comes from the fact that it makes more amenable the asking of questions that are particularly timely about sustainability, resilience, threshold events, and predictability (Bennett and McGinnis 2008). A particularly valuable consideration is the shift in focus from system elements to the *coupled* nature of these systems, thereby facilitating research on human–environment interactions (Berkes, Colding, and Folke 2003).

Facilitating does not mean necessarily making such work easier. On the contrary, modeling these coupled systems poses new challenges, as it involves human decisions at multiple spatial and temporal scales, landscape dynamics, ecological processes, and how they all interact simultaneously. Such models address important questions about system vulnerabilities, adaptation, resilience, feedback, nonlinearities and emergent properties otherwise observed with difficulty (Bolte et al. 2006). A particular challenge is posed by nonlinearities. While ecological phenomena normally vary within bounded ranges, rapid nonlinear changes can occur in complex systems when even small threshold values are exceeded. Thus, understanding intrinsic and extrinsic threshold values can result in system equilibrium resets (i.e. when a system is reset at a different equilibrium point), system collapse, and species extinctions. Under conditions of climate change, where the threshold values for different species' importance to the larger systems is unknown, and what its degrees of tolerance might be, and required interactions to maintain the system are unknown, the danger of crossing these thresholds is particularly high, and modeling these dynamics is a particular challenge (Burkett et al. 2005). Nonlinearity in complex systems leads to historical dependencies and multiple outcomes, and to the need to determine which environmental conditions or human decisions are the results of self-organization. Hidden within these possible trajectories lies the role of evolution in shaping ecosystem properties, whether systems become more resilient over time, and whether they tend towards chaotic behavior and restructuring as a mechanism of transformation (Levin 1998, 2000).

This transformation is best explained by concepts that view ecosystems, and our global environment, as complex adaptive systems (Levin 2005), in which patterns emerge from, and interact with, the actions of individual agents, and in which cooperation can develop and provide the regulation of local environments, and indeed impose regularity at higher levels (i.e. self-organization) (Levin 2005). Thus, the history of the earth's ecosystems is a history of coevolving organisms across space, time, and scales of complexity.

Pickett, Cadenasso, and Grove (2005) note that biocomplexity results from a "multiplicity of interconnected relationships and levels" but that no integrative framework yet exists to facilitate the application of this concept to coupled human–natural systems. They present a framework that focuses on linkages among different disciplines that are engaged in studies of coupled human–natural systems, including the ecological, physical, and socioeconomic sciences. The framework consists of three dimensions of complexity: spatial, organizational, and temporal. Spatial complexity increases as the focus changes from the type and number of the elements of spatial heterogeneity to an explicit configuration of the elements. Similarly, organizational complexity increases as the focus shifts from unconnected units to connectivity among functional units. Finally, temporal complexity increases as the current state of a system comes to rely more and more on past states, and therefore to reflect echoes, legacies, and evolving indirect effects of those states. This three-dimensional, conceptual notion of biocomplexity enables connections between models that derive from different disciplines to be drawn at an appropriate level of complexity for integration (Pickett, Cadenasso, and Grove 2005).

Plate 1 Overlay of property grid on a Landsat image for Altamira, Pará, Brazil, permitting analysis of changes over time at either individual properties (see Plate 3), or the entire landscape of 3,800+ properties

Source: ACT data, see publications in www.indiana.edu/~act

Cohort of Farm Property Occupancy

Cohorts

- < 1970
- 70 - 73
- 73 - 76
- 76 - 79
- 79 - 85
- 85 - 91
- 91 - 96
- Not Occ by 96

Plate 2 The overlay in Plate 1 was then used to develop a Stratified Sampling Frame to carry out a cohort analysis. Since the area had been all forest before 1972, it was possible to use time of initial clearing to define membership in cohorts and occupation of a property

Source: ACT data; see publications in www.indiana.edu/~act

Differences in Land Use Strategies Among Three Colonist Farms in the TransAmazon Highway, Altamira, Pará, Brazil.

(ACT Project: "Amazonian Deforestation and The Structure of Households: A GeoReferenced Approach")

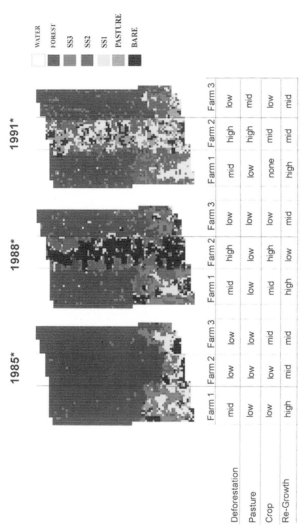

* Classification derived from Landsat TM images (1985, 1988, 1991)

Plate 3 Differences in the development of side-by-side properties in colonist farms in the Transamazon Highway, Altamira, Pará, Brazil. SS1, SS2, SS3 refer to stages of secondary succession
Source: ACT data; see publications in www.indiana.edu/~act

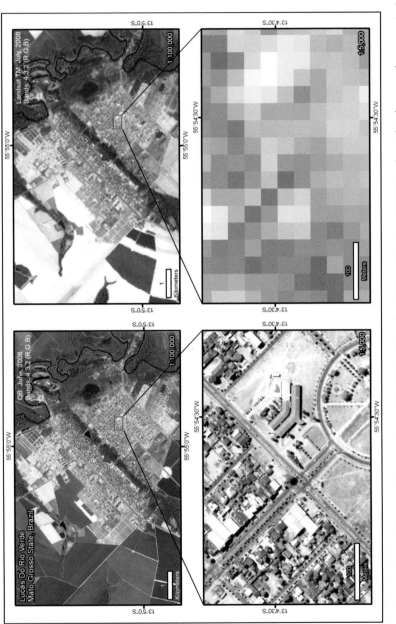

Plate 4 Comparison of the spatial resolution of Quickbird (on the left) and Landsat TM (on the right) for an urban area in Lucas de Rio Verde, Mato Grosso, Brazil. The images are for June and July 2008 respectively. Note that in zooming in on the Landsat image from 1:200.000 (above) to 1:10.000 (below) scale, we lose the ability to observe the urban area but see only pixels, whereas in the Quickbird image, it is possible to see individual houses and buildings, roads, and other details

Source: ACT lab acquisition and processing of images; www.indiana.edu/~act

The study of complex adaptive systems has recently become a major focus of interdisciplinary research in the social and natural sciences. Nonlinear systems are ubiquitous. Early phases of research on nonlinear systems focused on deterministic chaos, but more recent studies have investigated the properties of self-organizing systems or anti-chaos. For mathematicians and physicists, the biggest surprise is that complexity lurks within extremely simple systems. For biologists, it is the idea that natural selection is not the sole source of order in the biological world. For social scientists, it is ideas such as emergent phenomena – the idea that complex global patterns with new properties can emerge from local interactions – could have a comparable impact (Lansing 2003).

Spatially Explicit Processes in Ecological and Social Systems

The development of spatially explicit theory in ecology over the last twenty years has led to general recognition that spatial heterogeneity in the biophysical environment, together with the spatial dispersion of populations of organisms, are crucial elements in population dynamics (Tilman and Kareiva 1997; Bascompte and Sole 1998). Space is included, in the more abstract of the "spatially explicit" population models in ecology, by defining the environment as consisting of multiple locations and recognizing that organisms may move between localities. These relatively straightforward extensions of models of population dynamics have been sufficient to indicate that space plays a crucial role in the survival of individual species; in the joint survival of multiple species that compete for the same resources; in the stability of populations of predators and prey and hosts and parasites; and in the coevolution of species, including the evolution of cooperation (Axelrod 1984). Spatially explicit models address a wide range of issues in ecological theory, but this discussion will focus on those models that may improve understanding of the effects of habitat destruction and habitat fragmentation on biocomplexity.

Many of the most important results in spatial ecology have been obtained from the metapopulation framework, a general approach that is now well established in ecology (Hanski and Gilpin 1997). Metapopulation models treat populations of organisms as sets of distinct local populations, with each local population occupying a distinct patch of habitat. The patches form a network of "suitable habitats" that are locationally distinct from one another and that form intervening patches of territory that are not suitable as habitat. Members of local populations may disperse between patches of habitat and colonize unoccupied patches. Metapopulation models replace the extreme simplifications of nonspatial population models (in which all pairs of individuals are equally likely to interact and all individuals are equally likely to interact with any element of the environment) with a framework that leads to models that are reasonably tractable mathematically and computationally but that can still yield valuable results about the growth and extinction of populations in complex environments. Important results about the processes involved in species extinction have been obtained, for example, from models in which each patch in a network may be characterized simply as occupied or unoccupied and the growth and survival of a population depends on a balance between rates of local extinctions (in particular patches) and the rate at which unoccupied patches are colonized by populations that disperse from currently occupied patches.

Metapopulation models and other models in spatial ecology have yielded important theoretical results about how destruction and fragmentation of habitat are likely to affect biodiversity by leading to the extinction of populations, either globally or in local areas (Hanski 1998). Most of these results are general and abstract, and have been derived through general mathematical reasoning or through computational analysis of relatively simple environments, but they point to crucial directions for research on biodiversity. For example, these general results indicate that the relations between population survival and biodiversity on one hand, and habitat destruction and fragmentation on the other, are likely to be strongly nonlinear. That is, the quantity and fragmentation of habitat may range widely with little effect on the prospects for population survival, but those prospects for survival may deteriorate very suddenly once some critical threshold in the size or fragmentation of habitat is reached. Further, such critical thresholds are likely to depend heavily on the capacities of particular organisms to disperse between patches of habitat, a characteristic that is extremely difficult to observe and measure for most species. A second very general result obtained from mathematical reasoning and computation is the idea of an "extinction debt," which indicates that a population may survive for a considerable time, even in an environment that has changed in ways that doom the population to eventual extinction. Third, metapopulation models indicate that the destruction and fragmentation of habitat may alter the conditions for biodiversity by changing the competitive relations among species. For example, fragmentation of habitat may favor species whose capacity to disperse and colonize new areas exceeds that of competing species who are more competitive in other respects.

The most important contributions of spatially explicit ecological models to questions about the effects of habitat destruction and fragmentation on biodiversity and the extinction of species have been theoretical insights into the ways that ecosystems may respond to the stress of habitat destruction. These insights have been rather general and abstract and they have been gained mainly through mathematically based reasoning and through computational analyses of abstract and general situations. Experimental research and observation of the histories of particular systems have not been unimportant in spatial ecology and field observations of particular cases have yielded some important insights (Hanski and Gilpin 1997). Empirical evaluation and verification of the insights of spatially explicit theory present a very challenging set of problems, however. Experiments to test the implications of the theoretical models may require extremely large numbers of replications involving observations over very long time spans. Empirical models of spatial systems are also likely to require estimates of parameters that have proven difficult to estimate (especially parameters for species dispersal) and the structure of the models makes it likely that small errors in the estimates of these parameters will produce very large errors in model results (Steinberg and Kareiva 1997; Hartway Ruckelshaus, and Kareiva 1998; Harrison and Bruna 1999). The same problems will make it extremely difficult to develop models that have the capacity to predict the effects of particular environmental changes on the survival of populations and the maintenance of biodiversity. Consequently the major contributions of spatially explicit ecological models to the management of biodiversity are more likely to consist of general information about the nature of population processes in spatial environments and the ways that those processes respond to changes in habitats.

Much of the social science research on these questions is also being carried out within explicitly spatial frameworks but social scientists have been much less active in developing explicitly spatial theory (NRC 1999a). Rather, spatial frameworks are crucial as a means of organizing the information used in empirical research and environmental social scientists have been developing important capabilities in collecting information about changes in land use and land cover from a wide variety of sources and organizing that information in ways that make it possible to carry out a variety of explicitly spatial analyses of how habitat is lost and fragmented as land-use and land-cover undergoes human modification (Moran et al. 1994, 1999, 2000; Liverman et al. 1998; Walsh et al. 1999). Remote sensing technology, especially satellite-based remote sensing, has been crucial in gathering this information and the continuing development of geographic information systems has been a key factor in organizing and analyzing this information.

The capacity to organize detailed information about changes in land use over sizable regions has made it possible to carry out a variety of analyses of the ways that demographic, social, and economic variables are related to changes in land use, especially in environments where forest habitat is being destroyed by human activity (Lambin 1994; Entwisle et al. 1998; Moran et al. 1999). These analyses have mainly been concerned with examining hypotheses about the proximate social and economic determinants of changes in land use and land cover (e.g. deforestation, intensification of agriculture, urbanization, population growth). The destruction and fragmentation of habitat has not been a central issue in this research, although the connection with land-use and land-cover change allows advances to occur naturally from the existing work (Moran et al. 1994, 1996, 2000; Moran, Brondizio, and Mausel 1994). This work, however, has not incorporated to date the advances that have been made in nonlinear mathematical approaches even though social scientists have regularly pointed out that human ecosystem processes cannot be treated as if they behave in a linear fashion.

In order to advance the state of spatially explicit modeling of biodiversity we have to enter fully into the realm of processes of biocomplexity, where the properties of systems cannot be fully explained by understanding the component parts. These systems are characterized by nonlinearities, emergent properties, and positive feedbacks. Research on population dynamics is gradually being informed by the insights of nonlinear dynamics; however, these insights have been less fully integrated within a spatial framework, and have rarely taken into account the important role that human actions and institutions play in the dynamics of populations at various levels of analysis. One crucial step in integrating social and ecological processes is to identify common spatial and temporal scales in the operation of the two kinds of processes. That is, "to extract physical knowledge from a complex system, one must focus on the right level of description" (Goldenfeld and Kadanoff 1999). One might begin, for example, with a flexible unit, such as a landscape, which can contain human communities as well as communities of other organisms in interaction but which can be scaled up and down as appropriate. Landscapes can commonly be defined by watersheds or some similar integrated biophysical system within which human institutions also operate and affect all organisms to some degree. In this landscape, we can construct a preliminary dynamic model characterized by nonlinear dynamics but one that will include the role of human populations as their behavior affects other species. We can then seek to couple experiments and theory in computer simulations.

One important advance in this regard comes from the research produced by scientists funded by the coupled human–natural systems program at NSF. These studies (e.g. Liu et al. 2007a, 2007b) reveal complex patterns and processes not evident when studied by social or natural scientists separately. The coupling of human–natural systems varies across space, time, and organizational units. It also exhibits nonlinear dynamics with thresholds, feedback loops, time lags, heterogeneity and surprises. Perhaps even more importantly, past coupling seems to have legacy effects on present and future possibilities for coupled interactions. This leads to the necessity to pay close attention to past trajectories (environmental history), how people transformed the environment (historical ecology), and to how thresholds were crossed and why.

Walsh and McGinnis (2008) examine the nature of coupled human–natural systems by emphasizing biocomplexity, i.e. the interdisciplinary and integrated study of coupled human–natural systems to address the causes and consequences of landscape dynamics. Biocomplexity often views landscapes as complex systems, consisting of interactions of human and natural processes, in which landscape patterns are important emergent properties of complex dynamics. Moreover, they encompass the complex interactions within and among ecological systems, the physical systems on which they depend, and the human systems with which they interact (Michener et al. 2003; Walsh and McGinnis 2008). Along these same lines, Walsh et al. (2008) examine coupled human–natural systems in the Northern Ecuadorian Amazon, based on complexity theory linked to work in Cellular Automata (CA) in which land-use/land-cover change patterns were spatially simulated to examine deforestation and agricultural extensification of household farms. The basic intent was to understand linkages between people and the environment by explicitly considering pattern–process relationships and the nature of feedback mechanisms. The CA modeling approach emphasizes the human dimensions of land-use and land-cover change by including socioeconomic and demographic characteristics at the household level along with biophysical data that describe the resource endowments of farms, geographic accessibility of farms to roads and communities, and the evolving nature of human–environment interactions over time and space in response to exogenous and endogenous factors.

Similarly, work in Nang Rong District in North East Thailand uses cellular automata modeling to explore the land-cover consequences of alternative patterns of settlement in a setting where people establish dwelling units in nucleated villages and work in agricultural plots away from the villages (Entwisle et al. 2008). Forested land around the villages is converted to agricultural land in an inverse relationship to the distance from the village center, but frequently subjected to modification as a result of biophysical characteristics of the land. Land in the village may be reforested, in the form of shade and fruit trees, after the village is well established. The CA model finds that variability in land-cover change is more sensitive to the spatial reach of the households in the village than to their temporal reach, suggesting an unexpectedly important role for whether villagers walk or used motorized transit to get back and forth from their fields (Entwisle et al. 2008).

Advances have also taken place in considering both the direct and the indirect impacts of human activities in landscapes. Linderman et al. (2006) consider the spatiotemporal patterns of human impacts, forests, and bamboo episodic die-offs as they affect panda habitat in South West China. The model considers the direct consequences of local fuelwood collection, and household creation, on areas of critical panda habitat and the indirect impacts when coupled with vegetation dynamics. They find through the model simulations that over the next 30 years household impacts would result in the loss of up to 30% of the habitat relied on by pandas during past bamboo die-offs. Also affected would be the spatial distribution of understory bamboo (For further discussion of indirect effects in complex systems, see Wootton 2002.)

Land-use systems are characterized by complex interactions between human decision makers and their biophysical environment (see also discussion in Chapter 7). Mismatches between the scale of human drivers and the impacts of human decisions potentially threaten the ecological sustainability of these systems. Parker et al. (2008) and Parker, Hessl, and Davis (2008) review sources of complexity in land-use systems, moving from the human decision level to human interactions to effects over space, time, and scale. Selected challenges in modeling such systems and potential resolutions are discussed, including strategies to give empirical content to complex models, methods for linking models across human and natural systems, and the challenges to modeling indirect and cross-scale linkages and of the potential utility of complex models of land systems (Parker et al. 2008; Parker, Hessl, and Davis 2008). One important development along these lines has been the proliferation of agent-based models.

Agent-based Modeling of Complex Systems

The goal of most agent-based models is to understand how microdecisions and behavioral rules interact with environmental variables to *cause* the emergence of macro-patterns that are not reducible to those rules. Interactions between agents and the environment produce macro-patterns in ways that are not necessarily predictable given the characteristics of either alone. When these relationships are analytically intractable (as they often are when dealing with adaptive rather than strictly rational agents or with an environment/situation of marginal complexity), agent-based modeling provides a methodology for rigorously exploring relationships and patterns. This is especially useful for social scientists and natural scientists (e.g., ecologists, biologists, geneticists) whose subject matter is inherently historical. By endowing agents with characteristics and rules for interactions and creating a bioecological world that changes in light of their actions, it is possible to "see" how those rules and interactions produce patterns in a controlled fashion.

Scientists have used agent-based models to approach numerous subjects in both the social and natural sciences. Applications in economics, political science, and sociology have been especially prevalent with stock market, voting, alliance formation, cultural transmission, cooperation, and conflict models generating deep insights into human society (Arthur 1994; Holland

1995; Cederman 1997; Kollman, Miller, and Page 1997; Tesfatsion 1997). In biology and ecology, models of ecosystem evolution and species interaction/behavior have made inroads as well (Stein 1989; Nadel and Stein 1991, 1992, 1995; Belew and Mitchell 1996). Deadman and Gimblett (1994) have illustrated the usefulness of agent-based modeling in examining people–environment interactions in forested lands.

The land-use/land-cover change community has used various techniques for modeling complex social-ecological systems. Examples include spatial interaction models, cellular automata (Clarke and Gaydos 1998; Messina and Walsh 2001), and dynamic systems models (Evans et al. 2001). Agent-based modeling approaches have been used to explore the decision-making processes of land managers in the context of spatial and social interactions. Reviews of applications of agent-based models (ABMs) to land-cover change scenarios have demonstrated the utility of a local-level representation of land-use decision making (Berger and Parker 2002; Parker, Hessl, and Davis 2008; Parker et al. 2003, 2008). Early ABMs were comparatively abstract representations that explored fundamental aspects of spatially explicit systems but were not necessarily related to specific real-world applications (e.g. Epstein and Axtell 1996). Recent applications of ABMs have produced comparatively complex representations of social-ecological systems (Berger and Ringler 2002; Hoffmann, Kelley and Evans 2002; An et al. 2005; Brown et al. 2005). Berger and Parker (2002) characterize these models in terms of whether environmental and agent model components are empirically grounded or designed but not substantiated.

A fundamental reason why agent-based approaches may be an effective tool for exploring the complexities of biocomplex human–environment processes is the spatial pattern and heterogeneous nature of actors and the landscape. Landscape patterns are highly correlated with topographic distribution in many cases. However, in addition to these land suitability heterogeneities are the variety of landowner characteristics, histories, and experiences that contribute to the overall complexity in land-use/land-cover change dynamics. Koontz (2001) found that while the majority of landowners in a 1997 household-level survey noted nonmonetary reasons in their land-use decision making, the relative importance of nonmonetary factors varied by the size of the parcel owned by the landowner, household income, and educational attainment.

A particular challenge with modeling historical land-cover change is to develop an understanding of how path dependence and initial conditions determine specific future land-cover change trajectories. Previous research has explored the roles of initial conditions and path dependence in land-use modeling (Atkinson and Oleson 1996; Wilson 2000; Balmann 2001; Brown et al. 2005). In ABMs there are particular sensitivities in the initial conditions for land-use scenarios (Brown et al. 2005). Sensitivity analysis has proven a valuable tool to explore the impact of these historical uncertainties in the development of agent-based and other spatially explicit models of land-cover change.

In agent-based modeling, a major challenge is the development of explicit datasets to validate the agent interactions and heterogeneities in models (Manson 2002; Walker 2003; Pontius, Huffaker, and Denman 2004). Several disciplines have strong traditions of laboratory- or field-based experimental methods that have proven helpful in the design and development of behavioral models. The combination of ABMs with experimental approaches is one way to begin to validate and make modifications to the model. In particular, psychology and economics have considerable literatures drawing on controlled experimental scenarios to explore key aspects of decision-making processes such as risk, cognition, bargaining, and trust. To a lesser extent, experimental approaches have been applied in anthropology (Henrich et al. 2001; Bernard 2002), political science (e.g. Ostrom, Gardner and Walker 1994), and sociology (Kanazawa 1999). There has clearly been some reluctance over the adoption of experimental methods in disciplines such as anthropology (e.g. Chibnik 2005), but in each of these disciplines there is tacit acceptance of experimental methodologies within subdisciplinary fields. Two classic experimental designs are the Prisoner's Dilemma (e.g. Ostrom, Gardner and Walker 1994; Wedekind and Milinski 1996; Milinski and Wedekind 1998) and the Ultimatum Game (e.g. Henrich et al. 2001; Oosterbeek, Sloof, and Van De Kuilen et al. 2004), both of which have been conducted and replicated with varying subject populations and have resulted in numerous derivative experiments.

There are limited examples of spatial representation in experimental research. Spatial cognition research has employed the use of human subjects for experiments, integrating principles from psychology and geography, and there is considerable research in this particular area (e.g. Golledge 1999; Klatzky et al. 2002). However, the objective has focused on aspects of cognition and perception rather than the dynamics of economic contexts. One of the most widely cited examples of spatially explicit experimental research is Schelling's segregation model (1971, 1978). Despite the prevalence of spatial methods such as geographic information systems (GIS), cellular automata, and agent-based modeling in land-use/land-cover change research, and the contributions of economics to land-use theory, there are relatively few examples of experimental applications to land-use management in recent literature (the work of Bousquet et al. [2002], Wilke, Hutchinson, and Todd [2004], and Goldstone and Janssen [2005] is the exception). In management contexts, land-use decisions have an explicitly spatial outcome, so we have found the use of spatially explicit experiments is a valuable method to explore decision-making dynamics in questions of natural resource management.

This is still a relatively new form of modeling and scholars have voiced concerns with the agent-based model approach. One objection is that the modeling is somewhat inaccessible to non-computationally oriented scholars (Axelrod 1997). A second is that the models are not always readily applicable to empirical investigation, leaving scholars with deep, general insights that may or may not increase knowledge of actual events and patterns (Alker 1999). Finally, these models may be too simple to capture interesting social insights. Some scholars lament that these models ignore the very complexity of social life that they are attempting to capture.

One way to deal with the first objection is by making the documented programs available to others (i.e. to increase transparency) and by using the simulations in outreach activities with public officials and land owners. The second and third concerns are more serious, but recent work in agent-based modeling has begun to address them (Kohler and Carr 1996; Cederman 1997; Cohen, Riolo, and Axelrod 1999; Lustick 2000). In addition, as more scholars with empirical leanings and a desire to explore different questions begin to use these tools, the applicability, diversity, and complexity of the models will increase (e.g. Becu et al. 2003; Bousquet and LePage 2004; Bolte et al. 2006; Bennett and McGinnis 2008; Brown et al. 2008; Evans and Kelley 2008). The lacunae noted are not so much inherent in the approach as they are in the limited goals of the modelers to date.

Parker et al. (2003) present an overview of multi-agent system models of land-use/land-cover change (MAS/LUCC models). These models combine a cellular landscape model with agent-based representations of decision making, integrating the two components through specification of interdependencies and feedbacks between agents and their environment. The authors review alternative LUCC modeling techniques and discuss the ways in which MAS/LUCC models may overcome some important limitations of other techniques. They review ongoing MAS/LUCC modeling efforts and find that MAS/LUCC models are particularly well suited for representing complex spatial interactions under heterogeneous conditions and for modeling decentralized, autonomous decision making. Among the challenges still to be fully addressed by these models are validation and verification, application for policy analysis and scenario building, among others (see suggested validation approaches proposed by Pontius, Huffaker, and Denman 2004 and Walker 2003). Nevertheless, ABMs seem to be a productive approach to create fine-scale models focusing on human–environment interactions (Parker et al. 2003). Parker et al. (2008) and Parker, Hessl, and Davis (2008) provide a structured comparison of a variety of ABMs across sites focusing on frontier regions' land-change processes. This allows the authors to point to commonalities among the models in defining the frontier processes, while also discovering where the models differ from the expected sources of variation (e.g. whether owners own one parcel or multiple parcels; differences in size and parcel quality heterogeneity; differences in initial capital and labor; differences in exposure to market forces).

Hierarchical Modeling

Wu and David (2002) take a different approach coming from hierarchy theory. Ecological systems are characterized by a large number of diverse components, nonlinear interactions, scale multiplicity, and spatial heterogeneity. Hierarchy theory (Warren 2005), as well as empirical evidence, suggests that complexity often takes the form of modularity in structure and functionality. Therefore, a hierarchy perspective can be useful to understanding complex ecological systems. But, how can hierarchical thinking help with modeling spatially heterogeneous, nonlinear dynamic systems like landscapes, be they natural or human-dominated? Wu and David (2002) present a spatially explicit hierarchical modeling approach to studying the patterns and processes of heterogeneous landscapes. They discuss the theoretical basis for the modeling approach – the hierarchical patch dynamics paradigm and the scaling ladder strategy – and then describe the general structure of a hierarchical urban landscape model which is developed using this modeling approach. Further, they introduce a hierarchical patch dynamics modeling platform to facilitate the development of spatial hierarchical models and illustrate its utility through two examples: a hierarchical cellular automata model of land-use change and a spatial multi-species population dynamics model. A recent book (Banerjee, Carlin, and Gelfand 2004) provides a comprehensive discussion of hierarchical modeling for complex spatiotemporal data. Recent developments in Markov chain Monte Carlo computing now allow fully Bayesian analysis of multilevel models for complex geographically referenced data – and even for correction of misaligned geographic data in a GIS.

Conclusions

Four major research foci have been identified in understanding coupled human-natural systems: land, resources and the built environment; human health and the environment; freshwater resources, estuaries and coastal environments; and environmental services and valuation. Coupled human-natural systems seek to understand the complex web of environmental feedbacks at diverse temporal and spatial scales. They address how the environment functions, how people use the environment, how this changes the environment, and how these changes affect people (Pfirman and AC-ERE 2003). A key element in these decisions is the mediating role of institutions or organizations used to manage resources. Water rights, access to forests, and the status of protected areas are all handled by institutions and social organizations that can protect the environment, or fail to do so.

Integrated environmental resources management is a purposeful activity with the goal of maintaining and improving the state of an environmental resource affected by human activities. To achieve its goals, it has found it increasingly useful to turn to complex systems thinking. In many cases different goals are in conflict and the notion "integrated" clearly indicates that resources management should be approached from a broad perspective taking all potential trade-offs and different scales in space and time into account. The tradition of resources management and of dealing with environmental problems is characterized by a command and control approach. The increasing awareness of the complexity of environmental problems and of human-technology–environment systems has triggered the development of new management approaches. New management paradigms based on the insight that the systems to be managed are complex adaptive systems are needed, approaches that emphasize the role of social learning processes and the need to develop methods combining approaches from hard and soft systems analysis. Soft systems analysis focuses on the importance of subjective perceptions and socially constructed reality. Soft systems methods and group model building techniques are quite common in management science where the prime target of management has always been the social system. Resources management is still quite slow to take up such innovations that should follow as a logical consequence of adopting an integrated management approach (Pahl-Wostl 2007).

An integrative systems approach is essential to effective decision making (see next chapter) with regards to global sustainability (see Chapter 8), given how closely connected industrial, social, and ecological systems are. Yet, such a task is daunting given its modeling and computational requirements. A whole array of approaches must be explored – biocomplexity and ABM approaches, system dynamic modeling, thermodynamic analysis, hierarchical modeling, adaptational and resilience approaches, to name but a few – to investigate the impacts of ecological and human systems and of major shifts taking place – whether from climate change or anthropogenic change (Fiksel 2006).

7

Environmental Decision Making[1]

For environmental decisions we need the knowledge of both the natural and the social sciences. The natural sciences are well integrated as sources of information for decisions in policies regarding the environment. The social sciences are latecomers into these processes even though they offer a growing number of approaches that can improve environmental decision making at a variety of levels (NRC 2005b). Environmental decision making requires combining good environmental science with improved understanding of human–environment interactions and development of approaches that integrate sound science with consideration of human values and institutions so that decisions are responsible, competent, and socially acceptable. To achieve this one needs to develop criteria for improved quality of decisions, better tools for structuring decision processes, and creating effective analytic-deliberative processes (NRC 2005b:2–3).

Individuals, organizations, and human societies have significant effects on the natural environment, largely as a product of their decisions. Decisions, both small and large, can have cumulative effects and can alter the conditions of localities, communities, nations, and the planet. Decisions that affect the environment are particularly difficult to understand because they are characterized by structural complexity; multiple and often conflicting values; very long time horizons; different property rights schemes; incomplete and uncertain knowledge; are characterized by high stakes; and decisions must be made sometimes under conditions of high time pressure because of the deteriorating conditions of our planet (NRC 2005b:24). They are structurally complex because of the multi-scale nature of decisions and the often mismatched decisions diagnosed at one scale but targeted at a different scale by policy makers. Environmental values are deeply bound to cultural, economic, spiritual and other values, such as obligations to be

[1] I am grateful for the many substantive suggestions provided by Maria Claudia Lopez Perez on this chapter. Any errors, however, are my responsibility.

"good stewards" of our planet, that lead to highly variable willingness to compromise on priorities and to fight for or against different environmental policy options.

Whereas much of decision-making science has roots in psychology, it is economics that is most commonly looked to for useful approaches to understanding decisions. Economics has been noted to work on very short time horizons, even though environmental decisions have long-term consequences that make traditional estimation approaches inappropriate or unacceptable to individuals because of the above noted values that are inherently long term. Perhaps even more critical are the problems arising from calculating a given discount rate for environmental and social costs and benefits. Unlike many other objects of decisions, the environment is very much "open access" and it is difficult to exclude people from using or polluting it, and thereby putting the resource at risk of overuse (cf. the classic article pointing to this, that of Hardin 1968 on the "tragedy of the commons"). Methods for acting under conditions of incomplete and uncertain knowledge are needed because the deteriorating condition of environmental resources do not permit the luxury of postponing action, yet require flexibility in adjusting decisions made on a shifting state-of-knowledge (Funtowicz and Ravetz 1992; NRC 1996; Dietz and Stern 1998; Renn 2003; Tversky and Kahneman 1981; Slovic 1995; Kingdon 1987).

To deal with these difficult dimensions of environmental decision making, scientists have developed numerous analytical tools, among them mathematical models, spatial analytic techniques, risk analysis techniques, and cost-benefit approaches. Mathematical models of complex systems attempt to capture the multiple layers and linkages that are involved in environmental systems and how they are connected to structures of policy making (see discussion in the next chapter). Spatial sciences have developed sophisticated tools combining remote sensing with GIS to represent spatially explicit changes in the conditions of the environment (see Chapter 4). Risk analysis techniques, in contrast, focus on characterizing undesired outcomes, the uncertainties surrounding them and the probabilities of their occurrence (Bollig 2006; McCabe 2004). In this book the focus is on spatial analytic approaches, rather than on mathematical models, risk analysis, or cost-benefit analysis (CBA), but the latter is so widely used that some comment is called for. Economics has long used cost-benefit analysis as a tool that compares outcomes at different times in the future and estimates in the aggregate net societal outcome (e.g. Layard and Glaister 2004).

A cost-benefit analysis finds, quantifies, and adds all the positive factors. These are the benefits. Then it identifies, quantifies, and subtracts all the negatives, the costs. The difference between the two indicates whether the planned action is advisable. The real trick to doing a cost-benefit analysis well is making sure you include all the costs and all the benefits and properly quantify them. Doing so is less than straightforward, as it may be difficult to assign equal units of value to the costs and benefits; and it is essential that there be a way to assess both on an equal basis. In terms of environmental issues, we need to assign value to things in nature, which have been "free" for a very long time, and at this time what would be a fair value? And in human terms, assessing the benefits of goods and services provided by the environment to people is even harder. Much progress has been made since the Exxon Valdez Oil spill, an event of such huge magnitude economically and environmentally that considerable advances were necessary in calculating the costs to society and the environment over a variety of spatial and temporal dimensions. The issue is contentious enough that economists are deeply divided as a discipline between those who have one approach to valuation, and others who take a more ecological approach and turn to political economy rather than CBA to come up with an assessment of the economics of ecological policy problems.

Cost-benefit analysis seeks to translate all relevant considerations into monetary terms. Economists "monetize" both the costs of regulation, such as the money spent to install a scrubber on a power plant to reduce air pollution, and the benefits of regulation, such as saving human lives and preventing disease. When benefits of regulation will happen in the future, the economists first quantify those benefits in monetary terms. Then they "discount" their value to reflect how much we would have to invest today to have that much money when the benefit is delivered. The first step in a cost-benefit analysis is to calculate the costs of a public policy. The costs of protecting human health and the environment through the use of pollution control devices and other approaches are, by their very nature, measured in dollars or whatever currency is relevant. Thus, at least in theory, the cost side of cost-benefit analysis should be relatively straightforward – but rarely is. One has to consider the costs of including, or not, the environmental costs, and of implementing or not implementing different policy options. More problematic is the second step in the analysis: monetizing the benefits achieved by the regulation. Since there are no natural prices for a healthy environment, cost-benefit analysis requires the creation of artificial ones. Economists create artificial prices for health and environmental benefits by studying what people would be willing to pay for them, or what price they might be willing to accept. One popular method, called "contingent valuation," is essentially a form of opinion poll (Carson et al. 2003; Davis 1963). Researchers ask a cross-section of the affected population (and indeed, this presents a thorny problem of the method that might be used to choose a given affected population) how much they would be willing to pay to preserve or protect something that can't be bought in a store (Ackerman and Heinzerling 2002). Other techniques include price-based recreated preferences as a way of getting at these values (Hanemann 1994; Portney 1994).

The above approaches are an important part of the set of tools used, but they do not include some of the harder-to-deal-with dimensions, particularly how to deal with value conflicts and uncertainty. Many of the techniques often embody assumptions of value that are not always explicitly stated and can later impede the decisions that must be made. A growing number of studies recommend that processes integrate analysis with broadly based deliberative processes involving the range of parties interested or affected by decisions (NRC 1996). This is now often referred to, for short, as involvement of stakeholders in the analytic-deliberative process. This has already been seen at EPA and in the US Climate Change Program (US Climate Change Science Program 2003) and elsewhere. This means moving towards an environmental decision-making science approach (e.g. Raiffa 1968; Morgan and Henrion 1990; Keeney and Raiffa 1993; Clemen 1996) in which one considers objectives, ways to evaluate decisions and decision processes against those objectives, that identifies the questions and kinds of information needed, and that develops knowledge about which decision processes are likely to produce desired outcomes (NRC 2005b).

Good environmental decisions need to consider both physical and social phenomena and human values. This requires that one obtain competent and socially acceptable ways to integrate scientific information and values (Hammond, Keeney and Raiffa 1999; Slovic and Gregory 1999). In addition, environmental decision making involves diverse and conflicting values; substantial scientific uncertainty; and often the presence of coordination problems among stakeholders that can result in, among other things, mistrust. This results in hotly contested positions regardless of the scientific evidence because the acceptable outcomes (or objectives) may be themselves contested. Decision-making science approaches may help make these decisions by making these conflicts more explicit and structuring ways for stakeholders to reconsider their positions, and to shift in order to successfully reach attainable goals (e.g. Morgan and Henrion 1990; Clemen 1996; Suter 1993; Rodricks 1992; Travis 1988; NRC 1996).

Behavioral decision-making research coming out of psychology has shown that individuals typically omit key elements of good decision processes and that their decisions suffer as a result of such omissions (Slovic, Fischhoff and Lichtenstein 1977; cf. also Bowles 2004; Fehr and Gächter 2000, 2002). They may leave out emotions, existing preferences, past routines, and other elements that affect decisions. Individuals respond to complex tasks by simplifying in ways that seem adequate but that include predictable biases that distort the underlying information (Kahneman, Slovic and Tversky 1982), that show difficulty in clarifying objectives (March 1978), and that manifest difficulty in seeing all viable alternatives (Keeney 1992). In contrast, decision-making groups can identify more elements of any decision than individuals, and thereby correct individual's errors – yet, groups experience other sorts of problems such as mistrust among members based upon differences in social status (Hastie, Penrod, and Pennington 1983; David and Turner 1996), group norms regarding consensus or majority rule (Moscovici

1985), lack of participation by some members of the group which results in bias, and differences in tactics used to propose ideas (Turner 1991). Thus, depending on the nature of the problem individuals or group approaches to decisions may be needed or they should be used in combination.

One important task is to clarify values and preferences by helping people construct their preferences rather than simply revealing them. Perhaps the best known approach to this is the multi-attribute trade-off analysis (Keeney 1992) which yields a mathematical statement comprising a utility or value function that can be used to evaluate every alternative within the range of consequences foreseen by the decision maker. This approach, and others like it, offer many advantages but also many disadvantages such as the lack of trained people to direct the interview, the difficulty of evaluating the individual utility functions, and difficulties in expressing underlying values. Newer approaches have emerged that try to make the task cognitively simpler, more transparent, or more particular to specific types of decisions, among them: analytic hierarchy process (Saaty 1980, 1991); strategies that focus on a choice among alternatives in a given resource (McDaniels and Thomas 1999); methods that clarify preferences based on judgments of what may be "even swaps" (Hammond, Keeney and Raiffa 1999); value-focused thinking (Keeney 1992); and "satisficing" approaches (Payne et al. 1993) that seek less than optimal solutions. Work on revealed price preferences and hedonic prices is also relevant and their use is increasing (Bowles 2004; Camerer and Fehr 2004; Baland and Platteau 2000[1996]).

Findings from behavioral organization theory, behavioral decision theory, survey research, and experimental economics leave no doubt about the failure of rational choice as a descriptive model of human behavior (Jones 1999). But this does not mean that people and their politics are irrational. Thus, we need approaches for thinking about rational theory, among them "bounded rationality." Bounded rationality asserts that decision makers are intentionally rational; that is, they are goal-oriented and adaptive, but because of human cognitive and emotional architecture, they sometimes fail – even when they are making important decisions. Limits on rational adaptation are of two types: procedural limits, which limit how we go about making decisions, and substantive limits, which affect particular choices directly. Rational analysis in institutional contexts can serve as a standard for adaptive, goal-oriented human behavior. In relatively fixed task environments, such as asset markets or elections, we should be able to divide behavior into adaptive, goal-oriented behavior (that is, rational action) and behavior that is a consequence of processing limits, and we should then be able to measure the deviation. The extent of deviation is an empirical issue. These classes are mutually exclusive and exhaustive, and they may be examined empirically in situations in which actors make similar choices repeatedly. Another challenge is posed by uncertainty in the face of decisions that must be made. It has been said that people rather act under conditions of risk, than of uncertainty, as the latter tends to immobilize the decision maker (White 1974).

Characterizing uncertainties is another way to improve the decision-making process, and this has often involved methods that elicit probabilistic judgments and other sources of information (Morgan and Henrion 1990; Cullen and Frey 1999). Other methods have also been proposed that involve less demanding judgments: fuzzy set theory (Zadeh 1965) that assumes that it is not necessary to arrive at highly precise probabilities; scenario-building is increasingly used to characterize uncertainties and alternatives (Wack 1985a, 1985b); influence diagrams that help reveal the mental models of decision participants and the sources of their disagreements (Howard 1989; Clemen 1996), or those with different stakes (Morgan et al. 2002).

One of the most difficult environmental decisions is how to arrive at a societal preference in a collective action context because of the inherent difficulties in achieving coordination among stakeholders. There is no unique rule for aggregating the preferences of individuals with different values across a range of alternatives. This is particularly problematic for large-scale environmental problems involving long-time horizons, nonmarginal changes in human or environmental variables, deeply held values, and when issues of equity arise (NRC 1996). One effective way to deal with collective action problems is through institutional analysis.

Institutional Analysis

Human institutions – defined as ways of organizing activities – affect the resilience of the environment (Dietz, Ostrom, and Stern 2003). Locally evolved institutional arrangements governed by stable communities and buffered from outside forces have sustained resources successfully for centuries (Ostrom 1990; Baland and Platteau 2000[1996]), although they can fail when rapid change occurs after centuries of operating successfully. Ideal conditions for governance are increasingly rare. Critical problems, such as transboundary pollution, tropical deforestation, and climate change, are at larger scales than local communities have customarily dealt with, and involve nonlocal influences beyond their control. Part of the problem is that for environmental problems to be dealt with effectively by institutions requires that they have "well-defined boundaries" and this is very difficult with many of the above problems. Promising strategies for addressing collective action problems include dialogue among interested parties, officials, and scientists; complex, redundant, and layered institutions; a mix of institutional types; and institutional designs that facilitate experimentation, learning, and change.

According to Acheson (2006), many of the world's natural resources are in a state of crisis. His solution is to develop effective management institutions, but there is no consensus on what those institutions are. Some favor solving resource-management problems through the institution of private property; others advocate central government control; and others see local-level management as the solution. Acheson suggests that all these governance structures fail under certain conditions and that we need to learn to match the resource problems with governance institutions and specific management techniques if we are to manage resources effectively. This is a scale problem and one that is a persistent challenge to environmental management and decision making.

Among the most difficult environmental resources to manage are common-pool resources. We can define the concept of a common-pool source based on two attributes: the difficulty of excluding beneficiaries and the subtractability of use of the resource. Becker and Ostrom (1995) present similarities and differences among common-pool resources in regard to their ecological and institutional significance. More complex biological resources are a greater challenge to the design of sustainable institutions, but the same general principles appear to carry over to simpler systems. Extensive empirical evidence and theoretical developments in multiple disciplines stimulate a need to expand the range of rational choice models to be used as a foundation for the study of social dilemmas and collective action. Ostrom (1998) claims that individuals can achieve results that are "better than rational" by building preferences where reciprocity, reputation, and trust can help to overcome the strong temptations towards short-run self-interest. This constitutes a second-generation model of rationality and it is more consistent with optimizing behavior by individuals as members of communities who must take collective actions (see Ostrom 2006). This does not eliminate the temptation of having free riders come along, but it probably reduces its incidence.

According to Ostrom (1999), contemporary policy analysis of the governance of common-pool resources is based on three core assumptions: (a) resource users are norm-free maximizers of immediate gains, who will not cooperate to overcome the common dilemmas they face; (b) designing rules to change incentives of participants is a relatively simple analytical task; and (c) managing common-pool resources requires central or top-down direction. Ostrom finds, from laboratory experiments, that we need to use different assumptions, such as one asserting that humans are fallible, boundedly rational, and norm-using and that this is closer to the reality of how people deal with common-pool problems. Her research on complex adaptive systems suggests the need for a more realistic way of understanding how rules are changed as processes shift and the value of encouraging the evolution of polycentric governance systems. With regards to the design of rules, the challenge lies in how to monitor and ensure compliance with the rules – and the evidence is that many communities fail to comply with their own rules. The assumption of many (cf. since Hardin 1968) that top-down is the only way to ensure managing common-pool resources has been amply refuted (cf. Dietz, Rosa, and York 2007).

Sekher (2001) explores how different local organizations affect participatory management of common-pool resources (CPRs) in India. Building on the ideas of "interdependency" and "new institutionalism," along the lines of Elinor Ostrom's "design principles" and the "institutional analysis and development framework," the study attributes individual choice within collective-action strategies for CPR management to the incentives they face. The framework suggests that the participatory strategies are conditioned by three factors: the attributes of the resource, the attributes of the user-group, and the attributes of the institutional arrangements. Based on the user's perspective, Sekher makes a comparative analysis of three broad categories of local organizations operating in three villages, namely a nongovernmental people's organization (NGPO), a government-engineered people's organization (GEPO), and an indigenous participatory strategy (traditional management regime). Sekher (2001) argues that, depending on the process by which rules are made and interests internalized, that different organized participatory systems create restraints, provide opportunities, and confer legitimacy differently. A recent meta-analysis of a large body of work using Ostrom's design principles is now available that finds that the principles largely work, but that there are numerous conditions that can affect the degree to which they fail and why (Cox, Arnold, and Villamayor Tomas, in review). The following list contains the design principles as Ostrom (1990:90) originally formulated them:

1   Clearly defined boundaries: Individuals or households who have rights to withdraw resource units from the CPR must be clearly defined, as must the boundaries of the CPR itself.
2   Congruence between appropriation and provision rules and local conditions: Appropriation rules restricting time, place, technology, and/or quantity of resource units are related to local conditions and to provision rules requiring labor, material, and/or money.
3   Collective-choice arrangements: Most individuals affected by the operational rules can participate in modifying the operational rules.
4   Monitoring: Monitors, who actively audit CPR conditions and appropriator behavior, are accountable to the appropriators or are the appropriators.
5   Graduated Sanctions: Appropriators who violate operational rules are likely to be assessed graduated sanctions (depending on the seriousness and the context of the offense) by other appropriators, by officials accountable to these appropriators, or both.

6   Conflict-resolution mechanisms: Appropriators and their officials have rapid access to low-cost local arenas to resolve conflicts among appropriators or between appropriators and officials.
7   Minimal recognition of rights to organize: The rights of appropriators to devise their own institutions are not challenged by external governmental authorities.
8   Nested enterprise: Appropriation, provision, monitoring, enforcement, conflict resolution, and governance activities are organized in multiple layers of nested enterprises.

The primary role of the design principles was to explain under what conditions trust and reciprocity can be built and maintained in order to sustain collective action in the face of social dilemmas posed by common-pool resources.

Folke et al. (2005) explore the social dimensions that enable adaptive ecosystem-based management to work. They concentrate on experiences of adaptive governance of social-ecological systems during periods of abrupt change (crisis) and investigate social sources of renewal and reorganization. Such governance connects individuals, organizations, agencies, and institutions at multiple organizational levels. Key persons provide leadership, trust, vision, and meaning, and they help transform management organizations toward a learning environment. Adaptive governance systems often self-organize as social networks with teams and actor groups that draw on various knowledge systems and experiences for the development of a common understanding and policies. The emergence of bridging organizations seems to lower the costs of collaboration and conflict resolution, and enabling legislation and governmental policies can support self-organization while framing creativity for adaptive co-management efforts. A resilient social-ecological system may make use of crisis as an opportunity to transform into a more desired state (Folke et al. 2005).

Individual Behavior and Environmental Decisions

The activities of individuals and households have a profound impact on the environment (e.g. consumer expenditures account for two-thirds of GDP; NRC 2005b:69). Households account for nearly half of the US carbon emissions and large percentages of other noxious effluents (Stern and Gardner 1981; Cutter et al. 2002; Van den Burgh 2004; Stern 2007). Individual behaviors have significant and direct impact in the aggregate in areas such as transportation, housing, energy use, solid waste, water, and food. As citizens, individuals play an important role in influencing the environmental decisions of local communities, regions, and states. However, the behavior of individuals is not totally free – it is constrained by a whole constellation of social, economic, institutional, and technological systems within which they find themselves (Lutzenhiser, Harris, and Olsen 2001). For example, the desire to recycle may be constrained by the absence of curbside recycling pickup, thereby requiring driving a substantial distance to a recycling center, requiring the use of a car.

Environmental information can be effective in influencing behavior but to do so requires that information be appropriate, timely, and delivered in ways that facilitate implementation. Information is cognitively processed and weighed against individual's values, attitudes, and affective processes, against social norms, economic resources available, and against a technology which is affordable at the individual's level of income. Despite research over several decades, we are still only beginning to understand the ways individuals' values and preferences, constraints, and other factors shape environmentally significant behavior.

Evidence since the 1970s has noted a consistently high level of support for environmental protection, and support for regulations that go further to ensure conservation of natural resources (Dunlap and Scarce 1991; Dunlap 2002). This support is also evident in individual preferences for "smart growth" policies, community gardens, parks and nature reserves, farmers' markets, and other green products. However, this strong environmental concern and support is contradicted by the behavior of individuals who purchase large sports utility vehicles (SUVs), larger homes, and maintain levels of consumption inconsistent with their pronounced beliefs. Part of the problem lies in the difficulty for any individual in evaluating the environmental impact of their choices. Studies have shown that households hold mistaken beliefs about relative energy consumption of household appliances (Kempton et al.1985). Information, such as the energy-use indicators on appliances, has been found to poorly communicate with consumers (DuPont 2000; Shorey and Eckman 2000). Green labels have not been used widely in the US but in Europe they have had remarkable influence on individual behavior (Thøgerson 2002). In Sweden, eco-labeling of household chemicals, in the 1980s resulted in a drop of 15 percent in sales of cleaning and personal chemicals and in the replacement of 60 percent of chemicals in soap, shampoo, detergents, and cleaners with less harmful substances.

Clearly one of the important research tasks is to figure out how best to transmit information to individuals in ways that facilitate comprehension and provide action alternatives. Recent efforts by environmental NGOs to work with corporations to come up with actions they can take that can lead to more green outcomes have been effective in some cases. Even things such as economic incentives to purchase greener vehicles are often not taken advantage of because individuals do not understand the availability or benefits of the incentives (e.g. such as the tax write-off for buying a hybrid car, which reduces the total value paid for the car to well within that of nonhybrid cars). Many individuals continue to refer to hybrid vehicles as "more expensive" when in fact that is not the case when taking into account the tax benefits and the gas savings from the greater efficiency.

A better understanding of how information, incentives, and other instruments combined with individual values and social contexts shape consumer choices would go a long way to improving individual choices. Approaches that use community participation in bringing about change in environmental knowledge can be effective. Which contextual factors are more important, which incentives people respond to, and the effects of policies on individual choice remain areas rich for investigation (NRC 2005b:78). Studies have begun to shed light on these issues. Some have focused on aggregate scales of pro-environmental behavior (e.g. Kaiser 1998; Cottrell 2003). Others focus on particular consumer behaviors such as energy use (Black, Stern, and Elworth 1985), travel behaviors (Brown, Werner, and Kim 2003), and recycling behavior (do Valle et al. 2004). Others have compared different classes of behavior in different countries (Thøgerson 2004; Stern et al. 1999).

One of the most serious impediments to advances in this field is the persistence of disciplinary approaches and the lack of substantive interdisciplinarity (NRC 2005b:80). Scholars continue to read only partially across disciplines and are often unaware of the work in other fields that could inform their work. To arrive at a unified model of real-world situated choice, one needs sustained investment in interdisciplinary inquiries that overcome the current blind spots one finds in the development of individual decision making. Given the ever growing global economy, and how products are marketed and available in countries across the globe, one needs more comparative studies of how individuals in different societies respond to information, to prices, and to the variable contexts that shape their environmentally significant choices.

Decisions and Social Context

Over the last several decades, sociologists have investigated the public's increasing concern about the environment, but they have had little success explaining attitudes toward the environment or the adoption of pro-environment behaviors like recycling. Derksen and Gartrell (1993) examine the role of social context in the link between individual attitudes about the environment and recycling behavior by comparing communities that vary in their access to recycling programs. Results show that people with access to a structured recycling program have much higher levels of recycling than do people lacking such access. Furthermore, individual attitudes toward the environment affect recycling behavior only in the community with easy access to a structured recycling program. Individual concern about the environment enhances the effect of the recycling program, but does not overcome the barriers presented by lack of access.

What constitutes a good decision about the environment? Some research traditions offer concepts, theories, and methods intended to improve both individual and collective decision making about actions that will affect the environment. But there is relatively little explicit discussion of what would be appropriate criteria for calling an environmental decision a good choice. Five criteria for evaluating environmental decisions are suggested by Dietz (2003): human and environmental well-being; competence about facts and values; fairness in process and outcome; a reliance on human strengths rather than weaknesses; the opportunity to learn and act with greater efficiency.

Agency (i.e. the role of the individual decision maker) has long been an important topic in sociological theory and is central to several theories in anthropology (e.g. historical ecology, political ecology). Sociologists have devoted attention to new models of cultural evolution drawn from a variety of disciplines. Dietz and Burns (1992) examine the role of agency in evolutionary theory by distinguishing evolutionary theory from developmental theories that are usually identified with evolution in discussions of social theory. They then offer an approach to agency and to power grounded in social rule systems theory. These discussions provide a context to definition of agency as effective, intentional, unconstrained, and reflexive action by individual or collective actors (Dietz and Burns 1992).

To what extent are our decision making and learning processes influenced indirectly by others? To what extent are the opinions you hold simply a reflection of the opinions of those you associate with? Explanations of social influence usually focus on why people are persuaded by or conform to the opinions of others. Although important, this research has neglected the role of information collection in belief formation and how biased beliefs, as well as social influence, can emerge from biased search processes (Denrell 2008).

Dietz and Stern (1995) offer a boundedly rational model of choice that makes room for individual values and social influences in a process of preference construction. It takes from the expected utility model the notion that people assess their options in terms of expected outcomes, referenced to personal values, but it presumes that individuals assess sharply truncated lists of relevant options, outcomes, and values and apply a classification logic rather than a calculative one. Such a model is consistent with the nature of evolved human cognitive abilities. The model treats cognitive heuristics and various forms of social influence as determinants of selection of the truncated lists and it treats moral norms as classification rules activated when certain actions and outcomes become salient.

Research traditions across the social sciences have explored the drivers of individual behavior and proposed different models of decision making. Wilson and Dowlatabadi (2007) review several diverse perspectives: conventional and behavioral economics; technology adoption theory and attitude-based decision making; social and environmental psychology; and sociology. The individual decision models in these traditions differ axiomatically. Some are founded on informed rationality or psychological variables, and others emphasize physical or contextual factors from individual to social scales. Each perspective suggests particular lessons for designing interventions to change behavior. Throughout their review, these lessons are applied to decisions affecting residential energy use. They focus on examples drawn from both intuitive and reasoning-based types of decision as well as from a range of decision contexts that include capital investments in weatherization and repetitive behaviors such as appliance use.

Lambin et al. (2001) suggest that common understanding of the causes of land-use and land-cover change is dominated by simplifications which, in turn, underlie many environment-development policies. Cases reviewed support the conclusion that neither population nor poverty alone constitutes the sole and major underlying cause of land-cover change worldwide. Rather, people's responses to economic opportunities, as mediated by institutional factors, are what drives land-cover changes. Opportunities and constraints for new land uses are created by local as well as national markets and policies – yet, it is global forces that become the main determinants of land-use change, as they amplify or attenuate local factors.

Liu et al. (2008) call for more effective integration of science and decision making in environmental management. While scientists often complain that their input is ignored by decision makers, the latter have also expressed dissatisfaction that critical information for their decision making is often not readily available or accessible to them, or not presented in a usable form. Scientists need to produce more "usable" information with enhanced credibility, legitimacy, and saliency to ensure the adoption of research results. An example of this might be basin-scale management of coupled human–water systems, where water resources managers, like other decision makers, are frequently confronted with the need to make major decisions in the face of high system complexity and uncertainty. The integration of useful and relevant scientific information is necessary and critical to enable informed decision making. Liu et al. (2008) describe the main aspects of what has been learned in the process of supporting sustainable water resources planning and management in the semi-arid southwestern United States by means of integrated modeling. Their experience indicates that particular attention must be paid to the focus of the questions, explicit and participatory conceptual modeling, a suitable modeling strategy that is transparent to analysts and stakeholders alike, and a formal scenario-analysis approach in order to facilitate the development of "usable" scientific information for policy makers and stakeholders.

The drought in the southeast of England in 2004–6 generated important insights for contemporary interdisciplinary debates about what it means to build resilience in water management (Medd and Chappels 2007). First, there is a set of issues about the assessment and definition of drought at multiple levels of organization – local, regional, national – and consequently about the interaction between scales at which building resilience is to be established. Drawing on interviews with regional water company managers in southeast England and a selection of households within their jurisdictions, Medd and Chappels (2007) explore the contested framings of drought risk and the need to manage demand. They argue that definitions of drought are mediated by the institutional context of water management across different scales and by different disciplinary framings (from economics, geography, sociology, and environmental science). Second, chosen strategies of drought management reveal different disciplinary approaches to questions of scale. In particular, the debate about building resilience to ensure "security of supply" is framed or dominated largely by an engineering way of thinking in which technological fixes from the household level to large-scale reconfiguration of infrastructural networks are proposed as the best way to address the problem. By contrast, sociological approaches suggest the need to explore resilience through a reconceptualization of supply-and-demand as an ongoing process of co-management. These differences in framing constitute obstacles to dealing with the water crisis, and solutions will require more interactive, scale-sensitive approaches that use the right tools at the right scale. Other relevant cases can be found in our rapidly disappearing forests, and in how we go about protecting biodiversity.

Development of environmental decision support systems (EDSS) is rapidly progressing (Matthies, Giupponi, and Ostendorf 2007). The sustainable management of natural resources has grown in awareness of the complexity of interactions between sociocultural, economical and biophysical system components. As better data and methods become available, the complexity of the system representation is acknowledged. At the same time, realism and relevance are increasing and allowing direct support for management and policy development. Recent developments show a continuum between integrated assessment modeling and EDSS with varying levels of stakeholder participation in both EDSS development and application. There is a general tendency towards better utilization of interdisciplinary data, integration, and visualization of temporal and spatial results. Future developments appear directed towards better representation of reality in models, improving user-friendliness and their use in a group discussion context through participatory approaches.

The complexity of environmental problems makes necessary the development and application of new tools capable of processing not only numerical aspects, but also the experience from experts and wide public participation, which are all needed in decision-making processes (Poch et al. 2004). EDSSs are among the most promising approaches to confront this complexity. The fact that different tools (artificial intelligence techniques, statistical/numerical methods, GIS, and environmental ontologies) can be integrated under different architectures confers EDSSs the ability to confront complex problems, and the capability to support learning and decision-making processes. The flow diagram followed to build the EDSS is presented by Poch et al. (2004) for each of the systems, together with a discussion of the tasks involved in each step (problem analysis, data collection and knowledge acquisition, model selection, model implementation, and EDSS validation). In addition, the architecture used is presented, showing how the five levels on which it is based (data gathering, diagnosis, decision support, plans, and actions) have been implemented. In order to further advance the ability of EDSSs to cope with the complexity of environmental problems, one needs greater integration of data and knowledge, improvement of knowledge acquisition methods, new protocols to share and reuse knowledge, development of benchmarks, and involvement of end-users.

Conclusions

In order to make better decisions, one needs to begin by ensuring that decisions are made at the appropriate level (i.e. at the appropriate scale). Often decisions are made far from the resources and the people most affected by the use of those resources: see earlier discussion of the work of Rappaport (1979). In other words, decisions are made by government agencies, or companies, without input from citizens and communities affected. In some cases, it would be better to let communities decide what is best for them. But this may not be practical in many cases, and there is an important role that government agencies and higher level actors play – for example, to ensure that higher standards are applied than a given local community may be ready to accept without a fight. Generally speaking, the appropriate level for decision making should be determined by the scale of the resource system to be managed. The more localized the resources, the more the decision should be up to the local population, but the larger the area, and the more likely it is to have effects on other watersheds, the more the decision must involve a larger number of decision makers. Problems, such as acid rain, which involve movement of air pollutants across watersheds and even national boundaries, must necessarily involve cross-national decision making, international treaties, and other extra-local decision makers. Kyoto, REED, and other environmental treaties are efforts to provide this kind of higher level coordination, but implementation and compliance have been limited with few countries succeeding in living up to the Kyoto targets set, for example (Cole 2009). An important element of good environmental governance is to provide citizens with access to information and opportunities to participate in the decision-making process armed with that information. The Rio Declaration, from the 1992 global conference on the environment and development, which was adopted by 178 nations, defined that access has three components: access to information, access to decision making, and the opportunity to seek legal remedies. Without all three of these elements, there is a lack of public participation, and probably a lack of effective governance of resources. The information needed involves access to important data such as air and water quality in the local community (as this affects whether citizens drink the water or not); information about environmental trends through time (to see if things are degrading or improving); information on pollution from industrial facilities (to empower citizens and NGOs to pressure companies to behave responsibly); and information on how to deal with emergencies and risks present in their environment (e.g. if a large water impoundment is present, what the risks are that it may give way and flood the area). These should be minimum standards of information that citizens need to act responsibly in a democratic society. Access to decision making requires that citizens and other groups be able to influence national policies and plans, provincial and local policies and plans, and to take part in environmentally significant projects, such as licensing a power plant or a chemical plant. Access to legal remedies implies that it is possible for citizens and citizen organizations to seek legal remedies for irresponsible corporate behavior, ineffectiveness in the enforcement of pollution standards, and other failures in the decision-making process that endanger the public's health.

An important and growing element of citizen participation is through the proliferation of nongovernmental organizations (NGOs), such as environmental NGOs, which have more than doubled since 1985 with more than 40,000 officially recorded. These organizations have helped pressure government and corporations into opening up to public scrutiny and to allow greater citizen participation in decisions. On the other hand, NGOs themselves are caught in the larger political economy which does not question the foundations of uneven development, poverty, and inequality (for a critical analysis of these issues, see Bebbington 2004). Further, economic globalization has been effective in growing also very fast, as an increasing number of companies (more than 60,000 operate in the global marketplace) operate in a global market with few environmental strictures and little transparency. Some of these corporations, such as logging companies operating in Asia, remove trees illegally and work with corrupt officials who permit them to violate existing laws.

One of the proposed solutions to better environmental governance has been decentralization, or devolving decision making to local governments, but this alternative may not be possible in many cases. This solution is not a panacea to the problems noted above. More than 60 developing countries claim to be devolving power to local units – but few cases of true decentralization have been recorded, and rarely are adequate funds devolved to local agencies to permit them to operate effectively in monitoring the environment and in giving them power to prosecute those who violate local rules. In most cases, local agencies are charged with implementing decisions made elsewhere without local accountability. When done fully, decentralization can work (Andersson 2003, 2004; but see Andersson, Anda, and van Laerhoven 2008 for the many obstacles found and under what conditions it does not seem to work). In the next chapter, we discuss the emergence of a new field, variously called sustainability science and coupled human–natural systems.

8

Towards Sustainability Science

*The correlation between income and happiness is surprisingly weak,
observed University of Michigan researcher Ronald Inglehart in a
16-nation study of 170,000 people. Once comfortable, more money
provides diminishing returns. Lottery winners and the 100 wealthiest
Americans listed in Forbes express only slighter greater happiness than
the average American. While the average American made only $8,700
in today's dollars in 1957, and today makes $20,000, over this period
the number of Americans who say they are very happy has declined
from 35 to 32 percent. Meanwhile, the divorce rate has doubled, teen
suicide rates have tripled, violent crime has quadrupled, and more
people are depressed. Today, more than ever before, we have big
houses and broken homes, high incomes and low morale, secure rights
and diminishing civility. We celebrate our prosperity, but yearn for a
sense of purpose. In an age of plenty we are hungry for what money
cannot buy. Having secured human rights and affluence, we seek
purpose. One first step is to have less, and change the world into a
sustainable one.*

Myers 2000 (quoted in Moran 2005)

There is an urgent need to develop theories and methods for a science of
sustainability, based on the fundamental interactions between people and
the biophysical environment. This calls for new research and for a profound
level of multidisciplinary, multi-scale, multinational, and multi-temporal
integrative science that brings together the physical, biological, and social
sciences (Kaneshiro et al. 2005). Because such research runs counter to traditional disciplinary-based approaches that currently shape the education
and training of citizens as well as scholars, we need to develop the capacity
to speak across the disciplinary divides, understand the assumptions of others across the table, and learn to formulate questions, and approaches, that

are truly integrative. In this book I have tried to provide access for both natural and social scientists to the theory, methods, and jargon of the others with whom one is likely to work with, hoping thereby to facilitate this joint enterprise. It is only a first step in that direction, and surely many other useful approaches that are not discussed here will emerge from the field-based interactions of students, researchers, and civil society as they tackle complex human–environment dynamics.

According to Levin (2006) socioeconomic systems are, in fact, ecological systems characterized by familiar processes such as exploitation, cooperation, and parasitism, and ecological systems are economic systems in which competition for resources are central and in which individuals seek what is best for them, but which have emergent properties that have evolutionary and systemic consequence. Thus, they are complex adaptive systems in which patterns at the macro level emerge from interactions and selection processes at many lower levels of organization. Complexity theory can shed light on the interactions of these human–environment systems by focusing not only on its structurally complex characteristics but also on the management of the use of resources in such systems. Such management needs to be adaptive in its goals and approaches, seeking system sustainability and system self-organization, since, without the latter, the former is simply unattainable (Norberg and Cumming 2008).

Since the publication of *Our Common Journey* (NRC 1999e), research needs and priorities in sustainability science have continued to appear (e.g. Kates et al. 2001; Clark and Dickson 2003). Members of the National Academy of Science/National Research Council (NAS/NRC) Roundtable on Science and Technology for Sustainability and the Forum on Science and Innovation for Sustainable Development (http://sustainabilityscience.org) have been among the sources of research priorities (see also Swart et al. 2002, on critical challenges for sustainability science and a special issue of *PNAS (Proceedings of the National Academy of Science*, July 8, 2003, on science in support of sustainability). Challenges interconnecting human–environmental research with core disciplines in the behavioral and social sciences have been an issue always.

Disciplinary scientists have noted significant obstacles to engagement with environmental issues in sociology, psychology, and political science and a huge split between "ecological" and "environmental" economics that confuses those wishing to incorporate economics into an environmental research team (cf. the effort of Venkatachalam 2007 to bridge the two sides of economics of the environment). Environmental issues are closer to the core in anthropology and geography. In general, the discussion suggested that involvement of disciplinary social and behavioral scientists can be affected by the agendas and review practices of agencies such as the National Science Foundation (NSF) that provide major research support, especially to early-career scientists for whom an NSF grant can be an important career building block. NSF funding criteria and practices, including the composition of panels that review proposals, can help turn early-career scientists toward a focus either on established "core" disciplinary questions or on fundamental cross-disciplinary questions (CCSP 2008). A growing number of special requests for proposals (RFPs) have been issued by NSF in an effort to nudge scientists towards interdisciplinary research, and even within disciplinary programs we see evidence of doors opening for applications from other disciplines if the questions addressed are of core interest.

There are also important differences between stakeholders, and between North and South, in defining the most pressing problems of sustainable development and achieving sustainability (Clark and Dickson 2003). Clearly, it will have to involve both reducing hunger and poverty, while protecting the earth's life support systems and biodiversity. This makes the definition of sustainability very much a local and regional process, rather than a national or global one, if one is to address these different pressing problems from the stakeholders' perspective. Sustainability science will need to be fundamental research, but it will also have to be concerned with how to implement this basic science for the benefit of local people. The goal ultimately is to improve society's capacity to use the earth in ways that simultaneously meet the needs of the human population while sustaining the environmental foundations of our life support systems and substantially reducing poverty and hunger (NRC 1999e; Clark 2007).

Sustainability Science Research Priorities

Priorities for sustainability science dovetail with the priorities in other proximate areas of research such as human–environment interactions research, coupled systems, and the human dimensions of global change. All these areas are concerned with integrating the natural and social sciences in addressing the complex systems of which we are a part and which increasingly are at risk. By focusing on the dynamic interactions between nature and society, sustainability science becomes an integrative forum for research across a large array of disciplines (Clark and Dickson 2003). Among the priorities for research on sustainability one can name the following:

(1) *Improving the understanding of environmentally significant consumption.* For a decade or more, the sustainability science communities have been saying that the single biggest weakness in the knowledge base is a lack of understanding about human consumption linked to resource use (e.g. NRC 1997a, 1999a, 2005a; Kates 2000). Research on environmentally

significant consumption illuminates a fundamental human driver and builds understanding needed for effective mitigation responses. Part of the research agenda concerns understanding individual and household-level behavior (e.g. what motivates consumption; links among economic consumption, resource consumption, and human well-being, including the potential to satisfy basic needs and other demands with significantly less resource consumption; and the responsiveness of consumers to efforts to change their behavior through information, persuasion, incentives, and regulations. Another part of the research agenda concerns decisions in business organizations that affect environmental resource consumption, whether by the organizations themselves, by marketing to ultimate consumers, or through the structure of product and service chains. Examples of this are current efforts in universities to improve recycling and to form sustainability committees to look into all operations of the university.

(2) *Improving fundamental understanding of decision making.* Human response to climate change depends on decision making (e.g. NRC 1992, 1999a, 2005a). Anticipating or guiding human system responses to both perceived risks and opportunities related to climate change and its experienced and expected impacts requires a sophisticated understanding of how people and organizations handle incomplete and uncertain scientific information and incorporate, ignore, or reinterpret it in decision making. The research agenda includes both attention to individual cognition and to risk judgments and decision making in groups, organizations, and social institutions.

(3) *Improved understanding of how social institutions affect resource use.* This topic was identified as one of the eight "grand challenges in the environmental sciences" (NRC 2001) and has been repeatedly identified as a top priority (e.g. NRC 1999a; 2005a). The challenge is to understand how human use of natural resources is shaped by "markets, governments, international treaties, and formal and informal sets of institutions that are established to govern resource extraction, waste disposal, and other environmentally important activities" (NRC 2001:4). Institutions create contexts and rules that shape the human activities that drive climate change and that shape the realistic possibilities for mitigation and adaptation. The research agenda includes documenting the institutions shaping these activities from local to global levels, understanding the conditions under which the institutions can effectively advance mitigation and adaptation goals, and improving understanding of the conditions for institutional innovation and change. Fundamental research on resource institutions holds the promise of identifying more realistic behavioral models for designing responses to climate change (see discussion of institutions in Chapter 7).

(4) *Improving the understanding of socioeconomic change as context for climate change impacts and responses.* Assessing possible human-system

impacts of and responses to climate change calls for an understanding of changes in other driving forces affecting those systems over the time horizon of interest in future climates. Examples include demographic change, economic change, and institutional change. Three situations are high priorities: technological change, land-use change, and urbanization.

(a) One of the most significant and most difficult of socioeconomic changes to project beyond a period of one or two decades is *technological change*, which may or may not reduce the rate of climate change, reduce some of its impacts, and offer alternatives for adaptation to those impacts. Key practical applications of such research include projecting the rate of implementation of technologies for carbon capture and sequestration, seawater desalination, efficient cooling technologies for buildings, and finding ways to speed implementation of desired technologies. Fundamental research seeks improved understanding of what determines rates of technological innovation and adoption. The research agenda includes studies of the roles of incentives, of aspects of organizations that might develop and implement new technology, institutional forces promoting or resisting change, and the potential of both transformational and incremental change.

(b) A second kind of change, often a key in connecting human dimensions with earth-system modeling, is *land-use change*, which reflects interactions between human and natural systems. This is such a central issue for climate change – related to greenhouse gas emissions, emission sinks, impacts, and responses – that it seems remarkable that a capacity does not exist to project such changes beyond a decade or two. Largely because of limitations in the ability to project demographic and economic changes over a period of more than several decades, along with changes in institutional and policy contexts, however, projections of land-use change into the mid and longer terms are essentially unavailable at present. Needed research includes decomposing component factors influencing land-use change; improving fundamental understanding of the relationships among population, land-use change, and environment; and linkages across scales (NRC 1998a, 2005b).

A third kind of change is the shift of the world population towards cities and the rapid expansion of *urbanization* across the world. Ever larger cities make use of much larger amounts of fossil fuels, emit more carbon per capita, and transform landscapes from high-infiltration to low-infiltration surfaces that change the earth surface dynamics. Public health and demography are also deeply affected by urban living, with greater exposure to respiratory problems, rapid transmission of infection, high levels of trauma from vehicular traffic and crime, moderated by greater use of force by the state. Needed research in this area includes how to reduce the footprint of cities, facilitate the creation of green spaces, reduce the environmental costs of traffic and consumption by urbanites, and construct systems of transportation that reduce emissions, while at the same time facilitate the commute of urbanites to their places of work and leisure.

(5)   *Valuation of biodiversity and ecosystem goods and services.* In order to have a sustainable planet, and move towards a science of sustainability one needs to find ways to value biodiversity and ecosystem goods and services. Human economic systems inevitably weigh the value of all goods and services, and in this valuation, ecosystem goods and services have suffered, as they are often treated as free or common goods, and thus priced well below their true value. It is a form of discounting that favors polluting, high consumption, and wasteful behavior by consumers and industries. Integrative modeling and policy initiatives needs to have the scientifically-rigorous tools for valuing ecosystem goods and services over the short, medium and long-term so that purely short-term valuation does not trump long-term adaptive management.

(6)   *Educating a new generation of scientists in integrative sustainability science.* Scientists working in this integrative area regularly report at academic meetings and in panel reports that our universities are failing to provide the kind of multi-disciplinary training needed to address contemporary environmental problems. We need to develop better support that will induce the shift from disciplinary to multidisciplinary science. A new journal has begun that focuses on *Sustainability Science* (Komiyama and Takeuchi 2006). Other ones exist, such as *Global Environmental Change: Human and Policy Perspectives*, which encourage work across the disciplines. Scientists with a strong social science disciplinary background have a considerable learning curve before they can make serious contributions to understanding the climate problem, as do natural scientists in being able to work smoothly with social scientists and the human dimensions of climate change. More could be done to draw social scientists to climate change research, particularly at the predoctoral and early career stages. A 1992 NRC review devoted a chapter to human resource and organization issues and offered several recommendations for addressing the problem, including the creation of a transportable five-year package of dissertation, postdoctoral, and research support. The idea would be to facilitate career advancement for social scientists working in a field outside the core of their disciplines, which could help build the community of researchers and might strengthen interdisciplinary institutions working on climate change. As the most recent NRC (2007a:75) review noted, "The natural sciences may offer a successful model for building human dimensions capacity, especially programs to move young investigators into the arena and to support postdocs."

Scales of Sustainability

There is a need for a more systematic and concerted effort involving both natural and social scientists to build a balanced conceptualization of the earth's "socioecological system" (or coupled human–natural subsystems) that is more useful for exploring the relations between its dynamics, human development, and sustainability. The subject of sustainability science is not restricted to the planetary scale of "earth system" analysis. The inclusion of other scales, down to the local context and local communities, is part of the essence of sustainability science and, indeed, part of the conventional wisdom in the sustainable development agenda (i.e. that sustainability is addressed most effectively at local to regional scales). Several questions could focus scientific inquiry in this area: what are the appropriate units of analysis for the dynamics of the coupled human–natural system at different scales? What is the minimum set of elements and linkages that must be included for understanding the behavior of the system as a whole? How can the multilayered complexity of interactions between human and natural subsystems be understood and analyzed in terms of emerging properties and mutual co-evolutionary adaptations? How can we build models of coupled human–natural systems that allow for self-organization, structural change, and emergent properties? How can we incorporate nonquantifiable, but important, variables and understandings that often arise in the social realm into the conceptualization and modeling of coupled human–natural systems? How can we incorporate cross-scale interactions (e.g., between slow and fast variables, ecological and societal lags and inertia) into models and conceptualizations of coupled human–nature systems? (Gallopin, Sustainability Science Forum (http://sustainabilityscience.org).

Cities and Sustainability Science

Urban areas are "hot spots" of sustainability that drive environmental changes at a variety of scales and thus need to be a focus of sustainability science. Cities make huge demands on material goods, and have high levels of concentrated consumption, very large emissions, and huge amounts of waste to process. They alter land use and land cover, put pressure on biodiversity and water systems, and alter local and regional biogeochemical cycles and climate. Cities represent both the problems and the solutions to sustainability challenges of an increasingly urbanized world. Human–environment interactions in our ever growing cities may be driving environmental and climate change (Grimm et al. 2008).

The debates over sustainability have now reached discussion of our cities (Wakernagel and Rees 1996; Van den Berg, Hartig, and Staats 2007; see Wakernagel et al. 2006 for a discussion of the ecological footprint concept in promoting sustainability planning of cities; Olalla-Tarraga 2006). Historians have shown that cities not only shaped but were also shaped by nature (Mumford 1961; Cronon 1991; Gandy 2002; Colten 2005). Political ecologists have pointed to the environmental degradation and vulnerability of urban populations (Robbins, Poderman, and Birkenholtz 2001; Keil 2003; Desfor and Keil 2004). Geographers have a growing role in the urban planning area (see Wolch 2007 for a review of the issues for geographers). Ecologists are beginning to see that cities have an ecology and that issues such as biodiversity, energy, and material cycles are just as relevant to the ecology of cities as they are to natural systems (Platt, Rowntree, and Muick 1994; Pickett et al. 1997; Fernandez-Juricic 2000; Fernandez-Juricic and Jokimani 2001; Grimm and Redman 2004). Pickett and colleagues (2004) have proposed a "cities of resilience" notion to emphasize the role of heterogeneity in both social and ecological functioning of urban areas, and the adaptability of people and human institutions through learning to the challenges of urban living.

A sign of the growing importance of urban ecology and the human impact on ecosystems is the initiation of a series of urban long-term ecology research sites (LTER), www.lternet.edu, which complement a series of LTERs around the United States that were initiated more than twenty years ago to study the major natural ecosystems of the United States. In the late 1990s these expanded into a network of international sites as well. The bioecological community thereby acknowledged that the human dimensions of ecosystem structure and function are necessary to an understanding of these systems. Several traditional LTERs now include a human dimensions component and several are examining the history of their sites for clues on how early human use of those areas may have left legacy effects on the landscapes under study. The adaptability of our species to life in an increasingly urban world should indeed be researched. Air and water pollution are no less challenging to our species than cold or low biological productivity. Crime rates, crowding, and traffic jams are no less important pieces of information than proximity to good soils in affecting how we choose our settlements or location. In the past the complexity of urban ecosystems discouraged ecological scientists, who preferred to measure "natural" systems to the humanly constructed urban ones. This neglect shows signs of coming to an end with the development of urban LTERs. We now recognize that even natural systems were hardly ever pristine (see Foster and Aber 2004 on the history of Harvard Forest), and that the human imprint on all of the earth's systems is far from negligible and becomes more dominant each day. We can examine urban ecology and urban sustainability by looking at the ecology of cities, their use of energy, their spatial heterogeneity, and how they structure the behavior of their inhabitants (Moran 2006)

A number of issues have risen to the top of the agenda in urban ecology in recent years:

- the choice between compact but dense cities and the dispersed sprawl of so many areas, particularly in the United States;
- the greening of cities, creating more forests, green spaces, and green roofs;
- the need to reduce the number of cars and promote pedestrian traffic as a way to take people into the city center; and
- a more integrative view of cities linking the natural and the social spheres. (Moran 2006)

In the past three decades a more holistic view of urban environments as ecosystems has emerged (Berkowitz, Nilton and Hollweg 2003). The science of landscape ecology offers a spatially explicit perspective to urban ecosystem studies (Forman and Godron 1986). Barrett and colleagues (1997:534) have proposed a host–parasite analogy to describe the relationship between the heterotrophic urban area and the productive agricultural and natural landscape elements in which it is embedded. This view maintains a separation between rural and urban landscapes that is no longer tenable. Rural households include members who participate in urban life through schooling, banking, trading, and not infrequently through temporary, seasonal, and permanent residence. *Telecommuting* has further eroded the distance between the rural and the urban, as a growing number of people choose to leave the density of cities to live in rural settings, thereby linking the two in bonds of mutual interdependence. Even without telecommuting, a growing number of urbanites seek access to rural properties to escape growing urban dis-amenities like pollution, crime, noise, and solace from the uncertainties of a global economy undergoing transformation and creating job insecurity. Households are urban in terms of their lifestyle, goals, and decisions, but they also represent dimensions of a process of counter-urbanization already visible in several developed countries (Berry 1990:116). Relations between rural and urban components are dynamic; they take on different characteristics over time, and the city can be both a parasite and a positive force in reconstructing a degraded rural landscape (see McDonnell and Pickett 1990). This more dynamic perspective offers students of the environmental social sciences a ripe field of study. An emphasis on material cycling is also an important perspective given that millions of tons of raw materials are used each year to build or redevelop the built environment of cities (Graham 2002).

Urban areas and their surrounding rural landscapes represent a complex pattern of human–environmental systems open to continuous change. The rapidity and scale of land-use change associated with urban growth presents a unique opportunity to investigate interrelationships between urban land-use processes and ecosystem dynamics. Land-use processes, which are driven by socioeconomic, institutional, and cultural factors, influence natural ecosystem dynamics through events and activities that can be identified, monitored, and predicted (Haughton and Hunter 2003).

Human actions are expressed through a system of urban land uses. One way to proceed in the study of urban ecology is to examine salient aspects of land use that offer potential for investigating human–ecological interactions, for example, type and density of land use, land-use succession, scale, location, and pattern of development. A study by the Baltimore LTER found that hydrological changes associated with urbanization created riparian drought by lowering water tables, which in turn altered soil, vegetation, and microbial processes (Groffman et al. 2003). Type of activity (agricultural, residential, commercial, industrial, open space) can be described by variation in density. Land-use succession provides a way to address the phenomenon of increased intensity of urban use as the urban area grows and encroaches on previously rural land and as older urban areas change in character over time. A study of the Pearl River delta region of China suggests that this conversion is driven by the high returns from built-up land vis-à-vis the returns from farmland and forested lands (thirty times higher return) (Dai et al. 2005). However, in Europe farmers have developed agrotourism and other strategies to increase the economic return of their farmland, producing high quality organic foods and linking consumers to farmers in personal bonds of trust and reciprocity (Holloway et al. 2006).

Residential use may displace small agricultural producers or open space, while commercial land use may outbid urban residences for desirable urban locations. Scale of change is associated with migration into cities, rapid development, and new regional roles that lead to changes in scale or at a given sector. Given the need for environmental social science to be spatially explicit, location is an important dimension in urban ecology. Contagion and other approaches to proximity analysis can be used to understand how adjacent development affects areas such as parks and rural areas (Attwell 2000; Bryant 2006).

The pattern of development can describe variations in the clustering or dispersed nature of structures, and their relations to roads and other types of infrastructure. There are choices to be made between high-density urban dwellings and dispersed ones, notions of status and how it is displayed, and patterns of crime and social control that lead to suburban flight from the urban core area. How different households respond to urban growth is a dynamic, complex process that takes multiple forms and affects different social groups in diverse ways (Moran 2006).

Climate Change and Sustainability

Fundamental human dimensions research pursues questions driven by concerns with problems of climate change rather than resulting from the priorities of the social science disciplines (CCSP 2008). The relevance of disciplinary concepts to climate problems does not always seem the same from a disciplinary standpoint as from a climate problem perspective. For example, household energy consumption is an important contributor to global greenhouse gas emissions, but understanding it requires concepts from multiple disciplines. Efforts to explain it only in terms of environmental attitudes (psychology), social position (sociology), or household income (economics) are likely to seem naive or seriously incomplete to scientists who take a broader view of the climate research agenda.

The problem of linking the disciplines to climate questions is in part one of developing theories and methods. Issues such as environmentally significant consumption, land-use change, and valuation of environmental resources, among others, do not yield easily to discipline-specific concepts, theories, or methods. Arguably, multidisciplinary approaches are more likely to yield useful tools for answering questions about human–climate interactions. The roles of disciplinary tools must be worked out over time in research teams and the wider community. Without sufficient support for such teams to work together over time, progress will be slow. That has been a goal of this book by making theories and methods more accessible to both the natural and social sciences.

Climate change impacts and responses are observed in physical and ecological systems. Adaptation to these impacts is increasingly being observed in both physical and ecological systems as well as in human adjustments to resource availability and risk at different spatial and societal scales. One finds elements of effectiveness, efficiency, equity, and legitimacy that are important in judging success in terms of the sustainability of development pathways into an uncertain future. Adger, Arnell, and Tompkins (2005) argue that each of these elements of decision making is implicit within presently formulated scenarios of socioeconomic futures of both emission trajectories and adaptation, though with different weighting. The processes by which adaptations are to be judged at different scales involve new and challenging institutional processes. The future of the planet, and its sustainability, hang on whether we can successfully make changes from business-as-usual to sustainable practices and behavior at a variety of scales from local to global.

The link between climate change and sustainability science is fundamental. We can neither ignore climate change in the pursuit of sustainability, nor sustainability in the pursuit of dealing with climate change. In fact, climate

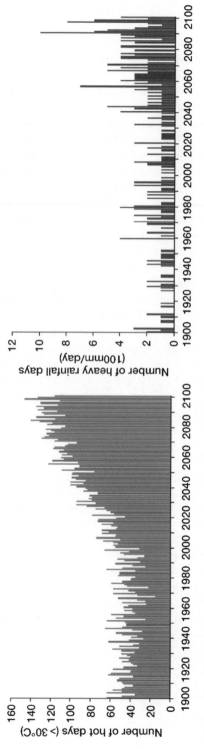

Figure 8.1 Changing pattern of temperature and precipitation for Japan
Source: Hasumi and Emori 2004

change research is one of the key areas that allows for the application of principles of sustainability science. Moreover, in both areas one has to deal with complex systems, and with a broad array of disciplines. Developed countries need to deal with emissions in a radical way, if they hope to bring along the developing countries. Moving towards more public transportation, more energy efficient buildings and residences, and changes in lifestyle are among the first things that come to mind in how we can move towards sustainability (Pachauri 2008). Another big area is moving towards agricultural sustainability (Ruttan 1999). Remarkably, as the world's population has increased, so has our capacity to produce food, and to avoid devastating famines (except for regions where political processes have limited people's access to food supplies intentionally). Yet, there is preliminary evidence of declines in agricultural research productivity and that yield increases have slowed down despite investments in research. Great hope is being placed in molecular biology and genetic engineering to lead us out of this bottleneck (Ruttan 1999:5962). Growing erosion worldwide, growing limitations on access to water, pest control, and climate change further limit the likely incremental yield gains from agriculture. While there is evidence that in some places, and up to some levels of CO_2 concentration, there could be a "fertilization effect" wherein there is a positive effect on the growth rate of plants from increasing carbon concentrations in the atmosphere, there is also evidence that not all plants respond favorably, and that some respond negatively – and that effects will vary across agroclimatic regions. The same can be said for predicted changes in temperature, with modest positive results around a 2.5 degree increase, but severely negative ones if the increase goes over 5 degrees C° above current levels (Ruttan 1999).

Current climate change and the anticipated changes represent a major impediment to sustainability (Swart, Raskin, and Robinson 2004). Climate change is expected to exacerbate the loss of biodiversity and increase the risk of extinctions. Water availability and quality are expected to decrease further in arid and semi-arid regions. The risk of flood and drought will increase, as will the inundation of coastal low-lying areas. Vector-borne diseases will spread with climate change beyond their current ranges, as will morbidity and mortality due to heat stress, as temperatures rise. Climate changes, and their downstream consequences, are expected to be without precedent and will test our capacity to adapt to these changes, and to develop anything resembling sustainability (Hay and Mimura 2006). Some regions will be challenged more than others. For example, the frequency of extreme high temperatures, and of heavy rainfall events, are expected to increase in Japan (see Figure 8.1). Glacial melt in the Himalayas will accelerate with global warming, and cause downstream flooding. Tropical cyclones are expected to increase 5–10% in intensity over the next four decades (Walsh 2004), and precipitation associated with these cyclones to increase by 25%. Millions of people will be negatively affected by the expected sea level rise and coastal flooding, with more than 10% of the population of Vietnam, Cambodia and Bangladesh affected, and many of the Pacific island countries. Sustainability is more likely to be achieved if one can increase the ability of societies to adapt to multiple stresses, including climate change. A proactive approach to adapting to forecasted climate change is likely to lead to more sustainable solutions and reduced human vulnerability.

In areas where vulnerability seems to be high, as in many parts of Africa due to a combination of environmental and human limitations, it is all the more imperative that sustainability science provide guidance to what should be priorities to move those regions towards sustainability: the existing infrastructure over many areas is inadequate to permit sustainable development, health conditions are precarious, access to education at all levels remains a problem, and there is poor enforcement of environmental regulations even when legislated. There is a need to put in place the sort of interdisciplinary sustainability science centers that can skip a generation and move young people to have the right tools to address the challenge of moving towards sustainability (Obasi 2004).

Conclusions

As we go forward in the twenty-first century, the fragile condition of our planet becomes ever more apparent, and the gap between what must be done and our ability to do it has increased. We must do better as scientists, as citizens, and as members of the human family, as we have a very large stake in ensuring that the environment that sustains all of us is able to provide food, fiber, and shelter for future generations. This means putting aside many things that we have held dear. It means putting aside purely national and regional interests, to ensure that processes that scale up globally contribute to a healthier planet rather than to its degradation. It means greater collaboration by segments of society, more robust institutions to address these problems, and better science for dealing with large and complex system problems. Sustainability science, or integrative human–environment research, is a viable approach to begin to deal with the challenges posed by coupled human–natural systems.

The topics covered in this book provide a set of resources to think about these issues. Hopefully they will help biological ecologists work with environmental social scientists in jointly addressing these issues, and advance our understanding of these biocomplex systems so that we can start moving towards sustainability. On our side we have a long developed capacity to adapt and respond to environmental challenges as a species. What worries many scientists is that the scale of the global and climate changes we have launched is without precedent, and that as individuals and members of nations we still do not grasp the urgency of solving these problems and stop our current business-as-usual unsustainable path. There is a need to continue to understand and propose ways to make better decisions about our environment, and to come up with integrative solutions that address human and environmental needs.

References

Acevedo, M. F., Urban, D. L., and Ablan, M. (1995) Transition and Gap Models of Forest Dynamics. *Ecological Applications* 5(4): 1040–55.

Achard, F., Eva, H. D., Stibig, H. J., et al. (2002) Determination of Deforestation Rates of the World's Humid Tropical Forests. *Science* 297: 999–1002.

Acheson, J. (2006) Institutional Failure in Resource Management. *Annual Review of Anthropology* 35: 117–34.

Ackerman, F., and Heinzerling, L. (2002) Pricing the Priceless: Cost-Benefit Analysis of Environmental Protection. *University of Pennsylvania Law Review* 150: 1569.

Adams, J. B., and Gillespie, A. R. (2006) *Remote Sensing of Landscapes with Spectral Images: A Physical Modeling Approach.* New York: Cambridge University Press.

Adger, W. N., Arnell, N. W., and Tompkins, E. L. (2005) Successful Adaptation to Climate Change across Scales. *Global Environmental Change* Part A 15(2): 77–86.

Adger, W. N., Brown, K., and Tompkins, E. (2005) The Political Economy of Cross-Scale Networks in Resource Co-Management. *Ecology and Society* 10(2): 9. http://www.ecologyandsociety.org/vol10/iss2/art9, accessed August 2009.

Adger, W. N., Agrawala, S., Mirza, M. M. Q., et al. (2007) Assessment of Adaptation Practices, Options, Constraints and Capacity. In M. L. Parry, O. F. Canziani, J. P. Palutikof, P. J. van der Linden and C.E. Hanson (eds.), *Climate Change 2007: Impacts, Adaptation and Vulnerability*. Contribution of Working Group II to the Fourth Assessment Report of the Intergovernmental Panel on Climate Change. Cambridge, UK: Cambridge University Press.

Adler, P. B., HilleRisLambers, J., and Levine, J. M. (2007) A Niche for Neutrality. *Ecology Letters* 10: 95–104.

Alcamo, J. R., Leemans, R., and Kreileman, E. (1998) *Global Change Scenarios of the 21st Century. Results from IMAGE 2.1 Model.* Oxford: Elsevier.

Alchian, A. (1950) Uncertainty, Evolution, and Economic Theory. *Journal of Political Economy* 58: 211–21.

Alexander, J. C., Giesen, B., Munch, R., and Smelser, N. J. (eds.) (1987) *The Micro-Macro Link*. Berkeley: University of California Press.

Alker, H. (1999) Ontological Reflections on Peace and War. Santa Fe Institute Working Paper 99-02-011. Santa Fe, New Mexico.

Alland, A. (1975) Adaptation. *Annual Review of Anthropology* 4: 59–73.

Allen, E. B. (ed.) (1988) *Reconstruction of Disturbed Arid Lands: An Ecological Approach*. Boulder, CO: Westview Press.

Allen, T. F. H., and Starr, T. B. (1982) *Hierarchy: Perspectives for Ecological Complexity*. Chicago: University of Chicago Press.

An, L., Linderman, M., Qi, J., Shortridge A., and Liu, J. (2005) Exploring Complexity in a Human–Environment System: An Agent-Based Spatial Model for Multidisciplinary and Multiscale Integration. *Annals of the Association of American Geographers* 95(1): 54–79.

Andelman, S. J., Bowles, C. M., Willig, M. R., and Waide, R. B. (2004) Understanding Environmental Complexity through a Distributed Knowledge Network. *BioScience* 54(3): 240–6.

Andersson, K. (2003) Can Decentralization Save Bolivia's Forests: An Institutional Analysis of Municipal Forest Governance. PhD diss. Political Science Department, Indiana University, Bloomington.

Andersson, K. (2004) Who Talks With Whom? The Role of Repeated Interactions in Decentralized Forest Governance. *World Development* 32(2): 233–49.

Andersson, K., Anda, G. G. de, and van Laerhoven, F. (2008) *Local Governments and Rural Development: Comparing Lessons from Brazil, Chile, Mexico, and Peru*. Tucson: University of Arizona Press.

Angelson, A., and Kaimowitz, D. (1999) Rethinking the Causes of Deforestation: Lessons from Economic Models. *The World Bank Research Observer* 14: 73–98.

Antrop, M. (2000) Background Concepts for Integrated Landscape Analysis. *Agriculture, Ecosystems and Environment* 77(1–2): 17–28.

Aronoff, S. (2005) *Remote Sensing for GIS Managers*. Redlands, CA: ESRI Press.

Arthur, W. B. (1994) *Increasing Returns and Path Dependence in the Economy*. Ann Arbor: University of Michigan Press.

Atkinson, G., and Oleson, T. (1996) Urban Sprawl as a Path Dependent Process. *Journal of Economic Issues* 30: 609–15.

Attwell, K. (2000) Urban Land Resources and Urban Planning: Case Studies from Denmark. *Landscape and Urban Planning* 52: 145–63.

Axelrod, R. (1984) *The Evolution of Cooperation*. New York: Basic Books.

Axelrod, R. (1997) Advancing the Art of Simulation in the Social Sciences: Obtaining, Analyzing and Sharing Results of Computer Models. *Complexity* 3(2): 16–22.

Bailey, S. (2007) Increasing Connectivity in Fragmented Landscapes: An Investigation of Evidence for Biodiversity Gain in Woodlands. *Forest Ecology and Management* 238: 7–23.

Baker, W. L., and Cai, Y. (1992) The R.le Programs for Multiscale Analysis of Landscape Structure using the GRASS Geographical Information System. *Landscape Ecology* 7(4): 291–302.

Baland, J.-M., and Platteau, J.-P. (2000[1996]) *Halting Degradation of National Resources: Is There a Role for Rural Communities?* Oxford: Clarendon Press.

Balée, W. (1994) *Footprints of the Forest: Ka'Apor Ethnobotany: The Historical Ecology of Plant Utilization by an Amazonian People*. New York: Columbia University Press.

Balée, W. (ed.) (1998) *Advances in Historical Ecology.* New York: Columbia University Press.

Balée, W., and Erickson, C. (eds.) (2006) *Time and Complexity in Historical Ecology: Studies in the Neotropical Lowlands.* New York: Columbia University Press.

Balmann, A. (2001) Modeling Land Use with Multi-Agent Systems: Perspectives for the Analysis of Agricultural Policies. *Proceedings of IIFET Conference Microbehavior and Macroresults.* Corvallis: Oregon State University.

Bamberg, S., and Schmidt, P. (1999) Regulating Transport: Behavioral Changes in the Field. *Journal of Consumer Policy* 22: 479–509.

Bamberg, S., Ajzen, I., and Schmidt, P. (2003) Choice of Travel Mode in the Theory of Planned Behavior: The Roles of Past Behavior, Habit, and Reasoned Action. *Basic and Applied Social Psychology* 25: 175–88.

Banerjee, S., Carlin, B. P., and Gelfand, A. E. (2004) *Hierarchical Modeling and Analysis for Spatial Data.* London: Chapman and Hall/CRC.

Barbieri, A., Bilsborrow, R., and Pan, W. (2005) Farm Household Lifecycles and Land Use in the Ecuadorian Amazon. *Population and Environment* 27(1): 1–27.

Barrett, G. W., Peles, J. D., and Odum, E. P. (1997) Transcending Processes and the Levels-of-Organization Concept. *BioScience* 47(8): 531–5.

Bascompte, J., and Sole, R. V. (eds.) (1998) *Modeling Spatio-Temporal Dynamics in Ecology.* Berlin, Germany: Springer-Verlag.

Bates, D. G., and Lees, S. H. (eds.) (1996) *Case Studies in Human Ecology.* New York: Plenum.

Batistella, M., and Moran, E. F. (eds.) (2008) *Geoinformação e Monitoramento Ambiental na América Latina.* São Paulo: Editora SENAC.

Bebbington, A. (2004) NGOs and Uneven Development: Geographies of Development Intervention. *Progress in Human Geography* 28(6): 725–45.

Becker, D. C., and Ostrom, E. (1995) Human Ecology and Resource Sustainability: The Importance of Institutional Diversity. *Annual Review of Ecology and Systematics* 26: 113–33.

Beckerman, S. (1991) Introduction. *Human Ecology* 19: 431–5.

Becu, N., Perez, P., Walker, A., Barreteau, O., and Le Page, C. (2003) Agent Based Simulation of a Small Catchment Water Management in Northern Thailand: Description of the CATCHSCAPE Model. *Ecological Modelling* 170: 319–31.

Behrens, C. (1990) Applications of Satellite Image Processing to the Analysis of Amazonian Cultural Ecology. *Conference Proceedings: Applications of Space Age Technology in Anthropology.* John C. Stennis Space Center, MS: NASA.

Behrens, C. (1994) Recent Advances in the Regional Analysis of Indigenous Land Use and Tropical Deforestation. Special Issue. *Human Ecology* 22(3): 243–413.

Behrens, C., Baksh, M., and Mothes, M. (1994) A Regional Analysis of Bari Land Use Intensification and Its Impact on Landscape Heterogeneity. *Human Ecology* 22: 279–316.

Belew, R. K., and Mitchell, M. (eds.) (1996) *Adaptive Individuals in Evolving Populations: Models and Algorithms.* Reading, MA: Addison-Wesley.

Bennett, J. (1976) *The Ecological Transition.* London: Pergamon Press.

Bennett, D., and McGinnis, D. (2008) Coupled and Complex: Human-Environment Interaction in the Greater Yellowstone Ecosystem, USA. *Geoforum* 39(2): 833–45.

Berger, T., and Parker, D. C. (2002) Introduction to Specific Examples of Research. In D. C. Parker, T. Berger and S. M. Manson (eds.), *Meeting the Challenge of Complexity: Proceedings of the Special Workshop on Agent-Based Models of Land-Use/Land-Cover Change.* CIPEC Collaborative Report No. CCR-3. Bloomington: Center for the Study of Institutions, Population, and Environmental Change (CIPEC), Indiana University.

Berger, T., and Ringler, C. (2002) Tradeoffs, Efficiency Gains, and Technical Change: Modeling Water Management and Land Use within a Multiple-Agent Framework. *Quarterly Journal of International Agriculture* 41(1/2): 119–44.

Bergin, M. S., West, J. J., Keating, T. J., and Russell, A. G. (2005) Regional Atmospheric Pollution and Transboundary Air Quality Management. *Annual Review of Environmental Research* 30: 1–37.

Berkes, F. (ed.) (1989) *Common Property Resources: Ecology and Community-Based Sustainable Development.* London: Belhaven Press.

Berkes, F. (2002) Cross-Scale Institutional Linkages: Some Promising Institutional Forms and Their Dynamics. In E. Ostrom, T. Dietz, N. Dolsak, P. C. Stern, S. Stonich, and E. Weber (eds.), *The Drama of the Commons.* Washington, DC: National Academy Press.

Berkes, F. (2006) From Community-Based Resource Management to Complex Systems: The Scale Issue and Marine Commons. *Ecology and Society* 11(1): 45.

Berkes, F., Colding, J., and Folke, C. (eds.) (2003) *Navigating Social-Ecological Systems: Building Resilience for Complexity and Change.* Cambridge: Cambridge University Press.

Berkowitz, A. R., Nilton, C. H., and Hollweg, K. S. (eds.) (2003) *Understanding Urban Ecosystems: A New Frontier for Science and Education.* New York: Springer.

Bernard, R. (2002) *Research Methods in Anthropology.* Walnut Creek, CA: Sage.

Berry, B. J. (1990) Urbanization. In B. L. Turner II, W. C. Clark, R. W. Kates, J. F. Richards, J. T. Mathews and W. B. Meyer (eds.), *The Earth as Transformed by Human Action.* New York: Cambridge University Press.

Bierregaard, R. O., Gascon, C., Lovejoy, T. E., and Mesquita, R. (eds.) (2001) *Lessons from Amazonia: The Ecology and Conservation of a Fragmented Forest.* New Haven, CT: Yale University Press.

Biersack, A. (1999) From the New Ecology to the New Ecologies. *American Anthropologist* 101: 5–18.

Bilsborrow, R. (1994) *Population, Development and Deforestation: Some Recent Evidence.* Population, Environment and Development. New York: United Nations.

Bilsborrow, R., Barbieri, A., and Pan, W. (2004) Changes in Population and Land Use over Time in the Ecuadorian Amazon. *Acta Amazonica* 34(4): 635–47.

Binswanger, H. P., and Ruttan, V. W. (1978) *Induced Innovation: Technology, Institutions and Development.* Baltimore, MD: Johns Hopkins University Press.

Black, J. S., Stern, P. C., and Elworth, J. T. (1985) Personal and Contextual Influences on Household Energy Adaptations. *Journal of Applied Psychology* 70: 3–21.

Blaikie, P., and Brookfield, H. (1987) *Land Degradation and Society.* London: Methuen.

Blasing, T. J., Broniak, C. T., and Marland, G. (2004) Estimates of Annual Fossil-Fuel CO_2 Emitted for Each State in the USA and the District of Columbia for Each Year from 1960 through 2001. In *Trends: A Compendium of Data on Global Change*. Carbon Dioxide Information Analysis Center, Oak Ridge National Laboratory.

Bodenhorn, B. (2000) It's Traditional to Change: A Case Study of Strategic Decision-Making. *Cambridge Anthropology* 22(1): 24–51.

Bohn, H., and Deacon, R. (2000) Ownership Risk, Investment, and the Use of Natural Resources. *American Economic Review* 90: 526–49.

Boken, V. K., Cracknell, A. P., and Heathcoate, R. L. (2005) *Monitoring and Predicting Agricultural Drought: A Global Study*. New York: Oxford University Press.

Bollig, M. (2006) *Risk Management in a Hazardous Environment: A Comparative Study of Two Pastoral Societies*. New York: Springer.

Bolstad, P. (2002) *GIS Fundamentals*. White Bear Lake, MN: Eider Press.

Bolte, J. P., Hulse, D. W. S., Gregory, V., and Smith, C. (2006) Modeling Biocomplexity: Actors, Landscapes and Alternative Futures. *Environmental Modelling and Software* 22(5): 570–9.

Booth, W. (1989) Monitoring the Fate of Forests from Space. *Science* 243: 1428–9.

Boserup, E. (1965) *The Conditions of Agricultural Growth*. Chicago: Aldine.

Boserup, E. (1981) *Population and Technological Change: A Study of Long-Term Trends*. Chicago: University of Chicago Press.

Boserup, E. (1983) The Impact of Scarcity and Plenty on Development. *Journal of Interdisciplinary History* 14: 383–407.

Boserup, E. (1990) *Economic and Demographic Relationships in Development*. Baltimore: Johns Hopkins University Press.

Boster, J. (1983) A Comparison of the Diversity of Jivaroan Gardens with that of the Tropical Forest. *Human Ecology* 11: 69–84.

Botkin, D. B., Janak, J. F. and Wallis, J. R. (1972) Some Ecological Consequences of a Computer Model of Forest Growth. *Journal of Ecology* 60(3): 849–72.

Boudon, R. (2003) Beyond Rational Choice Theory. *Annual Review of Sociology* 29:1–21.

Bousquet, F., and Le Page, C. (2004) Multi-Agent Simulations and Ecosystem Management: A Review. *Ecological Modelling* 176: 313–32.

Bousquet, F., Barreteau, O., D'Aquino, P., et al. (2002) Multi-Agent Systems and Role Games: Collective Learning Processes for Ecosystem Management. In M. A. Janssen (ed.), *Complexity and Ecosystem Management*. Cheltenham, UK/Northampton, MA: Edward Elgar Publishing.

Bowles, S. (2004) *Microeconomics: Behavior, Institutions and Evolution*. Princeton: Princeton University Press.

Braudel, F. (1973) *The Mediterranean and the Mediterranean World in the Age of Philip II*. 2 vols. New York: Harper and Row.

Brivio, P. A., and Zilioli, E. (2001) Urban Pattern Characterization through Geostatistical Analysis of Satellite Images. In J. P. Donnay, M. Barnsley and P. Longley (eds.), *Remote Sensing and Urban Analysis*. London: Taylor and Francis.

Broecker, W. S. (1991) The Great Ocean Conveyor Belt. *Oceanography* 4: 79–89.

Bromley, D. (ed.) (1992) *Making the Commons Work*. San Francisco: Institute for Contemporary Studies.

Brondizio, E. S. (1996) Forest Farmers: Human and Landscape Ecology of Caboclo Populations in the Amazon Estuary. PhD diss. Environmental Science Program, School of Public and Environmental Affairs, Indiana University.

Brondizio, E. S. (2005) Intraregional Analysis of Land-Use Change in the Amazon. In E. F. Moran and E. Ostrom (eds.), *Seeing the Forest and the Trees*. Cambridge, MA: MIT Press.

Brondizio, E. S. (2008) *The Amazonian Caboclo and the Açaí Palm: Forest Farmers in the Global Market*. New York: New York Botanical Garden Press.

Brondizio, E. S., and Moran, E. F. (2008) Human Dimensions of Climate Change: The Vulnerability of Small Farmers in the Amazon. *Philosophical Transactions of the Royal Society* B 363(1498):1803–9.

Brondizio, E. S., Moran, E. F., Mausel, P., and Wu, Y. (1994) Land Use Change in the Amazon Estuary: Patterns of Caboclo Settlement and Landscape Management. *Human Ecology* 22(3): 249–78.

Brondizio, E. S., Moran, E. F., Mausel, P., and Wu, Y. (1996) Land Cover in the Amazon Estuary: Linking of Thematic with Historical and Botanical Data. *Photogrammetric Engineering and Remote Sensing* 62(8): 921–9.

Brondizio, E. S., McCracken, S. E. F., Siqueira, A., Nelson, D., and Rodriguez-Pedraza, C. (2002) The Colonist Footprint: Towards a Conceptual Framework of Deforestation Trajectories Among Small Farmers in Frontier Amazonia. In C. H. Wood and R. Porro (eds.), *Patterns and Processes of Land Use and Forest Change in the Amazon*. Gainesville: University of Florida Press.

Brooks, N., and Adger, W. N. (2005) Assessing and Enhancing Adaptive Capacity. In B. Lim, E. Spanger-Siegfried, I. Burton, E. L. Malone and S. Huq (eds.), *Adaptation Policy Frameworks for Climate Change*. New York: Cambridge University Press.

Brosius, J. P. (1997) Endangered Forest, Endangered People. *Human Ecology* 25: 47–69.

Brosius, J. P. (1999) Green Dots, Pink Hearts: Displacing Politics from the Malaysian Rain Forest. *American Anthropologist* 101: 36–57.

Browder, J. O., and Godfrey, B. (1997) *Rainforest Cities: Urbanization, Development, and Globalization of the Brazilian Amazon*. New York: Columbia University Press.

Brown, B. B., Werner, C., and Kim, N. (2003) Personal and Contextual Factors Supporting the Switch to Transit Use: Evaluating a Natural Transit Intervention. Analyses of Social Issues and Public Policy 3: 139–60.

Brown, D. G., Page, S., Riolo, R., Zellner, M., and Rand, W. (2005) Path Dependence and the Validation of Agent-Based Spatial Models of Land Use. *International Journal of Geographical Information Science* 19(2): 153–74.

Brown, D. G., Robinson, D. T., An, L., et al. (2008) Exurbia from the Bottom-Up: Confronting Empirical Challenges to Characterizing a Complex System. *Geoforum* 39(2): 805–18.

Brown, J. C., and Purcell, M. (2005) There's Nothing Inherent about Scale: Political Ecology, the Local Trap, and the Politics of Development in the Brazilian Amazon. *Geoforum* 36(5): 607–24.

Bryant, M. M. (2006) Urban Landscape Conservation and the Role of Ecological Greenways at Local and Metropolitan Scales. *Landscape and Urban Planning* 76: 23–44.

Bryant, R. L., and Bailey, S. (1997) *Third World Political Ecology*. London: Routledge.

Buckley, W. F. (1968) *Modern Systems Research for the Behavioral Scientist*. Chicago: Aldine.

Burkett, V. R., Wilcox, D. A., Stottlemyer, R., et al. (2005) Nonlinear Dynamics in Ecosystem Response to Climatic Change: Case Studies and Policy Implications. *Ecological Complexity* 2(4): 357–94.

Butzer, K. (1976) *Early Hydraulic Civilization in Egypt: A Study in Cultural Ecology*. Chicago: University of Chicago Press.

Cadenasso, M. L., Pickett, S. T. A., and Grove, J. M. (2006) Dimensions of Ecosystem Complexity: Heterogeneity, Connectivity, and History. *Ecological Complexity* 3(1): 1–12.

Cadotte, M.W., Drake, J. A., and Fukami, T. (2005) Constructing Nature: Laboratory Models as Necessary Tools for Investigating Complex Ecological Communities. *Advancements in Ecological Research* 37: 333–53.

Camerer, C. (1998) Bounded Rationality in Individual Decision-Making. *Experimental Economics* 1: 163–83.

Camerer, C. (2003) *Behavioral Game Theory: Experiments in Strategic Interaction*. Princeton, NJ: Princeton University Press.

Camerer, C. F., and Fehr, E. (2004) Measuring Social Norms and Preferences Using Experimental Games: A Guide for Social Scientists. In J. Henrich, R. Boyd, S. Bowles, H. Gintis, E. Fehr and R. McElreath (eds.), *Foundations of Human Sociality – Experimental and Ethnograhic Evidence from 15 Small-Scale Societies*. New York: Oxford University Press.

Campbell, B. M., and Sayer, J. (2003) *Integrated Natural Resource Management: Linking Productivity, the Environment, and Development*. Wallingford, UK: CABI Publishers/CIFOR.

Campbell, J. B. (1987) *Introduction to Remote Sensing*. New York: Guilford Press.

Cancian, F. (1972) *Change and Uncertainty in a Peasant Economy*. Stanford, CA: Stanford University Press.

Carpenter, S. R., Kitchell, J. F., and Hodgson, J. R. (1985) Cascading Trophic Interactions and Lake Productivity. *BioScience* 35(10): 634–9.

Carson, R. T., Mitchell, R. C., Hanemann, W. M., Kopp, R. J., Presser, S., and Ruud, P. A. (2003) A Contingent Valuation Study of Lost Passive Use Values Resulting From the Exxon Valdez Oil Spill. *Environmental and Resource Economics* 25: 257–86.

Cash, D. W. (2000) Distributed Assessment Systems: An Emerging Paradigm of Research, Assessment and Decision-Making for Environmental Change. *Global Environmental Change* 10: 241–4.

Cash, D. W., and Moser, S. C. (2000) Linking Global and Local Scales: Designing Dynamic Assessment and Management Processes. *Global Environmental Change: Human and Policy Dimensions* 10(2): 109–20.

Cash, D. W., Adger, W. N., Berkes, F., et al. (2006) Scale and Cross-Scale Dynamics: Governance and Information in a Multi-Level World. *Ecology and Society* 11: 2–8.

Catton, W., and Dunlap, W. (1980) A New Ecological Paradigm for Post-Exuberant Sociology. *American Behavioral Scientist* 24(1): 15–47.

Caviedes, C. (2001) *El Niño in History: Storming Through the Ages*. Gainesville: University Press of Florida.

CCSP (2008) Weather and Climate Extremes in a Changing Climate. Regions of Focus: North America, Hawaii, Caribbean, and US Pacific Islands. A Report by the US Climate Change Science Program and the Subcommittee on Global Change Research. T. R. Karl, G. A. Meehl, C. D. Miller, S. J. Hassol, A. M. Waple, and W. L. Murray (eds.), Department of Commerce, NOAA's National Climatic Data Center, Washington, DC.

Cederman, L.-E. (1997) *Emergent Actors in World Politics: How States and Nations Develop and Dissolve*. Princeton, NJ: Princeton University Press.

Chase-Dunn, C. (1998) *Global Formation: Structures of the World Economy*. Lanham, MD: Rowman and Littlefield.

Chayanov, A. V. (1925[1966]) *The Theory of Peasant* Economy. C. Lane and R. E. F. Smith (trans.). D. Thorner, R. E. F. Smith, and B. Kerblay (eds.) Homewood, IL: Richard D. Irwin for American Economic Association.

Chesnais, J.-C. (1992) *The Demographic Transition: Stages, Patterns and Economic Implications*. New York: Clarendon.

Chibnik, M. (2005) Experimental Economics and Anthropology: A Critical Assessment. *American Ethnologist* 32(2): 198–209.

Chomitz, K. M., and Gray, D. A. (1996) Roads, Land Use, and Deforestation: A Spatial Model Applied to Belize. *World Bank Economic Review* 10(3): 487–512.

Chowdhury, R. R., and Turner, B. L. (2006) Reconciling Agency and Structure in Empirical Analysis: Smallholder Land Use in Southern Yucatan, Mexico. *Annals of the Association of American Geographers* 96(2): 302–22.

Clark, W. C. (2001) Research Systems for a Transition toward Sustainability. In W. Steffen, J. Jager, D. Carson, and C. Bradshaw (eds.), *Challenges of a Changing Earth*. Berlin: Springer-Verlag.

Clark, W. C. (2003) Urban Environments: Battlegrounds for Global Sustainability. *Environment* 45(7): 1.

Clark, W. C. (2007) Sustainability Science: A Room of Its Own. *Proceedings of the National Academy of Sciences* 104(6): 1737–8.

Clark, W. C., and Dickson, N. M. (2003) Sustainability Science: The Emerging Research Program. *Proceedings of the National Academy of Sciences* 100: 8059–61.

Clarke, K. C., and Gaydos, L. (1998) Loose Coupling a Cellular Automaton Model and GIS: Long-Term Growth Prediction for San Francisco and Washington/ Baltimore. *International Journal of Geographical Information Science* 12(7): 699–714.

Clemen, R. (1996) *Making Hard Decisions*, 2nd edn. Belmont, CA: Duxbury Press.

Clements, F. E. (1916) *Plant Succession: An Analysis of the Development of Vegetation*. Carnegie Institution of Washington Publication Number 242.

Clements, F. E. (1936) Nature and Structure of the Climax. *The Journal of Ecology* 24(1): 252–84.

Coale, A. J., and Watkins, S. C. (1986) *The Decline of Fertility in Europe*. Princeton, NJ: Princeton University Press.

Cochrane, M. A. (2000) Forest Fire, Deforestation and Landcover Change in the Brazilian Amazon. In L. F. Neuenschwander, K. C. Ryan, G. E. Gollberg and

J. D. Greer (eds.), *Crossing the Millennium: Integrating Spatial Technologies and Ecological Principles for a New Age in Fire Management*. Moscow: University of Idaho.

Cochrane, M. A. (2001) In the Line of Fire: Understanding the Impacts of Tropical Forest Fires. *Environment* 43: 28–38.

Cochrane, M. A., and Laurance, W. F. (2002) Fire as a Large-Scale Edge Effect in Amazonian Forests. *Journal of Tropical Ecology* 18: 311–25.

Cohen, J. E. (1995) Population Growth and Earth's Human Carrying Capacity. *Science* 269: 341–6.

Cohen, M., Riolo, R., and Axelrod, R. (1999) The Emergence of Social Organization in the Prisoner's Dilemma: How Context-Preservation and Other Factors Promote Cooperation. Santa Fe Institute Working Paper 99-01-002. Santa Fe, New Mexico.

Cole, D. H. (2009) Climate Change and Collective Action. In C. O'Cinneide and J. Holder (eds.), *Current Legal Problems*. New York: Oxford University Press.

Coleman, J. A. (1990) *Foundations of Social Theory*. Cambridge, MA: Harvard University Press.

Colten, C. (2005) *An Unnatural Metropolis: Wresting New Orleans from Nature*. Baton Rouge: Louisiana State University Press.

Conant, F. (1978) The Use of Landsat Data in Studies of Human Ecology. *Current Anthropology* 19: 382–4.

Conant, F. (1990) 1990 and Beyond: Satellite Remote Sensing and Ecological Anthropology. In E. F. Moran (ed.), *The Ecosystem Approach in Anthropology*. Ann Arbor: University of Michigan Press.

Conklin, H. C. (1980) *Ethnographic Atlas of Ifugao*. New Haven, CT: Yale University Press.

Connell, J. H. (1961) The Influence of Interspecific Competition and Other Factors on the Distribution of the Barnacle *Chthamalus stellatus*. *Ecology* 42(4): 710–23.

Connell, J. H., and Slatyer, R. O. (1977) Mechanisms of Succession in Natural Communities and Their Role in Community Stability and Organization. *American Naturalist* 111: 1119–44.

Constanza, R. (ed.) (1991) *Ecological Economics: The Science and Management of Sustainability*. New York: Columbia University Press.

Constanza, R., Wainger, L., Folke, C., and Maler, K. (1993) Modelling Complex Ecological Economic Systems. *BioScience* 43(8): 545–55.

Constanza, R., Low, B. S., Ostrom, E., and Wilson, J. (2001) *Institutions, Ecosystems and Sustainability*. Boca Raton, FL: Lewis Publishers.

Cottrell, S. (2003) Influence of Sociodemographics and Environmental Attitudes on General Responsible Environmental Behavior among Recreational Boaters. *Environment and Behavior* 35: 347–75.

Cowen, D. J., and Jensen, J. R. (1998) Extraction and Modeling of Urban Attributes Using Remote Sensing Technology. In D. Liverman, E. F. Moran, R. R. Rindfuss, and P.C. Stern (eds.), *People and Pixels: Linking Remote Sensing and Social Science*. Washington, DC: National Academy Press.

Cox, M., Arnold, G., and Villamayor Tomas, S. (in review) Evaluating Ostrom's Design Principles: A Meta-analysis of 112 Studies.

Cronon, W. (1991) *Nature's Metropolis: Chicago and the Great West*. New York: W. W. Norton.

Cropper, M. L., and Oates, W. E. (1992) Environmental Economics: A Survey. *Journal of Economic Literature* 30: 674–740.

Crumley, C. L. (ed.) (1994) *Historical Ecology: Cultural Knowledge and Changing Landscapes*. Santa Fe, NM: School of American Research Press.

Crutzen, P. (2002) Geology of Mankind. *Nature* 415: 23.

Cruz, R. V., Harasawa, H., Lal, M., et al. (2007) *Asia. Climate Change 2007: Impacts, Adaptation and Vulnerability*. Contribution of Working Group II to the Fourth Assessment Report of the Intergovernmental Panel on Climate Change. M. L. Parry, O. F. Canziani, J. P. Palutikof, P. J. van der Linden and C. E. Hanson (eds.) Cambridge, UK: Cambridge University Press.

Cullen, A. C., and Frey, H. C. (1999) *Probabilistic Techniques in Exposure Assessment*. New York: Plenum.

Cultural Survival (1995) Geomatics (Special Issue). *Cultural Survival Quarterly* (Winter).

Cutter, S. L., Mitchell, J. T., Hill, A., et al. (2002) Attitudes toward Reducing Greenhouse Gas Emissions from Local Places. In Association of American Geographers Global Change in Local Places (GCLP) Working Group, *Global Change and Local Places: Estimating, Understanding, and Reducing Greenhouse Gases*. Cambridge, UK: Cambridge University Press.

Cyert, R. M., and March, J. G. (1963) *A Behavioral Theory of the Firm*. Englewood Cliffs, NJ: Prentice-Hall.

Dai, E., Wu, S. H., Shi, W. Z., Cheung, C. K. and Shaker, A. (2005) Modeling Change-Patterns-Value Dynamics on Land Use: An Integrated GIS and Artificial Neural Network Approach. *Environment Management* 36: 576–91.

Dales, J. H. (1968) *Pollution, Property and Prices: An Essay in Policy-Making and Economics*. Toronto: University of Toronto Press.

Daly, H. E., and Cobb, J. B. (1994) *Un'Economia Per Il Bene Commune. Il Nuovo Paradigma Economico Orientato Verso la Communità, l'Ambiente e un Futuro Particolarmente Sostenibile. [An Economy for the Common Good: The New Economics Paradigm Looking Toward the Community, the Environment and a Sustainable Future]*. Como, Italy: RED Edizioni.

D'Antona, Á. O., Cak, A. D., and Tartalha do Nascimento, T. (in review) *Integrando Desenhos e Imagens de Satélite no Estudo de Mudanças no Uso e Cobertura da Terra. Ambiente e Sociedade. [Environment and Society]*.

Dasgupta, P., and Heal, G. M. (1979) *Economic Theory and Exhaustible Resources*. Cambridge, UK: Cambridge University Press.

David, B., and Turner, J. C. (1996) Studies in Self-Categorization and Minority Conversion: Is Being a Member of the Out-Group an Advantage? *British Journal of Social Psychology* 35: 179–99.

Davis, M. B. (1969) Climatic Changes in Southern Connecticut Recorded by Pollen Deposition at Rogers Lake. *Ecology* 50(3): 409–22.

Davis, R. (1963) Recreation Planning as an Economic Problem. *Natural Resources Journal* 3: 239–49.

Deacon, R. T. (1994) Deforestation and the Rule of Law in a Cross-Section of Countries. *Land Economics* 70(4): 414–30.

Deacon, R. T. (1995) Assessing the Relationship between Government Policy and Deforestation. *Journal of Environment Economics and Management* 28: 1–18.

Deadman, P. J. (1999) Modelling Individual Behavior and Group Performance in an Intelligent Agent-Based Simulation of the Tragedy of the Commons. *Journal of Environmental Management* 56(3): 159–72.

Deadman, P., and Gimblett, H. R. (1994) The Role of Goal-Oriented Autonomous Agents in Modeling People: Environment Interactions in Forest Recreation. *Mathematical and Computer Modelling* 20: 121–33.

Deadman, P. J., Robinson, D. T., Moran, E. F., and Brondizio, E. S. (2004) Effects of Colonist Household Structure on Land Use Change in the Amazon Rainforest: An Agent Based Simulation Approach. *Environment and Planning B: Planning and Design* 31: 693–709.

DeAngelis, D., and Gross, L. (eds.) (1992) *Individual-Based Models and Approaches in Ecology.* New York: Chapman and Hall.

Debinski, D. M., and Holt, R. D. (2000) A Survey and Overview of Habitat Fragmentation Experiments. *Conservation Biology* 14: 342–55.

De Haan, A. (1999) Livelihoods and Poverty: The Role of Migration: A Critical Review of the Migration Literature. *The Journal of Development Studies* 36(2): 1–47.

De Lisle, D. (1978) Effects of Distance Internal to the Farm: A Challenging Subject for North American Geographers. *Professional Geographer* 30: 278–88.

Demarest, A. (2004) *The Maya: The Rise and Fall of a Rain Forest Civilization.* Cambridge, UK: Cambridge University Press.

Demsetz, H. (1967) Toward a Theory of Property Rights. *American Economic Review* 62: 347–59.

Denrell, J. (2008) Organizational Risk Taking: Adaptation versus Variable Risk Preferences. *Industrial and Corporate Change* 17(3): 427–66.

Derksen, L., and Gartrell, J. (1993) The Social Context of Recycling. *American Sociological Review* 58(3): 434–42.

Desfor, G., and Keil, R. (2004) *Nature and the City: Making Environmental Policy in Toronto and Los Angeles.* Tucson: University of Arizona Press.

Diamond, J. (2005) *Collapse: How Societies Choose to Fail or Succeed.* New York: Viking.

Dietz, T. (2003) What is a Good Decision? Criteria for Environmental Decision Making. *Human Ecology Review* 10(1): 60–7.

Dietz, T., and Burns, T. R. (1992) Human Agency and the Evolutionary Dynamics of Culture. *Acta Sociologica* 35: 187–200.

Dietz, T., and Stern, P. C. (1995) Toward a Theory of Choice: Socially Embedded Preference Construction. *Journal of Socio-Economics* 24: 261–79.

Dietz, T., and Stern, P. C. (1998) Science, Values, and Biodiversity. *BioScience* 48(6): 441–4.

Dietz, T., Fitzgerald, A., and Shwom, R. (2005) Environmental Values. *Annual Review of Environment and Resources* 30: 335–72.

Dietz, T., Ostrom, E., and Stern, P. C. (2003) The Struggle to Govern the Commons. *Science* 302: 1907–12.

Dietz, T., Rosa, E. A., and York, R. (2007) Driving the Human Ecological Footprint. *Frontiers of Human Ecology* 5(1): 13–18.

do Valle, P.O, Reis, E., Manazes, J., and Rebelo, E. (2004) Behavioral Determinants of Household Recycling Participation: The Portuguese Case. *Environment and Behavior* 36: 505–40.

Dow, J. W. (1994) Anthropology: The Mapping of Cultural Traits from Field Data. *Social Science Computer Review* 12(4): 479–92.

Drury, W. H., and Nisbet, I. C. T. (1973) Succession. *Journal of the Arnold Arboretum* 54: 331–68.

Dunlap, R. E. (2002) An Enduring Concern: Light Stays Green for Environmental Protection. *Public Perspectives* (Sept./Oct.): 10–14.

Dunlap, R. E., and Scarce, R. (1991) The Polls/Poll Trends: Environmental Problems and Protection. *Public Opinion Quarterly* 55: 713–34.

DuPont, P. (2000) Communicating with Whom? The Effectiveness of Appliance Energy Labels in the U.S. and Thailand. *Proceedings, American Council for an Energy-Efficient Economy* 8.39–8.54.

Earle, T. C., Siegrist, M., and Gutscher, H. (2007) Trust, Risk Perception, and the TCC Model of Cooperation. In M. Siegrist, T. C. Earle and H. Gutscher (eds.), *Trust in Cooperative Risk Management: Uncertainty and Skepticism in the Public Mind*. London: Earthscan.

Easterling, W. E. (1997) Why Regional Studies are Needed in the Development of Full-Scale Integrated Assessment Modelling of Global Change Processes. Global Environmental Change Processes. *Global Environmental Change: Human and Policy Dimensions* 7: 337–56.

Eder, J. (1987) *On the Road to Tribal Extinction: Depopulation, Deculturation and Adaptive Well-Being*. Berkeley, CA: University of California Press.

Egler, F. E. (1954) Vegetation Science Concepts. I. Initial Floristic Composition: A Factor in Old-Field Vegetation Development. *Vegetatio* 4: 412–17.

Ehrhardt-Martinez, K. (1998) Social Determinants of Deforestation in Developing Countries: A Cross-National Study. *Social Forces* 77(2): 567–86.

Ehrhardt-Martinez, K., Crenshaw, E. M., and Jenkins, J. C. (2002) Deforestation and the Environmental Kuznets Curve: A Cross-National Investigation of Intervening Mechanisms. *Social Science Quarterly* 83: 226–43.

Eldredge, N., and Gould, S. J. (1972) Punctuated Equilibria: An Alternative to Phyletic Gradualism. In T. J. M. Schopf (ed.), *Models in Paleobiology*. San Francisco: Freeman and Cooper.

Ellen, R. (1990) Trade, Environment and the Reproduction of Local Systems in the Moluccas. In E. F. Moran (ed.), *The Ecosystem Approach in Anthropology*. Ann Arbor: University of Michigan Press.

Ellis, F. (1998) Household Livelihood Strategies and Rural Livelihood Diversification. *Journal of Development Studies* 35(1): 1–38.

Ellis, J. E., and Swift, D. M. (1988) Stability of African Pastoral Ecosystems: Alternate Paradigms and Implications for Development. *Journal of Range Management* 41: 450–9.

Ellis, J. E., Caughenour, M. B., and Swift, D. M. (1993) Climate Variability, Ecosystem Stability, and the Implications for Range and Livestock Development. In R. H. Behnke, I Scoones and C. Kerven (eds.), *Range Ecology at Disequilibrium: New Models of Natural Variability and Pastoral Adaptation in African Savannas*. London: ODI.

Entwisle, B., Walsh, S. J. Rindfuss, R. R., and Chamratrithirong, A. (1998) Land-Use/Land-Cover and Population Dynamics, Nang Rong, Thailand. In D. Liverman, E. F. Moran, R. R. Rindfuss, and P. C. Stern (eds.), *People and Pixels: Linking Remote Sensing and Social Science*. Washington, DC: National Academy Press.

Entwisle, B., Walsh, S. J., Rindfuss, R. R., and VanWey, L. K. (2005) Population and Upland Crop Production in Nang Rong, Thailand. *Population and Environment* 26(6): 449–70.

Entwisle, B., Rindfuss, R. R., Walsh, S. J., and Page, P. H. (2008) Population Growth and Its Spatial Distribution as Factors in the Deforestation of Nang Rong, Thailand. *Geoforum* 39(2): 879–97.

Epstein, J. M., and Axtell, R. (1996) *Growing Artificial Societies: Social Science from the Bottom Up*. Cambridge, MA: MIT Press (co-published with Brookings Institution).

Evans, T. P. (1998) Spatial Modeling of Community Boundaries in Northeast Thailand. Association of American Geographers Conference. Boston, MA.

Evans, T. P., and Kelley, H. (2004) Multi-Scale Analysis of a Household Level Agent-Based Model of Landcover Change. *Journal of Environmental Management* 72(1–2): 57–72.

Evans, T. P., and Kelley, H. (2008) Assessing the Transition from Deforestation to Forest Regrowth with an Agent-Based Model of Land Cover Change for South-Central Indiana (USA). *Geoforum* 39(2): 819–32.

Evans, T. P., and Moran, E. F. (2002) Spatial Integration of Social and Biophysical Factors Related to Land Cover Change. *Population and Development Review*. Supplement to 28: 165–86.

Evans, T. P., Green, G. M., and Carlson, L. A. (2001) Multi-Scale Analysis of Landcover Composition and Landscape Management of Public and Private Lands in Indiana. In A. Millington, S. Walsh, and P. Osborne (eds.), *GIS and Remote Sensing Applications in Biogeography and Ecology*. Boston: Kluwer.

Evans, T., Manire, A., de Castro, F., Brondizio, E., and McCracken, S. (2001) A Dynamic Model of Household Decision Making and Parcel-Level Land Cover Change in the Eastern Amazon. *Ecological Modelling* 143(1–2): 95–113.

Evans, T., Munroe, D. K., and Parker, D. C. (2005) Modeling Land-Use/Land-Cover Change: Exploring the Dynamics of Human- Environment Relationships. In E. Moran and E. Ostrom (eds.), *Seeing the Forest and the Trees: Human-Environment Interactions in Forest Ecosystems*. Cambridge, MA: MIT Press.

Evans, T., VanWey, L., and Moran, E. F. (2005) Human-Environment Research, Spatially Explicit Data Analysis, and Geographic Information Systems. In E. Moran and E. Ostrom (eds.), *Seeing the Forest and the Trees: Human-Environment Interactions in Forest Ecosystems*. Cambridge, MA: MIT Press.

Fang, J. Y., and Wang, Z. M. (2001) Forest Biomass Estimation at Regional and Global Levels, with Special Reference to China's Forest Biomass. *Ecological Research* 16(3): 587–92.

Fearnside, P. M. (1986) *Human Carrying Capacity of the Brazilian Rainforest*. New York: Columbia University Press.

Feeley, K. J., and Terborgh, J. W. (2006) Habitat Fragmentation and the Indirect Effects of Altered Herbivore (Red Howler Monkey, *Alouatta seniculus*) Abundance on Bird Species Richness. *Ecology* 87: 144–50.

Fehr, E., and Gächter, S. (2000) Fairness and Retaliation: The Economics of Reciprocity. *Journal of Economic Perspectives* 14: 159–81.

Fehr, E., and Gächter, S. (2002) Altruistic Punishment in Humans. *Nature* 415: 137–40.

Fernandez-Juricic, E. (2000) Avifaunal Use of Wooded Streets in an Urban Landscape. *Conservation Biology* 24: 513–21.

Fernandez-Juricic, E., and Jokimani, J. (2001) A Habitat Island Approach to Conserving Birds in Urban Landscapes: Case Studies from Southern and Northern Europe. *Biodiversity and Conservation* 10: 2023–43.

Ferraz, G., Nichols, J. D., Hines, J. E., Stouffer, P. C., Bierregaard, Jr., R. O., and Lovejoy, T. E. (2007) A Large-Scale Deforestation Experiment: Effects of Patch Area and Isolation on Amazon Birds. *Science* 315: 238–41.

Fiksel, J. (2006) Sustainability and Resilience: Toward a Systems Approach. Sustainability: *Science Practice and Policy* 2(2): 14–21.

Foley, J. A., DeFries, R., Asner, G. P., et al. (2005) Global Consequences of Land Use. *Science* 307: 570–4.

Folke, C., Hahn, T., Olsson, P., and Norberg, J. (2005) Adaptive Governance of Social-Ecological Systems. *Annual Review of Environment and Resources* 30: 441–73.

Foresman, T. W., Pickett, S. T. A., and Zipperer, W. C. (1997) Methods for Spatial and Temporal Land Use and Land Cover Assessment for Urban Ecosystems and Application in the Greater Baltimore-Chesapeake Region. *Urban Ecosystems* 1: 201–16.

Forman, R. T. T., and Godron, M. (1986) *Landscape Ecology*. New York: Wiley.

Foster, A. D., and Rosenzweig, M. R. (2003) Economic Growth and the Rise of Forests. *Quarterly Journal of Economics* 118(2): 601–37.

Foster, D., and Aber, J. (eds.) (2004) *Forests in Time: The Environmental Consequences of 1000 Years of Change in New England*. New Haven, CT: Yale University Press.

Foster, J. B. (1999) *Cannibals with Forks: Triple Bottom Line of 21st Century Business*. Gabriola Island, British Columbia, Canada: New Society Publishers.

Fox, J., Rindfuss, R., Walsh, S., and Mishra, V. (eds.) (2003) *People and the Environment: Approaches for Linking Household and Community Surveys to Remote Sensing and GIS*. Boston: Kluwer.

Frank, A. G. (1967) Capitalism and Underdevelopment in Latin America: Historical Studies of Brazil and Chile. New York: *Monthly Review*, 1969.

Freeman, A. M., III (1993) *The Measurement of Environmental and Resource Values: Theory and Methods*, 2nd edn. Washington, DC: Resources for the Future Press.

Funtowicz, S. O., and Ravetz, J. R. (1992) Three Types of Risk Assessment and the Emergence of Post-Normal Science. In S. Krimsky and D. Golding (eds.), *Social Theories of Risk*. Westport, CT: Praeger.

Gaines, S. W., and Gaines, W. M. (2000) Impact of Small-Group Decision-Making in Reducing Stress Conditions. *Journal of Anthropological Archeology* 19(1): 103–30.

Galvin, K. A., Thornton, P. K., Boone, R. B., and Sunderland, J. (2001) Impacts of Climate Variability on East African Pastoralists: Linking Social Science and Remote Sensing. *Climate Research* 19(2): 161–72.

Gandy, M. (2002) *Concrete and Clay: Reworking Nature in New York*. Cambridge, MA: MIT Press.

Gardner, G., and Stern, P. (1996) *Environmental Problems and Human Behavior*. New York: Allyn and Bacon.

Geertz, C. (1963) *Agricultural Involution*. Berkeley: University of California Press.

Geist, H., and Lambin, E. (2001) What Drives Tropical Deforestation? *Land Use Cover Change* Report Series No. 4, Louvain-la-Neuve.

Geist, H., and Lambin, E. (2002) Proximate Causes and Underlying Forces of Tropical Deforestation. *BioScience* 52(2): 143–50.

Gezon, L. (1997) Political Ecology and Conflict in Ankarana, Madagascar. *Ethnology* 36: 85–100.

Gezon, L. (1999) Of Shrimps and Spirit Possession: Toward a Political Ecology of Resource Management in Northern Madagascar. *American Anthropologist* 101: 58–67.

Gibson, C. C., Ostrom, E., and Ahn, T. (1998) Scaling Issues in the Social Sciences: A Report for the International Human Dimensions Programme on Global Environmental Change. *International Human Dimensions*. Programme Working Paper No. 1, Bonn, Germany.

Gibson, C. C., Ostrom, E., and Ahn, T. (2000) The Concept of Scale and the Human Dimensions of Global Change: A Survey. *Ecological Economics* 32(2): 217–39.

Gigerenzer, G., and Selten, R. (eds.) (2002) *Bounded Rationality: The Adaptive Toolbox*. Cambridge, MA: MIT Press.

Gigerenzer, G., Czerlinski, J., and Martignon, L. (2002) How Good are Fast and Frugal Heuristics? In R. Elio (ed.), *Common Sense, Reasoning and Rationality*. New York: Oxford University Press.

Gilbert, E. W. (1958) Pioneer Maps of Health and Disease in England. *The Geographical Journal* 124(2): 172–83.

Gleason, H. A. (1926) The Individualistic Concept of the Plant Association. *Bulletin of the Torrey Botanical Club* 53(1): 7–26.

Goldenfeld, N., and Kadanoff, L. P. (1999) Simple Lessons from Complexity. *Science* 284: 87–9.

Goldstone, R. L., and Janssen, M. A. (2005) Computational Models of Collective Behavior. *Trends in Cognitive Science* 9(9): 424–30.

Golledge, R. (1999) *Wayfinding Behavior: Cognitive Mapping and Other Spatial Processes*. Baltimore, MD: Johns Hopkins University Press.

Golley, F. (1984) Historical Origins of the Ecosystem Concept in Biology. In E. F. Moran (ed.), *The Ecosystem Concept in Anthropology*. Washington DC: American Association for Advancement of Science.

Gomes, M. P. (1988) *Os Índios e o Brasil*. Petrópolis: Vôzes. (Available in an English revised edition from the University of Florida Press.)

Goodchild, M. F. (1994) The Spatial Perspective: Geographic Information in Contemporary Social Science. *Mathematical Social Sciences* 27(1): 111–12.

Goodchild, M. F. (2003) Geographic Information Science and Systems for Environmental Management. *Annual Review of Environment and Resources* 28: 493–519.

Goodchild, M., and Janelle, D. (eds.) (2004) *Spatially Integrated Social Science*. Oxford: Oxford University Press.

Goodchild, M. F., Fu, P. D., and Rich, P. (2007) Sharing Geographic Information: An Assessment of the Geospatial One-Stop. *Annals of the Association of American Geographers* 97(2): 250–66.

Goodchild, M. F., Anselin, L., Appelbaum, R., and Harthorn, B. (2000) Toward Spatially Integrated Social Science. *International Regional Science Review* 23(2):139–59.

Goody, J. (1958) The Development Cycle in Domestic Groups. *Cambridge Papers in Social Anthropology, No. 1*. Cambridge, UK: Cambridge University Press for the Department of Archaeology and Anthropology.

Gordon, H. S. (1954) The Economic Theory of a Common-Property Resource: The Fishery. *Journal of Political Economy* 62: 124–42.

Gould, S. J. (2007) *Punctuated Equilibrium*. Cambridge, MA: Harvard University Press.

Gould, S. J., and Eldredge, N. (1977) Punctuated Equilibria: The Tempo and Mode of Evolution Reconsidered. *Paleobiology* 3: 115–51.

Gragson, T. L. (2005) Time in Service to Historical Ecology. *Ecological and Environmental Anthropology* 1(1): 2–9.

Graham, P. (2002) *Building Ecology: First Principles for a Sustainable Built Environment*. Oxford: Blackwell Science.

Granados, J., and Korner, C. (2002) In Deep Shade: Elevated CO_2 Increases the Vigor of Tropical Climbing Plants. *Global Change Biology* 8: 1109–17.

Green, G. M., Schweik, C. M., and Randolph, J. C. (2005a) Linking Disciplines Across Space and Time: Useful Concepts and Approaches for Land Cover Change Studies. In E. Moran and E. Ostrom (eds.), *Seeing the Forest and the Trees*. Cambridge, MA: MIT Press.

Green, G. M., Schweik, C. M., and Randolph, J. C. (2005) Retrieving Land Cover Change Information from Landsat Satellite Images by Minimizing Other Sources of Reflectance Variability. In E. Moran and E. Ostrom (eds.), *Seeing the Forest and the Trees*. Cambridge, MA: MIT Press.

Greenberg, J., and Park, T. (1994) Political Ecology. *Journal of Political Ecology* 1: 1–12.

Greene, R. P., and Pick, J. B. (2006) *Exploring the Urban Community: A GIS Approach*. Upper Saddle River, NJ: Pearson-Prentice Hall.

Grimm, N., and Redman, C. L. (2004) Approaches to the Study of Urban Ecosystems: The Case of Central Arizona-Phoenix. *Urban Ecosystems* 7: 199–213.

Grimm, V., Berger, U., Bastiansen, F., et al. (2006) A Standard Protocol for Describing Individual-Based and Agent-Based Models. *Ecological Modelling* 198(1–2): 115–26.

Grimm, N. B., Faeth, S. H., Golubiewski, N. E., et al. (2008) Global Change and the Ecology of Cities. *Science* 319 (5864): 756–60.

Groffman, P. M., Bain, D. J., Band, L. E., et al. (2003) Down by the Riverside: Urban Riparian Ecology. *Frontiers in Ecology and the Environment* 1: 315–21.

Gunderson, L. H., and Holling, C. S. (2002) *Panarchy: Understanding Transformations in Human and Natural Systems*. Washington, DC: Island Press.

Gutman, G., Janetos, A. C., Justice, C. O., et al. (eds.) (2004) *Land Change Science: Observing, Monitoring and Understanding Trajectories of Change on the Earth's Surface*. Dordrecht: Kluwer Academic Publishers.

Gutmann, M. P. (2000) Scaling and Demographic Issues in Global Change Research. *Climatic Change* 44: 377–91.

Gutmann, M., Parton, W., Cunfer, G., and Burke, I. (2005) Population and Environment in the US Great Plains. In B. Entwisle and P. Stern (eds.), *Population, Land Use and Environment*. Washington DC: National Academies Press.

Guyer, J., and Lambin, E. (1993) Land Use in an Urban Hinterland: Ethnography and Remote Sensing in the Study of African Intensification. *American Ethnologist* 95: 836–59.

Häfele, W. (1980) *Energy in a Finite World*. Cambridge, MA: Ballinger.

Haggett, P., Cliff, A. D., and Frey, A. (1977) *Locational Methods*. London: Arnold.

Hall, P. G. (1966) *Von Thünen's Isolated State*. Oxford: Pergamon Press.

Hammond, J., Keeney, R., and Raiffa, H. (1999) *Smart Choices*. Cambridge, MA: Harvard Business School Press.

Hanemann, W. K. (1994) Valuing the Environment through Contingent Valuation. *Journal of Economic Perspectives* 8: 19–43.

Hanski, I. (1998) Metapopulation Dynamic. *Nature* 396: 41–9.

Hanski, I., and Gilpin, M. (eds.) (1997) Metapopulation Biology: Ecology, Genetics and Evolution. Academic Press, London, UK.

Hardin, G. (1968) The Tragedy of the Commons. *Science* 1962: 1243–8.

Harrison, S., and Bruna, E. (1999) Habitat Fragmentation and Large-Scale Conservation: What Do We Know for Sure? *Ecography* 22: 225–32.

Hartway, C., Ruckelshaus, M., and Kareiva, P. (1998) The Challenge of Applying Spatial Explicit Models to a World of Sparse and Messy Data. In J. Bascompte and R. V. Sole (eds.), *Modeling Spatio-Temporal Dynamics in Ecology*. New York: Springer Verlag.

Harvell, C. D., Mitchell, C., Ward, J., et al. (2002) *Climate Warming and Disease Risks for Terrestrial and Marine Biota. Science* 296: 2158–62.

Harvey, D. (1973) *Social Justice and the City*. London: Edward Arnold.

Hastie, R., Penrod, S. D., and Pennington, N. (1983) *Inside the Jury*. Cambridge, MA: Harvard University Press.

Hasumi, H., and Emori, S. (2004) K-1 Coupled Model (MIROC) Description. K-1 Technical Report, Center for Climate System Research, University of Tokyo.

Haughton, G., and Hunter, C. (2003) *Sustainable Cities*. London: Taylor and Francis.

Hawley, A. H. (1986) *Human Ecology: A Theoretical Essay*. Chicago, Illinois: University of Chicago Press.

Hay, J., and Mimura, N. (2006) Supporting Climate Change Vulnerability and Adaptation Assessments in the Asia-Pacific Region: An Example of Sustainability Science. *Sustainability Science* 1: 23–35.

Hayami, Y., and Ruttan, V. W. (1987a) *Agricultural Development: An International Perspective*. Baltimore, MD: Johns Hopkins University Press.

Hayami, Y., and Ruttan, V. W (1987b) Population Growth and Agricultural Productivity. In D. G. Johnson and R. G. Lee (eds.), *Population Growth and Economic Development: Issues and Evidence*. Madison, WI: University of Wisconsin Press.

Heasley, L. (2003) Shifting Boundaries on a Wisconsin Landscape: Can GIS Help Historians Tell a Complicated Story? *Human Ecology* 31(2): 183–213.

Heijnen, L., and Kates, R. W. (1974) Northeast Tanzania: Comparative Observations Along a Moisture Gradient. In G. White (ed.), *Natural Hazards*. New York: Oxford University Press.

Henrich, J., Boyd, R., Bowles, S., et al. (2001) In Search of *Homo economicus*: Behavioral Experiments in 15 Small-Scale Societies. *American Economic Review* 91(2): 73–8.

Hess, L. L., Novo, E. M. L. M., Slaymaker, D. M., et al. (2002) Geocoded Digital Videography for Validation of Land Cover Mapping in the Amazon Basin. *International Journal of Remote Sensing* 23: 1527–56.

Hesse-Biber, S. N., and Leavy, P. (2006) *Emergent Methods in Social Research*. Thousand Oaks: Sage Publications.

Heynen, N., Kaika, M., and Swyngedouw, E. (eds.) (2006) *In the Nature of Cities: Urban Political Ecology and the Politics of Urban Metabolism*. London: Routledge.

Hibbard, K. A., Constanza, R., Crumley, C., et al. (2007) *Developing an Integrated History and Future of People on Earth*. IHOPE: Research Prospectus. Stockholm, Sweden: IGBP Secretariat.

Hoddinott, J. (1994) A Model of Migration and Remittances Applied to Western Kenya. Oxford *Economic Papers* 46: 459–76.

Hodell, D., Brenner, M., Curtis, J., and Guilderson, T. (2001) Solar Forcing of Drought Frequency in the Maya Lowlands. *Science* 292: 1367–73.

Hoffmann, M., Kelley, H., and Evans, T. (2002) Simulating Land-Cover Change in Indiana: An Agent-Based Model of De/Reforestation. In Marco Janssen (ed.) *Complexity and Ecosystem Management: The Theory and Practice of Multi-Agent Systems*. Cheltenham, UK/Northampton, MA: Edward Elgar Publishing.

Holland, J. H. (1995) *Hidden Order: How Adaptation Builds Complexity*. Reading, MA: Addison-Wesley.

Holling, C. S. (1973) Resilience and Stability of Ecological Systems. *Annual Review of Ecology and Systematics* 4: 1–23.

Holloway, L., Cox, R., Venn, L., Kneafsey, M., Dowler, E., and Tuomainen, H. (2006) Managing Sustainable Farmed Landscape through Alternative Food Networks: A Case Study from Italy. *Geographical Journal* 172: 219–29.

Hopfenberg, R. (2003) Human Carrying Capacity Is Determined by Food Availability. *Population and Environment* 25(2): 109–17.

Howard, R. (1989) Knowledge Maps. *Management Science* 35(8): 903–22.

Hubbell, S. P. (1979) Tree Dispersion, Abundance, and Diversity in a Tropical Dry Forest. *Science* 203: 1299–1309.

Hunter, M. L. (ed.) (1999) *Maintaining Diversity in Forest Ecosystems*. Cambridge, UK: Cambridge University Press.

Hurrell, J., Kushnir, Y., and Visbeck, M. (2001) The North Atlantic Oscillation. *Science* 291: 603–5.

Hurtt, G. C., Moorcroft, P. R., Pacala, S. W., and Levin, S. A. (1998) Terrestrial Models and Global Change: Challenges for the Future. *Global Change Biology* 4(5): 581–90.

Hutchinson, G. E. (1957) *A Treatise on Limnology. Vol. 1: Geography, Physics and Chemistry*. New York: John Wiley.

Hutchinson, G. E. (1959) Homage to Santa Rosalia or Why Are There So Many Kinds of Animals? *The American Naturalist* 93(870): 145–59.

Inoue, Y. (2003) Synergy of Remote Sensing and Modeling for Estimating Ecophysiological Processes in Plant Production. *Plant Production Science* 6(1): 3–16.

Interacademies (2000) *Transition to Sustainability in the 21st Century: The Contribution of Science and Technology*. Washington, DC: National Academies Press.

Intergovernmental Panel on Climate Change (IPCC) (2000) *Climate Change 2001: The Scientific Basis*. Cambridge: Cambridge University Press.

Jacobsen, J., and Firor, J. (eds.) (1992) *Human Impact on the Environment: Ancient Roots, Current Challenges*. Boulder: Westview Press.

Jarosz, L. (2004) Political Ecology as Ethical Practice. *Political Geography* 23(7): 917–27.

Jensen, J. (1983) Urban/Suburban Land Use Analysis. In J. E. Estes (ed.), *Manual of Remote Sensing*, 2nd edn. Vol.11. Falls Church, VA: American Society of Photogrammetry.

Jensen, J. (2005) *Introductory Digital Image Processing: A Remote Sensing Perspective*. 3rd edn. Upper Saddle River, NJ: Prentice Hall.

Jensen, J. (2007) *Remote Sensing of the Environment: An Earth Resource Perspective*. Upper Saddle River, NJ: Prentice Hall.

Jensen, J. R., Cowen, D. J., Halls, J., et al. (1994) Improved Urban Infrastructure Mapping and Forecasting for Bellsouth Using Remote Sensing and GIS Technology. *Photogrammetric Engineering and Remote Sensing* 60: 339–46.

Johnson, A. (1971) *Sharecroppers of the Sertão*. Stanford, CA: Stanford University Press.

Johnson, B. (1995) Human Rights and the Environment. *Human Ecology* 23: 111–23.

Jones, B. D. (1999) Bounded Rationality. *Annual Review of Political Science* 2: 297–321.

Jones, R. E. (1990) Understanding Paper Recycling in an Institutionally Supportive Setting: An Application of the Theory of Reasoned Action. *Journal of Environmental Systems* 19: 307–21.

Jordan. C. F. (ed.) (1987) *Amazonian Rain Forest*. New York: Springer-Verlag.

Kahneman, D., Slovic, P. and Tversky, A. (eds.) (1982) *Judgment under Uncertainty: Heuristics and Biases*. New York: Cambridge University Press.

Kaimowitz, D., and Angelson, A. (1998) *Economic Models of Deforestation*. Bagor: CIFOR.

Kaiser, F. G. (1998) A General Measure of Ecological Behavior. *Journal of Applied Social Psychology* 28: 395–422.

Kanazawa, S. (1999) Testing Macro Organizational Theories in Laboratory Experiments. *Social Science Research* 28(1): 66–87.

Kaneshiro, K. Y., Chinn, P., Duin, K. N., Hood, A. P., Maly, K., and Wilcox, B. A. (2005) Hawai'i's Mountain-to-Sea Ecosystems: Social-Ecological Microcosms for Sustainability Science and Practice. *EcoHealth* 2(4): 349–60.

Kates, R. (2000) Population and Consumption: What We Know, What We Need to Know. *Environment* 10: 12–19.

Kates, R., and Parris, T. (2003) Long-Term Trends and a Sustainability Transition. *Proceedings of the National Academy of Science* 10(14):8062–7.

Kates, R., Clark, W.C., Corell, R., et al. (2001) Sustainability Science. *Science* 292: 641–2.

Katzev, R., and Johnson, T. (1983) A Social Psychological Analysis of Residential Electricity Consumption: The Impact of Minimal Justification Techniques. *Journal of Economic Psychology* 3: 267–84. (Reprinted in P. Ester, G. Gaskell, B. Joerges, G. Midden, F. van Raaij and T. Vries (eds.), *Consumer Behavior and Energy Policy*. Amsterdam: North-Holland, 1984).

Katzev, R., and Johnson, T. (1987) *Promoting Energy Conservation: An Analysis of Behavioral Approaches*. Boulder, CO: Westview Press.

Keeling, C. D., and Whorf, T. P. (2000) Atmospheric CO_2 Records from Sites in the SIO Air Sampling Network. In US Department of Energy (ed.), *Trends: A Compendium of Data on Global Change*. Carbon Dioxide Information Analysis Center, Oak Ridge National Laboratory, US Department of Energy, Oak Ridge, TN.

Keeney, R. L. (1992) *Value-Focused Thinking: A Path to Creative Decision Making*. Cambridge, MA: Harvard University Press.

Keeney, R. L., and H. Raiffa (1993) *Decisions with Multiple Objectives*, 2nd edn. New York: Cambridge University Press.

Keil, R. (2003) Urban Political Ecology. *Urban Geography* 24: 723–38.

Kempton, W., Harris, C. K., Keith, J. G., and Weihl, J. S. (1985) Do Consumers Know "What Works" in Energy Conservation? *Marriage and Family Review* 9: 115–33.

Kingdon, J. (1987) *Agendas, Alternatives and Public Policies*. Boston, MA: Addison Wesley.

Kirch, P. V. (2005) Archaeology and Global Change: The Holocene Record. *Annual Review of Environment and Resources* 30: 409–40.

Kirk, D. (1996) Demographic Transition Theory. *Population Studies* 50: 361–87.

Klatzky, R., Lippa, Y., Loomis, J., and Golledge, R. (2002) Learning Directions of Objects Specified by Vision, Spatial Audition, or Auditory Spatial Language. *Learning and Memory* 9(6): 364–7.

Klein, R., Sathaye, J., and Wilbanks, T. (eds.) (2007) Challenges in Integrating Mitigation and Adaptation as Responses to Climate Change, Special Issue. *Mitigation and Adaptation Strategies for Global Change* 12(5): 639–962.

Klein Goldwijk, C. G. M., and Battjes, J. J. (1997) *One Hundred Year Database for Integrated Environmental Assessments*. (RIVM), Bilthoven: National Institute for Public Health and Environment.

Koch, T., and Denike, K. (2004) Medical Mapping: The Revolution in Teaching- and Using- Maps for the Analysis of Medical Issues. *Journal of Geography* 103: 76–85.

Kohler, H. P. (2000) Fertility Decline as a Coordination Problem. *Journal of Development Economics* 63: 231–63.

Kohler, T. A., and Carr, E. (eds.) (1996) Swarm Based Modelling of Prehistoric Settlement Systems in Southwestern North America. *Proceedings of Colloquium II, UISPP XIIIth Congress*. Forli, Italy.

Kollman, K., Miller, J. H., and Page, S. E. (1997) Political Institutions and Sorting in a Tiebout Model. *American Economic Review* 87(5): 977–92.

Komiyama, H., and Takeuchi, K. (2006) Sustainability Science: Building a New Discipline. *Sustainability Science* 1: 1–6.

Koontz, T. M. (1997) Federalism and Natural Resource Policy: Comparing State and National Management of Public Forests. PhD diss. Indiana University.

Koontz, T. M. (2001) Money Talks-But to Whom? Financial v. Non-Monetary Motivations in Land Use Decisions. *Society and Natural Resources* 14: 51–65.

Kottak, C. (1999) The New Ecological Anthropology. *American Anthropologist* 101: 19–35.

Krugman, P. (1995) *Development, Geography, and Economic Theory*. Cambridge, MA: MIT Press.

Lambin, E. F. (1994) Modelling Deforestation Processes: A Review. Trees Publications Series B: Research Report, No. 1. European Commission, EUR 15744 EN.

Lambin, E. F., and Geist, H. J. (eds.) (2006) *Land Use and Land Cover Change: Local Processes and Global Impacts*. IGBP Springer Book Series, No. 9. Heidelberg: Springer.

Lambin, E. F., Baulies, X., Bockstael, N., et al. (1999) Land-Use and Land-Cover Change (LUCC) – Implementation Strategy. A Core Project of the International Geosphere-Biosphere Programme and the International Human Dimensions Programme on Global Environmental Change (= IGBP Report; 48/IHDP Report; 10). – IGBP Secretariat: Stockholm & IHDP Secretariat: Bonn.

Lambin, E. F., Turner B. L., II, Geist, H. J., et al. (2001) The Causes of Land-Use and Land-Cover Change: Moving Beyond the Myths. *Global Environmental Change* 11(4): 261–9.

Langton, C. (ed.) (1997) *Artificial Life: An Overview*. Cambridge, MA: MIT Press.

Lansing, S. (1991) *Priests and Programmers*. Chicago: University of Chicago Press.

Lansing, S. (2003) Complex Adaptive Systems. *Annual Review of Anthropology* 32: 183–204.

Laurance, W., and Bierregaard, R. O., Jr. (eds.) (1997) *Tropical Forest Remnants: Ecology, Management, and Conservation of Fragmented Communities*. Chicago: University of Chicago Press.

Laurance, W., Cochrane, M., Bergen, S., et al. (2001) The Future of the Brazilian Amazon. *Science* 291: 438–42.

Laurance, W., Nascimento, H. E. M., Laurance, S. G., et al. (2006) Rapid Decay of Tree-Community Composition in Amazonian Forest Fragments. *Proceedings of the National Academy of Sciences* 103(50): 19010–14.

Lave, L. B. (1996) Benefit-Cost Analysis: Do the Benefits Exceed the Costs? *In* R. Hahn (ed.), *Risks, Costs, and Lives Saved: Getting Better Results from Regulation*. Oxford: Oxford University Press

Layard, R., and Glaister, S. (2004) *Cost Benefit Analysis*. Cambridge, UK: Cambridge University Press.

LeBars, M., Attonaty, J. M., Pinson S., and Ferrard, N. (2005) An Agent-Based Simulation Testing of the Impact of Water Allocation on Farmers' Collective Behaviors. *Simulation-Transactions of the Society for Modeling and Simulation International* 81(3): 223–35.

Lees, S., and Bates, D. (1990) The Ecology of Cumulative Change. In E. F. Moran (ed.), *The Ecosystem Approach in Anthropology*. Ann Arbor: University of Michigan Press.

Leibenstein, H. (1976) *Beyond Economic Man*. Cambridge, MA: Harvard University Press.

Levin, R. I., and Kirkpatrick, C. A. (1975) *Quantitative Approaches to Management*, 3rd edn. New York: McGraw-Hill.

Levin, S. (1992) The Problem of Pattern and Scale in Ecology. *Ecology* 73(6): 1943–67.

Levin, S. (1998) Ecosystem and the Biosphere as a Complex Adaptive System. *Ecosystems* 1(5): 431–6.

Levin, S. (2000) *Fragile Dominion: Complexity and the Commons*. Reading: Perseus.

Levin, S. (2005) Self-Organization and the Emergence of Complexity in Ecological Systems. *Bioscience* 55(12): 1075–9.

Levin, S. (2006) Learning to Live in a Global Commons: Socioeconomic Challenges for a Sustainable Environment. *Ecological Research* 21(3): 328–33.

Libecap, G. (1995) The Conditions for Successful Collective Action. In R. O. Keohane and E. Ostrom (eds.), *Local Commons and Global Interdependence: Heterogeneity and Cooperation in Two Domains*. London: Sage.

Lillesand, T. M., and Kiefer, R. W. (1994) *Remote Sensing and Image Interpretation*, 3rd edn. New York: John Wiley.

Lindblom, C. (1964) The Science of Muddling Through. In W. J Gore and J. W. Dyson (eds.), *The Making of Decisions*. New York: Free Press.

Linderman, M. A., An, L., Bearer, S., He, G., and Liu, J. (2006) Interactive Effects of Natural and Human Disturbances on Vegetation Dynamics Across Landscapes. *Ecological Applications* 16(2): 452–63.

Little, M., and Morren, G. (1976) *Ecology, Energetics and Human Variability*. Dubuque, IA: William C. Brown.

Liu, J., Daily, G., Ehrlich, P., and Luck, G. (2003) Effects of Household Dynamics on Resource Consumption and Biodiversity. *Nature* 21: 530–3.

Liu, J., An, L., Batie, S., et al. (2005) Beyond Population Size: Examining Intricate Interactions among Population Structure, Land Use and Environment in the Wolong Nature Reserve, China. In B. Entwisle and P. Stern (eds.), *Population, Land Use and Environment*. Washington, DC: National Academies Press.

Liu, J., Dietz, T., Carpenter, S. R., et al. (2007a) Complexity of Coupled Human and Natural Systems. *Science* 317: 1513–16.

Liu, J., Dietz, T., Carpenter, S. R., et al. (2007b) Coupled Human and Natural Systems. *Ambio* 36: 639–49.

Liu, Y., Gupta, H. V., Springer, E., and Wagener, T. (2008) Linking Science with Environmental Decision Making: Experiences from an Integrated Modeling Approach to Support Sustainable Water Resources Management. *Environmental Modelling and Software* 23(7): 846–58.

Liverman, D., Moran, E. F., Rindfuss, R. R., and Stern, P. C. (eds.) (1998) *People and Pixels: Linking Remote Sensing and Social Science*. Washington, DC: National Academy Press.

Livi Bacci, M. (2001) *A Concise History of World Population*. Malden, MA: Blackwell.

Lo, C. P., and Yeung, A. K. W. (2002) *Concepts and Techniques in Geographic Information Systems*. Upper Saddle River, NJ: Prentice Hall.

Loreau, M., Naeem, S., Inchausti, P., et al. (2001) Biodiversity and Ecosystem Functioning: Current Knowledge and Future Challenges. *Science* 294: 804–8.

Loris, V., and Damiano, G. (2006) Mapping the Green Herbage Ratio of Grasslands Using Both Aerial and Satellite Derived Spectral Reflectance. *Agriculture, Ecosystems and Environment* 115(1–4): 141–9.

Lubchenco, J. (1998) Entering the Century of the Environment: A New Social Contract for Science. *Science* 279: 491–7.

Lucas, R. E. B., and Stark, O. (1985) Motivations to Remit: Evidence from Botswana. *Journal of Political Economy* 93(5): 901–18.

Luken, J. O. (1990) *Directing Ecological Succession*. London: Chapman and Hall.

Lustick, I. S. (2000) Agent-Based Modelling of Collective Identity: Testing Constructivist Theory. *JASSS-Journal of Artificial Societies and Social Simulation* 3(1): 1–29.

Lutzenhiser, L., Harris, C., and Olsen, M. (2001) Energy, Society and Environment. In R. Dunlap and W. Michaelson (eds.), *Handbook of Environmental Sociology*. Westport, CT: Greenwood Press.

Lyons, T., Inglis, M., and Hitchcock, R. (1972) The Application of Space Imagery to Anthropology. In *Proceedings of the Third Annual Conference on Remote Sensing in Arid Lands*. Tucson: University of Arizona, Office of Arid Land Studies.

MacArthur, R. H., and Wilson, E. O. (1967) *The Theory of Island Biogeography*. Princeton: Princeton University Press.

Mackay, D. M. (1968) Towards an Information-Flow Model of Human Behavior. In W. Buckley (ed.), *Modern Systems Research for the Behavioral Scientist*. Chicago: Aldine.

Mackellar, F. L., Lutz, W., Prinz, C., and Goujon, A. (1995) Population, Households, and Carbon Dioxide Emissions. *Population and Development Review* 21(4): 849–65.

Macy, M. W., and Willer, R. (2002) From Factors to Actors: Computational Sociology and Agent-Based Modeling. *Annual Review of Sociology* 28: 143–66.

Madhavan, B. B., Kubo, S., Kurisaki, N. T., and Sivakumar, V. L. N. (2001) Appraising the Anatomy and Spatial Growth of the Bangkok Metropolitan Area Using a Vegetation-Impervious-Soil Model through Remote Sensing. *International Journal of Remote Sensing* 22: 789–806.

Malthus, T. R. ([1803]1989) *An Essay on the Principle of Population*. Reprint with the variorums of 1806, 1807, 1817, and 1826. P. James (ed.) Cambridge, UK: Cambridge University Press.

Mann, M. E., Bradley, R. S., and Hughes, M. K. (1999) Northern Hemisphere Temperatures during the Past Millennium: Inferences, Uncertainties and Limitations. *Geophysical Research Letters* 26(6): 759–62.

Manson, S. (2002) Validation and Verification of Multi-Agent Systems. In M.A. Janssen (ed.), *Complexity and Ecosystem Management*. Northampton, MA/ Cheltenham, UK: Edward Elgar Publishing.

Manson, S. (2008) Does Scale Exist? An Epistemological Scale Continuum for Complex Human-Environment Systems. *Geoforum* 39(2): 776–88.

Marceau, D. J. (1999) The Scale Issue in Social and Natural Science. *Canadian Journal of Remote Sensing* 25(4): 347–56.

March, J. (1978) Bounded Rationality, Ambiguity and the Engineering of Choice. *Bell Journal of Economics* 9(2): 587–608.

March, J. G., and Simon, H. A. (1958) *Organizations*. New York: John Wiley.

Marston, S. (2000) The Social Construction of Scale. *Progress in Human Geography* 24(2): 219–42.

Martin, D., and Bracken, I. (1993) The Integration of Socioeconomic and Physical Resource Data for Applied Land Management Information Systems. *Applied Geography* 13: 45–53.

Mason, K. O. (1997) Explaining Fertility Transitions. *Demography* 34: 443–54.

Massey, D. S., Arango, J., Hugo, G., Kouaouci, A., Pellegrino, A., and Taylor, J. E. (1993) Theories of International Migration: A Review and Appraisal. *Population and Development Review* 19(3): 431–66.

Mather, A. (1992) The Forest Transition. *Area* 24(4): 367–79.

Matthies, M, Giupponi, C., and Ostendorf, B. (2007) Environmental Decision Support Systems: Current Issues, Methods and Tools. *Environmental Modelling and Software* 22(2): 123–7.

Mausel, P., Wu, Y., Li, Y., Moran, E. F., and Brondizio, E. S. (1993) Spectral Identification of Successional Stages Following Deforestation in the Amazon. *Geocarto International* 8: 61–71.

McCabe, J. T. (2004) *Cattle Bring Us to Our Enemies: Turkana Ecology, Politics, and Raiding in a Disequilibrium System*. Ann Arbor: University of Michigan Press.

McCay, B., and Acheson, J. (eds.) (1987) *The Question of the Commons: The Culture and Ecology of Communal Resources*. Tucson: University of Arizona Press.

McConnell, W. J., and Keys, E. (2005) Meta-Analysis of Agricultural Change. In E. F. Moran and E. Ostrom (eds.), *Seeing the Forest and the Trees: Human–Environment Interactions in Forest Ecosystems*. Cambridge, MA: MIT Press.

McCoy, R. M. (2005) *Field Methods in Remote Sensing*. New York: Guilford Press.

McCracken, S., Brondizio, E. S., Nelson, D., Moran, E. F., Siqueira, A. D., and Rodriguez-Pedraza, C. (1999) Remote Sensing and GIS at the Farm Property Level: Demography and Deforestation in the Brazilian Amazon. *Photogrammetric Engineering and Remote Sensing* 65(11): 1311–20.

McCracken, S., Siqueira, A., Moran, E., and Brondizio, E. (2002) Land Use Patterns on an Agricultural Frontier in Brazil: Insights and Examples from a Demographic Perspective. In D. Wood and R. Porro (eds.), *Deforestation and Land Use in the Amazon*. Gainesville: University Press of Florida.

McDaniels, T., and Thomas, K. (1999) Eliciting Public Preferences for Local Land Use Alternatives: A Structured Value Referendum with Approval Voting. *Journal of Policy Analysis and Management* 18(2): 264–80.

McDonnell, M. J., and Pickett, S. T. A. (1990) The Study of Ecosystem Structure and Function Along Urban-Rural Gradients: An Unexploited Opportunity for Ecology. *Ecology* 71: 1231–7.

McKean, M. A. (1992) Management of Traditional Commons Lands (*Iriaichi*) in Japan. In D. W. Bromley, D. Feeny, M. McKean, P. Peters, J. Gilles, R. Oakerson,

C. F. Runge and J. Thomson (eds.), *Making the Commons Work: Theory, Practice, and Policy*. San Francisco: ICS Press.

McQueen, D. J., Johannes, M. R. S., and Post, J. R. (1989) Bottom-Up and Top-Down Impacts on Freshwater Pelagic Community Structure. *Ecological Monographs* 59(3): 289–309.

Meadows, D. H., Meadows, D. L., Randers J., and Behrens W., III (1972) *The Limits to Growth*. New York: Universe Books.

Medd, W., and Chappells, H. (2007) Drought, Demand and Scale: Fluidity and Flexibility in the Framing of Water Relations. *Interdisciplinary Science Reviews* 32(3): 233–48.

Meffe, G. K., and Carroll, C. R. (1997) Conservation Reserves in Heterogenous Landscapes. In G. K. Meffe, and C. R. Carroll (eds.), *Principles of Conservation Biology*, 2nd edn. Sunderland, MA: Sinauer Associates.

Meggers, B. (1971) *Amazonia*. Chicago: Aldine.

Mesquita, R. C. G., Ickes, K., Ganade, G., and Williamson, G. B. (2001) Alternative Successional Pathways in the Amazonian Basin. *Journal of Ecology* 89: 528–37.

Messina, J. P., and Walsh, S. J. (2001) 2.5D Morphogenesis: Modeling Land Use and Land Cover Dynamics in the Ecuadorian Amazon. *Plant Ecology* 156(1): 75–88.

Meyer, W., and Turner, B. L., II (1994) *Changes in Land Use and Land Cover: A Global Perspective*. Cambridge, UK: Cambridge University Press.

Michener, W. K., Baerwald, T. J., Firth, P., et al. (2003) Defining and Unraveling Biocomplexity. *Bioscience* 51(12): 1018–23.

Milinski, M., and Wedekind, C. (1998) Working Memory Constrains Human Cooperation in the Prisoner's Dilemma. *Proceedings of the National Academy of Sciences of the United States of America* 95(23): 13755–8.

Millennium Ecosystem Assessment (2003) Dealing with Scale. Conceptual Framework. *Millennium Ecosystem Assessment*: 107–26. Kuala Lumpur: Island Press.

Miller, B. (2005) Environmental Risk in Water Resources Management in the Mekong Delta: A Multi-Scale Analysis. In T. Tvedt and E. Jakobsson (eds.), *History of Water. Vol. 1: Control and River Biographies*. London and New York: I. B. Tauris.

Miller, D., and de Roo, G. (eds.) (2005) *Urban Environmental Planning: Policies, Instruments, and Methods in an International Perspective*. Aldershot, UK: Ashgate Publishing.

Mitsch, W., and Day, J. (2004) Thinking Big with Whole Ecosystem Studies and Ecosystem Restoration: A Legacy of H. T. Odum. *Ecological Modelling* 178 (1–2): 133–55.

Moorcroft, P. R., Hurtt, G. C., and Pacala, S. W. (2001) A Method for Scaling Vegetation Dynamics: The Ecosystem Demography Model (ED). *Ecological Monographs* 71(4): 557–86.

Moran, E. F. (1976) *Agricultural Development along the Transamazon Highway*. Center for Latin American Studies Monograph Series. Bloomington: Center for Latin American Studies, Indiana University.

Moran, E. F. (1979) *Human Adaptability*. N. Scituate, MA: Duxbury Press. Reissued by Westview Press, 1982.

Moran, E. F. (1981) *Developing the Amazon.* Bloomington: Indiana University Press.

Moran, E. F. (1982a) Ecological, Anthropological and Agronomic Research in the Amazon Basin. *Latin American Research Review* 17: 3–41.

Moran, E. F. (1982b) The Evolution of Cape Verde's Agriculture. *African Economic History* 11: 63–86.

Moran, E. F. (1988) Following the Amazonian Highways. In J. Denslow and C. Padoch (eds.), *People of the Rain Forest.* Berkeley, CA: University of California Press/Smithsonian Institute.

Moran, E. F. (ed.) (1990) *The Ecosystem Approach in Anthropology: From Concept to Practice.* Ann Arbor: University of Michigan Press.

Moran, E. F. (1993) Deforestation and Land Use in the Brazilian Amazon. *Human Ecology* 21: 1–21.

Moran, E. F. (1995) *The Comparative Analysis of Human Societies: Toward Common Standards for Data Collection and Reporting.* Boulder: Lynne Rienner.

Moran, E. F. (2000) Theory and Practice in Environmental Anthropology. In C. Hill and M. Baba, (eds.), *The Unity of Theory and Practice in Anthropology: Rebuilding a Fractured Synthesis.* Washington, DC: National Association for the Practice of Anthropology Bulletin 18: 132–46.

Moran, E. F. (2005) New Directions in Human-Environment Interactions and Land Use/Land Cover Research. In E. Moran and E. Ostrom (eds.), *Seeing the Forest and the Trees.* Cambridge, MA: MIT Press.

Moran, E. F. (2006) *People and Nature: An Introduction to Human Ecological Relations.* New York: Blackwell.

Moran, E. F. (2007) *Human Adaptability: An Introduction to Ecological Anthropology,* 3rd edn. Boulder: Westview Press.

Moran, E. F., and Brondizio, E. S. (1998) Land-Use Change After Deforestation in Amazonia. In Liverman et al. (eds.), *People and Pixels: Linking Remote Sensing and Social Science.* Washington, DC: National Academy Press.

Moran, E. F., and Brondizio, E. S. (2001) Human Ecology from Space: Ecological Anthropology Engages the Study of Global Environmental Change. In E. Messer and M. Lambeck (eds.), *Ecology and the Sacred: Engaging the Anthropology of Roy Rappaport.* Ann Arbor: University of Michigan Press.

Moran, E. F., and Ostrom, E. (eds.) (2005) *Seeing the Forest and the Trees: Human-Environment Interactions in Forest Ecosystems.* Cambridge, MA: MIT Press.

Moran, E. F., Brondizio, E. S., and Mausel, P. (1994) Secondary Succession. *Research and Exploration* 10(4): 458–76.

Moran, E. F., Brondizio, E. S., and McCracken, S. (2002) Trajectories of Land Use: Soils, Succession, and Crop Choice. In C. H. Wood and R. Porro (eds.), *Deforestation and Land Use in the Amazon.* Gainesville, FL: University of Florida Press.

Moran, E. F., Brondizio, E. S., and VanWey, L. (2005) Population and Environment in Amazonia: Landscape and Household Dynamics. In B. Entwisle and P. Stern (eds.), *Population, Land Use and Environment.* Washington, DC: The National Academies Press.

Moran, E. F., McCracken, S., and Brondizio, E. S. (2001) *The Development Cycle of Domestic Groups and Its Impact on Deforestation and Land Use in the Amazon.* Presented at the Population Association of America 66th Annual Meeting, Washington, DC, March 29–31.

Moran, E. F., Ostrom, E., and Randolph, J. C. (2002) Ecological Systems and Multitier Human Organizations. In *UNESCO/Encyclopedia of Life Support Systems.* Oxford, UK: EOLSS Publishers.

Moran, E. F., Brondizio, E. S., Mausel, P., and Wu, Y. (1994) Integrating Amazonian Vegetation, Land Use, and Satellite Data. *Bioscience* 44(5): 329–38.

Moran, E. F., Packer, A., Brondizio, E. S., and Tucker, J. (1996) Restoration of Vegetation Cover in the Eastern Amazon. *Ecological Economics* 18: 41–54.

Moran, E. F., McCracken, S., Brondizio, E., Nelson, D., Siqueira, A., and Rodriguez-Pedraza, C. (1999) Remote Sensing and GIS at Farm Property Level: Demography and Deforestation in the Brazilian Amazon. *Photogrammetric Engineering and Remote Sensing* 65(11): 1311–20.

Moran, E. F., Brondizio, E. S., Tucker, J., da Silva-Forsberg, M. C., McCracken, S., and Falesi, I. (2000) Effects of Soil Fertility and Land-Use on Forest Succession in Amazonia. *Forest Ecology and Management* 139: 93–108.

Moran, E. F., Adams, R. T., Bakoyema, B., Fiorini, S., and Boucek, B. (2006) Human Strategies for Coping with El Niño Related Drought in Amazônia. *Climatic Change* 77: 343–61.

Morgan, M. G., and Henrion, M. (1990) *Uncertainty.* Cambridge, UK: Cambridge University Press.

Morgan, M. G., Kandlikar, M., Risbey, J., and Dowlatabadi, H. (1999) Why Conventional Tools of Policy Analysis are Often Inadequate for Problems of Global Change. *Climatic Change* 41: 271–81.

Morgan, M. G., Fischhoff, B., Bostrom, A., and Atman, C. (2002) *Risk Communication: A Mental Models Approach.* Cambridge, UK: Cambridge University Press.

Morgenstern, R. D. (ed.) (1997) *Economic Analysis at the EPA.* Washington, DC: Resources for the Future Press.

Moscovici, S. (1985) Innovation and Minority Influence. In G. Lindzey and E. Aronson (eds.), *Handbook of Social Psychology,* Vol. 2. New York: Random House.

Muller, D. (2005) Stata in Space: Economic Analysis of Spatially Explicit Raster Data. *The Stata Journal* 5(2): 224–38.

Muller, P. O. (1973) Trend Surfaces of American Agricultural Patterns: A Macro-Thünen Economy. *Geographical Analysis* 24: 228–42.

Mumford, L. (1961) *The City in History: Its Origin, Its Transformation and Its Prospects.* New York: Harcourt, Brace and World.

Myers, H. (2000) Options for Appropriate Development in Nunavut Communities. *Inuit Studies* 24(1): 25–40.

Nadel, L., and Stein, D. (eds.) (1991) *Lectures in Complex Systems.* Reading, MA: Addison-Wesley.

Nadel, L., and Stein, D. (1992) *Lectures in Complex Systems.* Redwood City, CA: Addison-Wesley.

Nadel, L., and Stein, D. (1995) *1993 Lectures in Complex Systems: Lectures Vol. VI.* Santa Fe Institute, New York: Addison-Wesley.

Nagendra, H. (2001) Using Remote Sensing to Assess Biodiversity. *International Journal of Remote Sensing* 22(12): 2377–400.

Nagendra, H. (2002) Tenure and Forest Conditions: Community Forestry in the Nepal Terai. *Environmental Conservation* 29: 530–9.

Nagendra, H., Munroe, D. K., and Southworth, J. (2004) *From Pattern to Process: Landscape Fragmentation and the Analysis of Land Use/Land Cover Change.*

National Science Board (1989) *Loss of Biological Diversity.* Washington, DC: National Scientific Board Committee on International Science.

National Science Foundation (2003) *Complex Environmental Systems: Synthesis for Earth, Life and Society in the 21st Century.* Arlington, VA: NSF

Nepstad, D., Moreira, A., and Alencar, A. (1999) *Flames in the Rainforest: Origins, Impacts and Alternatives to Amazonian Fire.* Brazilia, Brazil: The Pilot Program to Conserve the Brazilian Rain Forest.

Nepstad, D., Capobianco, J. P., Barros, A. C., et al. (2000) *Avança Brasil: Os Custos Ambientais Para a Amazônia.* [*Forward Brazil: The Environmental Costs for the Amazon*]. Belém, Brazil: Gráfica e Editora Alves.

Netting, R. (1968) *Hill Farmers of Nigeria.* Seattle: Washington University Press.

Netting, R. (1981) *Balancing on an Alp.* New York: Cambridge University Press.

Netting, R. (1993) *Smallholders, Householders: Farm Families and the Ecology of Intensive Sustainable Agriculture.* Stanford: Stanford University Press.

Netting, R., Stone, G., and Stone, P. (1995) The Social Organization of Agrarian Labor. In E. F. Moran (ed.), *The Comparative Analysis of Human Societies.* Boulder: Lynne Rienner.

Nicholaides, J. J., III, and Moran, E. F. (1995) Soil Indices for Comparative Analysis of Agrarian Systems. In E. F. Moran (ed.), *The Comparative Analysis of Human Societies.* Boulder: Lynne Rienner.

Nilsson, S., and Schopfhauser, W. (1995) The Carbon-Sequestration Potential of a Global Afforestation Program. *Climatic Change* 30(3): 267–93.

Norberg, J., and Cumming, G. S. (eds.) (2008) *Complexity Theory for a Sustainable Future.* New York: Columbia University Press.

Norby, R. J., Hanson, P. J., O'Neill, E. G., et al. (2002) Net Primary Productivity of a CO_2- Enriched Deciduous Forest and the Implications for Carbon Storage. *Ecological Applications* 12: 1261–6.

Nordhaus, W. D. (1997) Do Real Wage and Output Series Capture Reality? The History of Lighting Suggests Not. In T. Bresnahan and R. Gordon (eds.) *The Economics of New Goods.* Chicago: University of Chicago Press.

North, D. C. (1990) *Institutions, Institutional Change and Economic Performance.* New York: Cambridge University Press.

NRC (National Research Council) (1984) *Energy Use: The Human Dimension.* New York: Freeman.

NRC (National Research Council) (1985) *Energy Efficiency in Buildings: Behavioral Issues.* Washington, DC: National Academy Press.

NRC (National Research Council) (1989) *Improving Risk Communication.* Washington, DC: National Academy Press.

NRC (National Research Council) (1990) *Research Strategies for the US Global Change Research Program.* Washington, DC: National Academy Press.

NRC (National Research Council) (1992) *Global Environmental Change: Understanding the Human Dimensions.* Washington, DC: National Academy Press.

NRC (National Research Council) (1993) *Science Priorities for the Human Dimensions.* Washington, DC: National Academy Press.

NRC (National Research Council) (1994a) *Research Needs and Modes of Support for the Human Dimensions of Global Change.* Washington, DC: National Academy Press.

NRC (National Research Council) (1994b) *Science Priorities for the Human Dimensions of Global Change.* Washington, DC: National Academy Press.

NRC (National Research Council) (1996) *Understanding Risk: Informing Decisions in a Democratic Society.* P.C. Stern and H.V. Fineberg (eds.) Committee on Risk Characterization. Commission on Behavioral and Social Sciences and Education. Washington, DC: National Academy Press.

NRC (National Research Council) (1997a) *Environmentally Significant Consumption: Research Issues. Committee on the Human Dimensions of Global Change.* Washington, DC: National Academy Press.

NRC (National Research Council) (1997b) *NOAA's Arctic Research Initiative: Proceedings of a Workshop.* Washington, DC: National Academy Press.

NRC (National Research Council) (1998a) *People and Pixels: Linking Remote Sensing and Social Science. Committee on the Human Dimensions of Global Change.* Washington, DC: National Academy Press.

NRC (National Research Council) (1998b) *Decade-to-Century-Scale Climate Variability and Change: A Science Strategy.* Commission on Geosciences, Environment and Resources. Washington, DC: National Academy Press.

NRC (National Research Council) (1999a) *Global Environmental Change: Research Pathways for the Next Decade. Committee on Global Change Research.* Washington, DC: National Academy Press.

NRC (National Research Council) (1999b) *Human Dimensions of Global Environmental Change: Research Pathways for the Next Decade.* Washington, DC: National Academy Press.

NRC (National Research Council) (1999c) *Making Climate Forecasts Matter.* Washington, DC: National Academy Press.

NRC (National Research Council) (1999d) *Nature's Numbers: Expanding the National Economic Accounts to Include the Environment.* Washington DC: National Academy Press

NRC (National Research Council) (1999e) *Our Common Journey: A Transition toward Sustainability.* Washington, DC: National Academy Press.

NRC (National Research Council) (2001) *Grand Challenges in Environmental Sciences.* Report from the Committee on Grand Challenges in Environmental Sciences. Washington, DC: National Academy Press.

NRC (National Research Council) (2002a) *The Drama of the Commons.* Washington, DC: National Academy Press.

NRC (National Research Council) (2002b) *New Tools for Environmental Protection: Education, Information, and Voluntary Measures.* Washington, DC: National Academy Press.

NRC (National Research Council) (2002c) *Human Interactions with the Carbon Cycle: Summary of a Workshop.* Washington, DC: National Academy Press.

NRC (National Research Council) (2004) *Implementing Climate and Global Change: A Review of the Final US Climate Change Science Program Strategic Plan.* Washington, DC: National Academy Press.

NRC (National Research Council) (2005a) *Population, Land Use and Environment: Research Directions. Committee on theHuman Dimensions of Global Change.* Washington, DC: National Academies Press.

NRC (National Research Council) (2005b) *Decision Making for the Environment: Social and Behavioral Science Research Priorities.* Washington, DC: National Academy Press.

NRC (National Research Council) (2005c) *Valuing Ecosystem Services: Toward Better Environmental Decision-Making.* Washington, DC: National Academies Press.

NRC (National Research Council) (2006) *Facing Hazards and Disasters: Understanding Human Dimensions.* Washington, DC: National Academy Press.

NRC (National Research Council) (2007a) *Evaluating Progress of the US Climate Change Science Program: Methods and Preliminary Results.* Washington, DC: National Academy Press.

NRC (National Research Council) (2007b) *Understanding Multiple Environmental Stresses: Report of a Workshop.* Washington, DC: National Academy Press.

NRC (National Research Council) (2008) *Research and Networks for Decision Support in the NOAA Sectoral Applications Research Program.* Washington, DC: National Academy Press.

Nyerges, A., and Green, G. (2000) The Ethnography of Landscape: GIS and Remote Sensing in the Study of Forest Change in West African Guinea Savanna. *American Anthropologist* 102(2): 271–89.

Obasi, G. (2004) Embracing Sustainability Science: The Challenges for Africa. *Environment* 44(4): 8–19.

Odum, E. (1969) The Strategy of Ecosystem Development. *Science* 164: 262–70.

Odum, E. (1971) *Fundamentals of Ecology*, 3rd edn. Philadelphia: Saunders. Originally published in 1959.

Odum, H. T. (1971) *Energy, Power and Society.* New York: Wiley InterScience.

Okabe, A. (2006) *GIS-Based Studies in the Humanities and Social Sciences.* Boca Raton, FL: CRC/Taylor and Francis.

O'Kelly, M., and Bryan, D. (1996) Agricultural Location Theory: von Thünen's Contribution to Economic Geography. *Progress in Human Geography* 20: 457–75.

Olalla-Tarraga, M. A. (2006) A Conceptual Framework to Assess Sustainability in Urban Ecological Systems. International *Journal of Sustainable Development and World Ecology* 13: 1–15.

Olson, M. (1965) *The Logic of Collective Action: Public Goods and the Theory of Groups.* Cambridge: Harvard University Press.

Olsson P., Folke, C. and Berkes, F. (2004) Adaptive Co-Management for Building Social-Ecological Resilience. *Environmental Management* 34: 75–90.

Oosterbeek, H., Sloof, R., and Van De Kuilen, G. (2004) Cultural Differences in Ultimatum Game Experiments: Evidence from a Meta-Analysis. *Experimental Economics* 7(2): 171–88.

Openshaw, S. (1994) Computational Human Geography: Towards a Research Agenda. *Environment and Planning* 26: 499–508.

Openshaw, S. (1995) Human Systems Modeling on a Grand New Area in Science: What Happened to theScience in Social Science? *Environment and Planning* 27: 159–64.

Orford, S., Harris, R., and Dorling, D. (1999) Geography: Information Visualization in the Social Sciences- A State-of-the-Art Review. *Social Science Computer Review* 17(3): 289–304.

Ostrom, E. (1990) *Governing the Commons: The Evolution of Institutions for Collective Action.* New York: Cambridge University Press.

Ostrom, E. (1992) *Crafting Institutions for Self-Governing Irrigation Systems.* San Francisco: ICS Press.

Ostrom, E. (1998) The Institutional Analysis and Development Approach. In E. T. Loehman and D. M. Kilgour (eds.), *Designing Institutions for Environmental and Resource Management.* Cheltenham, UK: Edward Elgar.

Ostrom, E. (1999) Coping with Tragedies of the Commons. *Annual Review of Political Science* 2: 493–535.

Ostrom, E. (2005) *Understanding Institutional Diversity.* Princeton, NJ: Princeton University Press.

Ostrom, E. (2006) Multiple Institutions for Multiple Outcomes. In A. Smajgl and S. Larson (eds.), *Adapting Rules for Sustainable Resource Use.* Townsville, Australia: SCIRO Sustainable Ecosystems.

Ostrom, E., and Walker, J. (2003) *Trust and Reciprocity: Interdisciplinary Lessons from Experimental Research.* New York: Russell Sage Foundation.

Ostrom, E., Gardner, R., and Walker, J. (1994) *Rules, Games and Common Pool Resources.* Ann Arbor: University of Michigan Press.

Ostrom, E., Janssen, M. A., and Anderies, J. M. (eds.) (2007) Going Beyond Panaceas. Special Feature. *Proceedings of the National Academy of Sciences* 104: 15176–223.

Pacala, S. W., Canham, C. D., Saponara, J., Silander, J. A., Jr., Kobe, R. K., and Ribbens, E. (1996) Forest Models Defined by Field Measurements: Estimation, Error Analysis and Dynamics. *Ecological Monographs* 66(1): 1–43.

Pachauri, R. (2008) Climate Change and Sustainability Science. *Sustainability Science* 3: 1–3.

Padgett, J. P., Steinemann, A. C., Clarke, J. H., and Vandenbergh, M. P. (2008) A Comparison of Carbon Calculators. *Environmental Impact Assessment Review* 28(2–3): 106–15.

Pahl-Wostl, C. (2007) The Implications of Complexity for Integrated Resources Management. *Environmental Modelling and Software* 22(5): 561–9.

Paine, R. T. (1969) A Note on Trophic Complexity and Community Stability. *American Naturalist* 100: 65–75.

Palerm, A. (1968) The Agricultural Basis of Urban Civilization in Mesoamerica. In Y. Cohen (ed.), *Man in Adaptation.* Chicago: Aldine.

Pan, W., and Bilsborrow, R. (2005) A Multilevel Study of Fragmentation of Plots and Land Use in the Ecuadorian Amazon. *Global Planetary Change* 47: 232–52.

Parker, D. C., Hessl, A., and Davis, S. C. (2008) Complexity, Land-Use Modeling, and the Human Dimension: Fundamental Challenges for Mapping Unknown Outcome Spaces. *Geoforum* 39(2): 789–804.

Parker, D., Manson, S., Janssen, M., Hoffmann, M., and Deadman, P. (2003) Multi-Agent Systems for the Simulation of Land Use and Land Cover Change: A Review. *Annals of the Association of American Geographers* 93(2): 316–40.

Parker D. C., Entwisle, B., Rindfuss, R. R., et al. (2008) Case Studies, Cross-Site Comparisons, and the Challenge of Generalization: Comparing Agent-Based Models of Land-Use Change in Frontier Regions. *Journal of Land Use Science* 3(1): 41–72.

Pataki, D. E., Ehleringer, J. R., Flanagan, L. B., et al. (2003) The Application and Interpretation of Keeling Plots in Terrestrial Carbon Cycle Research. *Global Biogeochemical Cycles* 17(1): 1022.

Patenaude, G., Milne, R., and Dawson, T. P. (2005) Synthesis of Remote Sensing Approaches for Forest Carbon Estimation: Reporting to the Kyoto Protocol. *Environmental Science and Policy* 8(2): 161–78.

Payne, J., Bettman, J., and Johnson, E. (1993) *The Adaptive Decision Maker*. New York: Cambridge.

Peck, D. L. (1990) *Our Changing Planet: The FY 1991 US Global Change Research Program*. Washington, DC: Office of Science and Technology Policy, Committee on Earth Sciences.

Peet, R., and Watts, M. (1994) Development Theory and Environmentalism in an Age of Market Triumphalism. *Economic Geography* 69: 227–53.

Peet, R. and Watts, M. (eds.) (1996) *Liberation Ecologies: Environment, Development, Social Movements*. London: Routledge.

Penuelas, J. and Filella, I. (2001) Responses to a Warming World. *Science* 294: 793–5.

Peres, C. A., and Dolman, P. M. (2000) Density Compensation in Neotropical Primate Communities: Evidence from 56 Hunted and Nonhunted Amazonian Forests of Varying Productivity. *Oecologia* 122: 175–89.

Perz, S. G. (2001) Household Demographic Factors as Life Cycle Determinants of Land Use in the Amazon. *Population Research and Policy Review* 20: 159–86.

Peterson, R. O. (1999) Wolf–Moose Interaction on Isle Royale: The End of Natural Regulation? *Ecological Applications* 9: 10–16.

Petit, J. R., Jouzel, J., and Raynaud, D. (1999) Climate and Atmospheric History of the Past 420,000 Years from the Vostok Ice Core, Antarctica. *Nature* 399: 429–36.

Pfirman, S., and the AC-ERE (2003) *Complex Environmental Systems: Synthesis for Earth, Life and Society in the 21st Century*. Washington, DC: National Science Foundation.

Pfirman, S., and NACFERA Education (2005) *Complex Environmental Systems: Pathways to the Future: 1–16*. NSF's Follow-Up Report to Their January 2003 Release: Complex Environmental Systems: Synthesis for Earth, Life, and Society in the 21st Century.

Pickett, S. T. A. (1976) Succession: An Evolutionary Interpretation. *American Naturalist* 110: 107–19.

Pickett, S. T. A. (1982) Population Patterns through Twenty Years of Oldfield Succession. *Vegetatio* 49: 45–59.

Pickett, S., Cadenasso, M., and Grove, J. (2004) Resilient Cities: Meaning, Models and Metaphor for Integrating the Ecological Socio-Economic and Planning Realms. *Landscape and Urban Planning* 69: 369–84.

Pickett, S. T. A., Cadenasso, M. L., and Grove, J. M. (2005) Biocomplexity in Coupled Natural–Human Systems: A Multidimensional Framework. *Ecosystems* 8(3): 225–32.

Pickett, S. T. A., Collins, S. L., and Armesto, J. J. (1987) Models, Mechanisms and Pathways of Succession. *The Botanical Review* 53: 335–71.

Pickett, S., Burch, W., Jr., Dalton, S., Foresman, T., Grove, J., and Rowntree. R. (1997) A Conceptual Framework for the Study of Human Ecosystems in Urban Areas. *Urban Ecosystems* 1: 185–99.

Pietsch, S., and Hasenauer, H. (2002) Using Mechanistic Modeling within Forest Ecosystem Restoration. *Forest Ecology and Management* 159(1–2): 111–31.

Platt, R. H., Rowntree, R. A., and Muick, P. C. (eds.) (1994) *The Ecological City: Preserving and Restoring Urban Biodiversity*. Boston: University of Massachusetts Press.

Poch, M., Comas, J., Rodríguez-Roda, I., Sànchez-Marrè, M., and Cortés, U. (2004) Designing and Building Real Environmental Decision Support Systems. *Environmental Modelling and Software* 19: 857–73.

Polanyi, K. (1944) *The Great Transformation: The Political and Economic Origins of Our Time*. New York: Rinehart.

Pontius, R. G., Huffaker, D., and Denman, K. (2004) Useful Techniques of Validation for Spatially Explicit Land Change Models. *Ecological Modelling* 179(4): 445–61.

Portney, P. R. (1994) The Contingent Valuation Debate: Why Economists Should Care. *Journal of Economic Perspectives* 8: 3–17.

Potter, C. (1999) Terrestrial Biomass and the Effects of Deforestation on the Global Carbon Cycle. *BioScience* 49: 769–78.

Powell, R. L., Roberts, D., and Hess, L. (2001) Long-Term Monitoring of Urbanization in the Brazilian Amazon Using Optical Remote Sensing. Poster presented at Human Dimensions of Global Change Conference, Rio de Janeiro, Brazil, Oct. 6–8.

Prakash, A., and Potoski, M. (2006) *The Voluntary Environmentalists: Green Clubs, ISO 14001, and Voluntary Environmental Regulations*. Cambridge, UK: Cambridge University Press.

Prance, G. T. (ed.) (1986) *Tropical Rain Forests and the World Atmosphere*. Boulder, CO: Westview Press.

Pretty, J. N. (2002) *Agri-Culture: Reconnecting People, Land, and Nature*. London: EarthScan.

Proceedings of the National Academy of Sciences of the United States of America (2003) *Science and Technology for Sustainable Development*. Special Feature. PNAS 100(14): 8059–91.

Ragin, C. C. (1987) *The Comparative Method*. Berkeley: University of California Press.

Rahmstorf, S., and Stocker, T. F. (2003) Thermohaline Circulation: Past Changes and Future Surprises. In W. Steffen (ed.), *Global Change and the Earth System*. Springer: IGBP Series.

Raiffa, H. (1968) *Decision Analysis: Introductory Lectures on Choice under Uncertainty*. Reading, MA: Addison-Wesley.

Rapport, D., and Turner, J. (1977) Economic Models in Ecology. *Science* 195: 367–73.

Rapport, D. J., and Whitford, W. G. (1999) How Ecosystems Respond to Stress. *BioScience* 49(3): 193–203.

Rappaport, R. (1968) *Pigs for the Ancestors*. New Haven, CT: Yale University Press.

Rappaport, R. (1977) Ecology, Adaptation and the Ills of Functionalism. *Michigan Discussions in Anthropology* 2: 138–90.

Rappaport, R. (1979) *Ecology, Meaning and Religion*. Richmond, VA: North Atlantic Books.

Rappaport, R. (1993) The Anthropology of Trouble. *American Anthropologist* 95: 295–303.

Rapport, D. J., and Whitford, W. G. (1999) How Ecosystems Respond to Stress. *BioScience* 49(3): 193–203.

Raven, P. (2002) Science, Sustainability, and the Human Prospect. *Science* 297: 954–8.

Redclift, M. (1996) *Wasted: Counting the Costs of Global Consumption*. London: EarthScan.

Redford, K. H. (1992) The Empty Forest. *BioScience* 42: 412–22.

Redman, C. L. (1999) *Human Impact on Ancient Environments*. Tucson: University of Arizona Press.

Redman, C. L. (2005) The Urban Ecology of Metropolitan Phoenix: A Laboratory for Interdisciplinary Study. In B. Entwisle and P. Stern (eds.), *Population, Land Use and Environment*. Washington, DC: National Academies Press.

Redman, C. L., James, S. R., Fish, P. R., and Rogers, J. D. (eds.) (2004) *The Archeology of Global Change*. Washington, DC: Smithsonian Press.

Reid, W., Berkes, F., Wilbanks, T., and Capistrano, D. (eds.) (2006) *Bridging Scales and Knowledge Systems: Linking Global Science and Local Knowledge in Assessment*. Washington, DC: Island Press.

Reining, P. (1973) *ERTS Image Analysis of a Site North of Segon, Mali, W. Africa*. Springfield, VA: NTIS.

Renn, O. (2003) The Challenge of Integrating Deliberation and Expertise: Participation and Discourse in Risk Management. In T. McDaniels and M. J. Small (eds.), *Risk Analysis and Society: An Interdisciplinary Characterization of the Field*. Cambridge, UK: Cambridge University Press.

Repetto, R. (1989) Economic Incentives for Sustainable Production. In G. Schramm and J. J. Warford (eds.), *Environmental Management and Economic Development*. Washington, DC: The World Bank.

Richerson, P. J. (1977) Ecology and Human Ecology: A Comparison of Theories in the Biological and Social Sciences. *American Ethnologist* 4(1): 1–26.

Richerson, P. J., and Boyd, R. (1997/1998) Homage to Malthus, Ricardo and Boserup: Toward a General Theory of Population, Economic Growth, Environmental Deterioration, Wealth and Poverty. *Human Ecology Review* 4: 85–90.

Ridd, M. K. (1995) Exploring a V-I-S (Vegetation-Impervious Surface-Soil) Model for Urban Ecosystem Analysis through Remote Sensing: Comparative Anatomy for Cities. *International Journal of Remote Sensing* 12(12): 2165–85.

Rindfuss, R., Walsh, S., Mishra, V., Fox, J., and Dolcemascolo, G. (2003) Linking Household and Remotely Sensed Data: Methodological and Practical Problems. In J. Fox, S. Walsh and V. Mishra (eds.), *People and the Environment: Approaches for Linking Household and Community Surveys to Remote Sensing and GIS*. Dordrecht: Kluwer.

Robbins, P., Poderman, A., and Birkenholtz, T. (2001) Lawns and Toxins: An Ecology of the Cities. *Cities* 18: 369–80.

Roberts, D. A., Batista, G. T., Pereira, J. L. G., Waller, E. K., and Nelson, B. W. (1998) Change Identification Using Multitemporal Spectral Mixture Analysis: Applications in Eastern Amazônia. In R. S. Lunetta and C. D. Elvidge (eds.), *Remote Sensing Change Detection: Environmental Monitoring Methods and Applications*. Ann Arbor, MI: Ann Arbor Press.

Rodricks, J. V. (1992) *Calculated Risks: Understanding the Toxicity and Human Health Risks of Chemicals in our Environment*. Cambridge, UK: Cambridge University Press.

Roe, G. H., and Baker, M. B. (2007) Why is Climate Sensitivity so Unpredictable? *Science* 318: 629–32.

Rogers, E. M. (1969) *Diffusion of Innovations: Educational Change in Thai Government Secondary Schools*. Michigan State University Report, East Lansing Collection of Communication Arts No. RR-2.

Roosevelt, A. (1989) Natural Resource Management in Amazonia before the Conquest: Beyond Ethnographic Projection. *Advances in Economic Botany* 7: 30–62.

Rudel, T. K. (1989) *Situations and Strategies in Land Use Planning*. New York: Cambridge University Press.

Rudel, T. K. (1998) Is There a Forest Transition? Deforestation, Reforestation, and Development. *Rural Sociology* 63(4): 533–52.

Rudel, T. K. (2005) *Tropical Forests: Regional Paths of Destruction and Regeneration in the Late Twentieth Century*. New York: Columbia University Press.

Rudel, T. K., Coomes, O. T., Moran, E., et al. (2005) Forest Transitions: Towards a Global Understanding of Land Use Change. *Global Environmental Change Part A* 15(1): 23–31.

Ruttan, V. (1999) The Transition to Agricultural Sustainability. *PNAS* 96(11): 5960–7.

Saaty, T. L. (1980) *The Analytical Hierarchy Process*. New York: McGraw Hill.

Saaty, T. L. (1991) *Multicriteria Decision Making: The Analytical Hierarchy Process, Extended Edition*. Pittsburgh, PA: RWS Publishers.

Saldarriaga, J. G., West, D. C., Tharp, M. L., and Uhl, C. (1988) Long-Term Chronosequence of Forest Succession in the Upper Rio Negro of Colombia and Venezuela. *Journal of Ecology* 76: 938–58.

Samuelson, P. A. (1983) Thünen at Two Hundred. *Journal of Economic Literature* 21: 1468–88.

Sanford, R., Saldarriaga, J., Clark, K., Uhl, C., and Herrera, R. (1985) Amazon Rain Forest Fires. *Science* 227: 53–5.

Sassen, S. (1988) *The Mobility of Labor and Capital: A Study in International Investment and Labor Flow*. Cambridge: Cambridge University Press.

Sauer, C. (1958) Man in the Ecology of Tropical America. *Proceedings of the Ninth Pacific Science Congress* 20: 104–10.

Schelhas, J., and Greenberg, R. (eds.) (1996) *Forest Patches in Tropical Landscapes*. Washington, DC: Island Press.

Schelling, T. (1971) Dynamic Models of Segregation. *Journal of Mathematical Sociology* 1: 143–86.

Schelling, T. (1978) *Micromotives and Macrobehavior*. New York: W. W. Norton.

Schiller, A. (2003) A Framework for Vulnerability Analysis in Sustainability Science. *Proceedings of the National Academy of Sciences* 100: 8074–9.

Schlager, E. (1990) Model Specification and Policy Analysis: The Governance of Coastal Fisheries. PhD diss. Indiana University, Bloomington

Schmink, M. (1984) Household Economic Strategies: Review and Research Agenda. *Latin American Research Review* 19(3): 87–101.

Schnaiberg, A. (1980) *The Environment: From Surplus to Scarcity*. New York: Oxford University Press.

Schneider, H. K. (1974) *Economic Man*. New York: Free Press.

Schwartz, H. H. (2000) *Rationality Gone Awry? Decision-Making Inconsistent with Economic and Financial Theory*. Westport, CT: Praeger.

Schweik, C. (1998) The Spatial and Temporal Analysis of Forest Resources and Institutions. CIPEC Dissertation Series, No. 2. Bloomington: Center for the Study of Institutions, Population and Environmental Change, Indiana University.

Schweik, C. (2000) Optimal Foraging, Institutions, and Forest Change: A Case from Nepal. In C. C. Gibson, M. A. McKean, and E. Ostrom (eds.), *People and Forests: Communities, Institutions, and Governance*. Cambridge, MA: MIT Press.

Schweik, C., Nagendra, H., and Sinha, D. (2003) Using Satellite Imagery to Locate Innovative Forest Management Practices in Nepal. *Ambio* 32(4): 312–19.

Scott, A. D. (1955) The Fishery: The Objectives of Sole Ownership. *Journal of Political Economy* 63: 116–24.

Scott, R. E. (2006) The Law and Economics of Incomplete Contracts. *Annual Review of Law and Social Science* 2: 279–97.

Sekher, M. (2001) Organized Participatory Management: Insights from Community Forestry Practices in India. *Forest Policy and Economics* 3: 137–54.

Seto, K. C. (2005) Economies, Societies, and Landscapes in Transition: Examples from the Pearl River Delta, China and the Red River Delta, Vietnam. In B. Entwisle (ed.), *Population, Land Use and Environment: Research Directions*. Washington DC: National Academy Press.

Shapley, D., and Roy, R. (1985) *Lost at the Frontier: US Science and Technology Policy Adrift*. Philadelphia: ISI Press.

Sheppard, E., and McMaster, R. (2004*) Scale and Geographic Inquiry: Nature, Society and Method*. Oxford, UK: Blackwell.

Sheridan, T. (1988) *Where the Dove Calls: The Political Ecology of a Peasant Corporate Community*. Tucson: University of Arizona Press.

Shorey, E., and Eckman, T. (2000) *Appliances and Global Climate Change: Increasing Consumer Participation in Reducing Greenhouse Gases*. Arlington, VA: Pew Center on Global Climate Change.

Shugart, H. H., and West, D. C. (1977) Development of an Appalachian Deciduous Forest Succession Model and Its Application to Assessment of the Impact of the Chestnut Blight. *Journal of Environmental Management* 5: 161–79.

Siegrist, M., Earle, T. C., and Gutscher, H. (2007) *Trust in Cooperative Risk Management: Uncertainty and Skepticism in the Public Mind*. London: Earthscan.

Silvertown, J. (2004) Plant Coexistence and the Niche. *Trends in Ecological Evolution* 19: 605–11.

Simberloff, D. S., and Wilson, E. O. (1969) Experimental Zoogeography of Islands: The Colonization of Empty Islands. *Ecology* 50(2): 278–96.

Simon, H. (1985) Human Nature in Politics: The Dialogue of Psychology with Political Science. *American Political Science Review* 79: 293–304.

Simon, H. (1997) *Models of Bounded Reality: Empirically Grounded Economic Reason*. Cambridge, MA: MIT Press.

Simon, L. (1981) *The Ultimate Resource*. Princeton, NJ: Princeton University Press.

Singh, N. M. (2002) Federations of Community Forest Management Groups in Orissa: Crafting New Institutions to Assert Local Rights. *Forests, Trees and People Newsletter* 46: 35–45.

Siqueira, A., McCracken, S. D., Brondizio, E. S., and Moran, E. F. (2003) Women and Work in a Brazilian Agricultural Frontier. In G. Clark (ed.), *Gender at Work in Economic Life*. New York: Altamira Press.

Siqueira, A. D., D'Antona, A. O., D'Antona, M. F., and Moran, E. F. (2007) Embodied Decisions: Reversible and Irreversible Contraceptive Methods among Rural Women in the Brazilian Amazon. *Human Organization* 66(2): 185–95.

Skole, D., and Tucker, C. (1993) Tropical Deforestation and Habitat Fragmentation in the Amazon: Satellite Data from 1978 to 1988. *Science* 260: 1905–10.

Slovic, P. (1995) The Construction of Preference. *American Psychologist* 50: 364–71.

Slovic, P. (1999) Trust, Emotion, Sex, Politics, and Science: Surveying the Risk-Assessment Battlefield. *Risk Analysis* 19: 689–701.

Slovic, P., and Gregory, R. (1999) Risk Analysis, Decision Analysis and the Social Context for Risk Decision Making. In J. Shanteau, B. A. Mellers and D. A. Schum (eds.), *Decision Science and Technology: Reflections on the Contributions of Ward Edwards*. Boston, MA: Kluwer Academic.

Slovic, P., Fischhoff, B., and Lichtenstein, S. (1977) Behavioral Decision Theory. *Annual Review of Psychology* 28: 1–39.

Slovic, P., Kunreuther, H., and White, G. (1974) Decision Processes, Rationality and Adjustment to Natural Hazards. In G. White (ed.), *Natural Hazards*. New York: Oxford University Press.

Smit, B., and Wandel, J. (2006) Adaptation, Adaptive Capacity and Vulnerability. *Global Environmental Change* 16: 282–92.

Smith, B. D. (1989) Origins of Agriculture in Eastern North America. *Science* 246: 1566–71.

Smith, N. (1982) Colonization Lessons from the Rainforest. *Science* 212: 755–61.

Smith, N. L. (2002) Species Extinction. At www.whole-systems.org/extinctions. html. Accessed January 24, 2003.

Smith, T. M., and Urban, D. L. (1988) Scale and Resolution of Forest Structural Pattern. *Vegetatio* 74(2–3): 143–50.

Sober, E., and Wilson, D. S. (1998) *Unto Others: The Evolution and Psychology of Unselfish Behavior*. Cambridge, MA: Harvard University Press.

Southworth, J., and Tucker, C. (2001) The Roles of Accessibility, Local Institutions, and Socioeconomic Factors Influencing Forest Cover Change in the Mountains of Western Honduras. *Mountain Research and Development* 21(3): 276–83.

Spooner, B. (ed.) (1972) *Population Growth: Anthropological Implications*. Cambridge, MA: MIT Press.

Stark, O. (1991) *The Migration of Labor*. Cambridge, MA: Basil Blackwell.

Stark, O., and Bloom, D. E. (1985) The New Economics of Labor Migration. *American Economic Review* 75: 173–8.

Stark, O., and Levhari, D. (1982) On Migration and Risk in LDCs. *Economic Development and Cultural Change* 31: 191–6.

Stark, O., and Lucas, R. E. B. (1988) Migration, Remittances, and the Family. *Economic Development and Cultural Change* 36(3): 465–81.

Steffen, W., Sanderson, A., Tyson, P., et al. (eds.) (2003) *Global Change and the Earth System: A Planet under Pressure*. New York: Springer-Verlag.

Stein, D. (ed.) (1989) *Lectures in the Science of Complexity*. New York: Addison-Wesley.

Steinberg, E. K., and Kareiva, P. (1997) Challenges and Opportunities for Empirical Evaluation of Spatial Theory. In D. Tilman and P. Kareiva (eds.), *Spatial Ecology: The Role of Space in Population Dynamics and Interspecific Interactions*. Princeton University Press.

Steinberg, S. J., and Steinberg, S. L. (2006) *GIS: Geographic Information Systems for the Social Sciences: Investigating Space and Place*. Thousand Oaks, CA: Sage Publications.

Steininger, M. K. (1996) Tropical Secondary Forest Regrowth in the Amazon: Age, Area and Change Estimation with Thematic Mapper Data. *International Journal of Remote Sensing* 17: 9–27.

Stern, N. (2007) *The Economics of Climate Change: The Stern Review*. Cambridge, UK: Cambridge University Press.

Stern, P. C. (1993) A Second Environmental Science: Human–Environment Interactions. *Science* 260: 1897–9.

Stern, P. C. (2000) Psychology and the Science of Human-Environment Interactions. *American Psychologist* 55: 523–30.

Stern, P. C., and Gardner, G. T. (1981) The Place of Behavior Change in Managing Environmental Problems. *Zeitschrift für Umweltpolitik* 2: 213–39.

Stern, P. C., Dietz, T., and Black, J. S. (1986) Support for Environmental Protection: The Role of Moral Norms. *Population and Environment* 8(3/4): 204–22.

Stern, P. C., Dietz, T., Kalof, L., and Guagnano, G. A. (1995) Values, Beliefs and Pro-Environmental Action: Attitude Formation toward Emergent Attitude Objects. *Journal of Applied Social Psychology* 25: 1611–36.

Stern, P., Dietz, T., Abel, T., Guagnano, C., and Kaloff, L. (1999) A Social Psychological Theory of Support for Social Movements: The Case of Environmentalism. *Human Ecology Review* 6: 81–97.

Steward, J. (1936) The Economic and Social Basis of Primitive Bands. In *Essays in Anthropology Presented to A. L. Kroeber and R. Lowie* (eds.) Berkeley: University of California Press.

Steward, J. (1938) Basin-Plateau Aboriginal Sociopolitical Groups. Bulletin 120, Bureau of American Ethnology. Washington, DC: Smithsonian Institution.

Steward, J. (1955) *The Theory of Culture Change*. Urbana: University of Illinois Press.

Sussman, R., Green, G. M., and Sussman, L. (1994) Satellite Imagery, Human Ecology, Anthropology and Deforestation in Madagascar. *Human Ecology* 22(3): 333–54.

Suter, G. (1993) *Ecological Risk Assessment*. Boca Raton, FL: Lewis Publishers, an imprint of CRC Press.

Swart, R. J., Raskin, P., and Robinson, J. (2004) The Problem of the Future: Sustainability Science and Scenario Analysis. *Global Environmental Change* 14: 137–46.

Swart, R., Raskin, P., Robinson, J., Kates, R., and Clark, W. C. (2002) Critical Challenges for Sustainability Science. *Science* 297: 1994–5.

Szreter, S. (1996) *Fertility, Class and Gender in Britain, 1860–1940*. New York: Cambridge University Press.

Tang, S. Y. (1992) *Institutions and Collective Action: Self-Governance in Irrigation*. San Francisco: ICS Press.

Terborgh, J., Lopez, L., Nuñez, P., et al. (2001) Ecological Meltdown in Predator-Free Forest Fragments. *Science* 294: 1923–6.

Terborgh, J., Nuñez-Iturri, G., Pitman, N. C. A., et al. (2008) Tree Recruitment in an Empty Forest. *Ecology* 89(6): 1757–68.

Tesfatsion, L. (1997) How Economists Can Get a Life. In W. B. Arthur, S. Durlaf, and D. Lane (eds.), *The Economy as an Evolving Complex System II*. Reading, MA: Addison-Wesley.

Thøgerson, J. (2002) Promoting "Green" Consumer Behavior with Eco-Labels. In T. Dietz and P. C. Stern (eds.), *New Tools for Environmental Protection: Education, Information, and Voluntary Measures*. National Research Council, Committee on the Human Dimensions of Global Change. Division of Behavioral and Social Sciences and Education. Washington, DC: National Academy Press.

Thøgerson, J. (2004) A Cognitive Dissonance Interpretation of Consistencies and Inconsistencies in Environmentally Responsible Behavior. *Journal of Environmental Psychology* 24: 93–103.

Tilman, D. (1999) Ecological Consequences of Biodiversity: A Search for General Principles. *Ecology* 80: 1455–74.

Tilman, D. (2001) Effects of Diversity and Composition on Grassland Stability and Productivity. In M. Press et al. (eds.), *Ecology: Achievement and Challenge*. New York: Cambridge University Press.

Tilman, D., and Kareiva, P. (eds.) (1997) *Spatial Ecology*. Princeton, NJ: Princeton University Press.

Tilman, D., J. Fargione, B., Wolff, C., et al. (2001) Forecasting Agriculturally Driven Global Environmental Change. *Science* 282: 281–4.

Travis, C. (1988) *Carcinogen Risk Assessment*. New York: Plenum Press.

Treitz, P. M., Howard, P. J., and Gong, P. (1992) Application of Satellite and GIS Technologies for Land-Cover and Land-Use Mapping at the Rural–Urban Fringe: A Case Study. *Photogrammetric Engineering and Remote Sensing* 58: 439–48.

Tucker, C. (1999) Private vs. Communal Forests: Forest Conditions and Tenure in a Honduran Community. *Human Ecology* 27(2): 201–30.

Tucker, C., and Ostrom, E. (2005) Multidisciplinary Research Relating Institutions and Forest Transformations. In E. Moran and E. Ostrom (eds.), *Seeing the Forest and the Trees*. Cambridge, MA: MIT Press.

Tucker, C., and Southworth, J. (2005) Processes of Forest Change at the Local and Landscape Levels in Honduras andGuatemala. In E. Moran and E. Ostrom (eds.), *Seeing the Forest and the Trees*. Cambridge, MA: MIT Press.

Tucker, J., Brondizio, E., and Moran, E. F. (1998) Rates of Forest Regrowth in Eastern Amazônia: A Comparison of Altamira and Bragantina Regions, Pará State, Brazil. *Interciencia* 23(2): 64–73.

Tucker, C., Munroe, D., Nagendra, H., and Southworth, J. (2005) Comparative Spatial Analyses of Forest Conservation and Change in Honduras and Guatemala. *Conservation and Society* 3(1): 174–200.

Turner, B. L. (1989) The Human Causes of Global Environmental Change. In R. S. DeFries and T. F. Malone (eds.), *Global Change and Our Common Future*. Papers from a Forum. Washington, DC: National Academy of Sciences.

Turner, B. L., II, Hyden, G., and Kates, R. (1993) *Population Growth and Agricultural Change in Africa: Studies from Densely Settled Areas of Sub-Saharan Africa*. Gainesville: University Press of Florida.

Turner, B. L., II, Meyer, W. B., and Skole, D. L. (1994) Global Land Use/Land Cover Change: Toward an Integrated Program of Study. *Ambio* 23: 91–5.

Turner, B. L., Kasperson, R. E. Matson, P. A. et al. (1989) Predicting Across the Scales: Theory Development and Testing. *Landscape Ecology* 3: 245–52.

Turner, B. L., II, Clark, W. C., Kates, R. W., Richards, J. F., Mathews, J. T., and Meyer, W. B. (eds.) (1990) *The Earth as Transformed by Human Action*. New York: Cambridge University Press.

Turner, J. C. (1991) *Social Influence*. Pacific Grove, CA: Brooks-Cole.

Turner, M. G., Gardner, R. H., and O'Neill, R. V. (2001) *Landscape Ecology in Theory and Practice*. New York: Springer-Verlag.

Tversky, A., and Kahneman, D. (1981) The Framing of Decisions and the Psychology of Choice. *Science* 211: 453–8.

Udehn, L. (2002) The Changing Face of Methodological Individualism. *Annual Review of Sociology* 28: 479–507.

UNEP (2000) *Global Environmental Outlook 2000*. United Nations Environment Programme, Nairobi, Kenya.

United Nations (1994) Programme of Action of the 1994 International Conference on Population and Development (A/CONF.171/13). Reprinted in *Population and Development Review* 21(1): 187–213 and 21(2): 437–61.

US Bureau of the Census (2000) International Database. At www.census.gov/ipc/www/worldpop.htm, accessed May 10, 2000.

US Climate Change Science Program and Subcommittee on Global Change Research (2003) Strategic Plan for the US Climate Change Science Program. Washington, DC: US Climate Change Science Program and Subcommittee on Global Change Research.

Van den Berg, A. E., Hartig, T., and Staats, H. (2007) Preference for Nature in Urbanized Societies: Stress, Restoration, and the Pursuit of Sustainability. *Journal of Social Issues* 63: 79–96.

Van den Burgh, M. P. (2004) From Smokestack to SUV: The Individual as Regulated Entity in the New Era of Environmental Law. *Vanderbilt Law Review* 57: 515–628.

Van der Leeuw, S. E. (1998) The Archaeomedes Project: Understanding the Natural and Anthropogenic Causes of Land Degradation and Desertification in the Mediterranean. Luxemburg: Office for Official Publications of the European Union.

Vandermeer, J. H. (2003) *Tropical Agroecosystems*. Boca Raton, FL: CRC Press.

VanWey, L. K. (2003) Land Ownership as a Determinant of Temporary Migration in Nang Rong, Thailand. *European Journal of Population* 19: 121–45.

VanWey, L. K. (2005) Land Ownership as a Determinant of International and Internal Migration in Mexico and Internal Migration in Thailand. *International Migration Review* 39(1): 141–72.

Vayda, A. P. (1974) Warfare in Ecological Perspective. *Annual Review of Ecology and Systematics* 5: 183–93.

Vayda, A. P. (1976) *Warfare in Ecological Perspective*. New York: Plenum.

Vayda, A. P. (1983) Progressive Contextualization: Methods for Research in Human Ecology. *Human Ecology* 11(3): 265–81.

Vayda, A. P., and Rappaport, R. (1976) Ecology, Cultural and Noncultural. In P. Richerson and J. McEvoy (eds.), *Human Ecology*. North Scituate, MA: Duxbury Press.

Vayda, A. P., and Walters, B. (1999) Against Political Ecology. *Human Ecology* 27(1): 167–80.

Veldkamp, T., Verburg, P., Kok, K., de Joning, F., and Soepboer, W. (2002) Spatial Explicit Land use Change, Scenarios for Policy Purposes: Some Applications of the CLUE Framework. In S. Walsh and K. Crews-Meyer (eds.), *Linking People, Place and Policy: A GIScience Approach*. Boston: Kluwer.

Venkatachalam, L. (2007) Environmental Economics and Ecological Economics: Where Can They Converge? *Ecological Economics* 61: 550–8.

Verberg, P. H., Eickhout, B., and Van Meijl, H. (2008) A Multi-Scale, Multi-Model Approach for Analyzing the Future Dynamics of European Land Use. *Annals of Regional Science* 42(1): 57–77.

Visser, S. (1982) On Agricultural Location Theory. *Geographical Analysis* 14: 167–76.

Vitousek, P. M. (1994) Beyond Global Warming: Ecology and Global Change. *Ecology* 75: 1861–76.

Vitousek, P. M., and Reiners, W. A. (1975) Ecosystem Succession and Nutrient Retention: A Hypothesis. *BioScience* 25(6): 376–81.

Vitousek, P., Mooney, H., Lubchenco, J., and Melillo, J. (1997) Human Domination of Earth's Ecosystems. *Science* 277: 494–9.

Vogt, E. (ed.) (1974) *Aerial Photography in Anthropological Field Research.* Cambridge, MA: Harvard University Press.

Wack, P. (1985a) Scenarios: Uncharted Waters Ahead. *Harvard Business Review* 63(5): 72–89.

Wack, P. (1985b) Scenarios: Shooting the Rapids. *Harvard Business Review* 63(6): 139–50.

Wade, R. (1994) *Village Republics: Economic Conditions for Collective Action in South India.* San Francisco: ICS Press.

Wakernagel, M., and Rees, W. (1996) *Our Ecological Footprint.* Philadelphia: New Society Publishers.

Wakernagel, M., Kitzes, J., Moran, D., Goldfinger, S., and Thomas, M. (2006) The Ecological Footprint of Cities and Regions: Comparing Resource Availability with Resource Demand. *Environment and Urbanization* 18: 103–12.

Walker, B. H., and Steffen, W. (1997) An Overview of the Implications of Global Change for Natural and Managed Terrestrial Ecosystems. *Conservation Ecology* 1(2): 2.

Walker, D. M., Perez-Barberia, F. J., and Marion, G. (2006) Stochastic Modelling of Ecological Processes Using Hybrid Gibbs Samplers. *Ecological Modelling* 198: 40–52.

Walker, R. T. (2003) Evaluating the Performance of Spatially Explicit Models. *Photogrammetric Engineering and Remote Sensing* 69(11): 1271–8.

Walker, R. T., and Homma, A. K. O. (1996) Land Use and Land Cover Dynamics in the Brazilian Amazon: An Overview. *Ecological Economics* 18: 67–80.

Walker, R., Moran, E. F., and Anselin, L. (2000) Deforestation and Cattle Ranching in the Brazilian Amazon: External Capital and Household Processes. *World Development* 28(4): 683–99.

Wallerstein, I. (1974) *The Modern World-System.* Vol. 1. New York: Academic Press.

Walsh, K. (2004) Tropical Cyclones and Climate Change: Unresolved Issues. *Climate Research* 27: 77–83.

Walsh, S., and Crews-Meyer, K. (eds.) (2002) *Linking People, Place and Policy: A GIScience Approach.* Boston: Kluwer.

Walsh, S. J., and McGinnis, D. (2008) Biocomplexity in Coupled Human–Natural Systems: The Study of Population and Environment Interactions. *Geoforum* 39(2): 773–5.

Walsh, S., Evans, T., Welsh, W., Entwisle, B., and Rindfuss, R. (1999) Scale Dependent Relationships Between Population and Environment in Northeastern Thailand. *Photogrammetric Engineering and Remote Sensing* 65(1): 97–105.

Walsh, S. J., Rindfuss, R., Prasartkukl, P., Entwisle, B., and Chamratrithrirong, A. (2005) Population Change and Landscape Dynamics: The Nang Rong Thailand Studies. In B. Entwisle and P. Stern (eds.), *Population, Land Use and Environment.* Washington, DC: National Academies Press.

Walsh, S. J., Messina, J. P., Mena, C. F., and Page, P. (2008) Complexity Theory, Spatial Simulation Models, and Land Use Dynamics in the Northern Ecuadorian Amazon. *Geoforum* 39(2): 867–78.

Warren, W. A. (2005) Hierarchy Theory in Sociology, Ecology, and Resource Management: A Conceptual Model for Natural Resource or Environmental Sociology and Socioecological Systems. *Society & Natural Resources* 18(5): 447–66.

Wätzold, M., Drechsler, C. W., Armstrong, S., et al. (2006) Ecological–Economic Modelling for Biodiversity Management: Potential, Pitfalls, and Prospects. *Conservation Biology* 20(4): 1034–41.

Webber, M. J. (1973) Equilibrium of Location in an Isolated State. *Environment and Planning* 5: 751–9.

Wedekind, C., and Milinski, M. (1996) Human Cooperation in the Simultaneous and the Alternating Prisoner's Dilemma: Pavlov versus Generous Tit-for-Tat. *Proceedings of the National Academy of Sciences of the United States of America* 93(7): 2686–9.

Welch, W. P. (1983) The Political Feasibility of Full Ownership Property Rights: The Cases of Pollution and Fisheries. *Policy Sciences* 16: 165–80.

Wernick, I. (1997) *Consuming Materials: The American Way. Environmentally Significant Consumption: Research Directions.* Washington, DC: National Academies Press.

Wessman, C. (1992) Spatial Scales and Global Change: Bridging the Gap from Plots to GCM Grid Cells. *Annual Review of Ecology and Systematics* 23: 175–200.

Weyant, J., Cline, W., Fankhauser, S., et al. (1996) Integrated Assessment of Climate Change: An Overview and Comparison of Approaches and Results. In J. P. Bruce, H. Lee, and E. F. Haites (eds.), *Climate Changes, 1995: Economic and Social Dimensions of Climate Change.* Contribution of Working Group III to the Second Assessment Report of the Intergovernmental Panel on Climate Change. New York: Cambridge University Press.

White, G. (1974) *Natural Hazards.* Chicago: University of Chicago Press.

Whyte, A. (1985) Ecological Approaches to Urban Systems. *Nature and Resources* 21(1): 13–20.

Widegren, Ö. (1998) The New Environmental Paradigm and Personal Norms. *Environment and Behavior* 30: 75–100.

Wiens, J. (1977) On Competition and Variable Environments. *American Scientist* 65: 590–7.

Wiens, J. (1984) On Understanding a Non-Equilibrium World: Myth and Reality in Community Patterns and Processes. In D. R. Strong, D. Simberloff, L. G. Abele, and A. B. Thistle (eds.), *Ecological Communities: Conceptual Issues and the Evidence.* Princeton University Press, NJ: Princeton University Press.

Wilbanks, T. J. (2007) Scale and Sustainability. *Climate Policy* 7/4: 278–87.

Wilbanks, T. J., and Kates, R. (1999) Global Change in Local Places. *Climatic Change* 43(3): 601–28.

Wilbanks, T. J., Kane, S. M., Leiby, P. N., et al. (2003) Possible Responses to Global Climate Change: Integrating Mitigation and Adaptation. *Environment* 45(5): 28–38.

Wilk, R. (1990) Household Ecology: Decision-Making and Resource Flows. In E. F. Moran (ed.), *The Ecosystem Approach in Anthropology.* Ann Arbor: University of Michigan Press.

Wilke, A., Hutchinson, J. M. C., and Todd, P. M. (2004) Testing Simple Rules for Human Foraging in Patchy Environments. In K. Forbus, D. Gentner, and T. Regier (eds.), *Proceedings of the 26th Annual Conference of the Cognitive Science Society*. Mahwah, NJ: Erlbaum.

Wilkie, D. (1994) Remote Sensing Imagery for Resource Inventories in Central Africa: The Importance of Detailed Data. *Human Ecology* 22: 379–404.

Wilmsen, E. (1989) *Land Filled with Flies: A Political Economy of the Kalahari*. Chicago: University of Chicago Press.

Wilson, A. G. (2000) *Complex Spatial Systems: The Modelling Foundations of Urban and Regional Analysis*. New York: Pearson.

Wilson, C., and Dowlatabadi, H. (2007) Models of Decision Making and Residential Use. *Annual Review of Environment and Resources* 32: 169–203.

Wilson, D. S. (1980) *The Natural Selection of Populations and Communities*. Menlo Park, CA: Benjamin/Cumings.

Wilson, D. S. (1983) The Group Selection Controversy: History and Current Status. *Annual Review of Ecology and Systematics* 14: 159–88.

Wilson, E. O. (1998) *Consilience*. New York: Alfred A. Knopf.

Winterhalder, B. (1994) Concepts in Historical Ecology: The View from Evolutionary Ecology. In C. Crumley (ed.), *Historical Ecology*. Santa Fe, NM: School of American Research Press.

With, K. A., and King, A. W. (1999) Dispersal Success on Fractal Landscapes: A Consequence of Lacunarity Thresholds. *Landscape Ecology* 14: 73–82.

Wojtkowski, P. A. (2004) *Landscape Agroecology*. New York: Food Products Press.

Wolf, E. (1982) *Europe and the People without History*. Berkeley: University of California Press.

Wolf, E. (1999) *Envisioning Power*. Berkeley: University of California Press.

Wolch, J. (2007) Green Urban Worlds. *Annals of the Association of American Geographers* 97(2): 373–84.

Wood, C. H., and Perz, S. (1996) Population and Land Use Change in the Brazilian Amazon. In S. Ramphal and S. Sindig (eds.), *Population Growth and Environmental Issues*. Westport, CT: Praeger.

Wood, C., and Porro, R. (eds.) (2002) *Deforestation and Land Use in the Amazon*. Gainesville: University Press of Florida.

Wood, C., and Skole, D. (1998) Linking Satellite, Census, and Survey Data to Study Deforestation in the Brazilian Amazon. In D. Liverman et al. (eds.), *People and Pixels: Linking Remote Sensing and Social Science*. Washington, DC: National Academy Press.

Wooster, D. (ed.) (1984) History as Natural History: An Essay on Theory and Method. *Pacific Historical Review* 3: 1–19.

Wootton, J. T. (2002) Indirect Effects in Complex Ecosystems: Recent Progress and Future Challenges. *Journal of Sea Research* 48: 157–72.

Wu, F. (1998) SimLand: A Prototype to Simulate Land Conversion through the Integrated GIS and CA with AHP-Derived Transition Rules. *International Journal of Geographic Information Science* 12: 63–82.

Wu, J., and David, J. L. (2002) A Spatially Explicit Hierarchical Approach to Modeling Complex Ecological Systems: Theory and Applications. *Ecological Modelling* 153: 7–26.

Xu, C. L., and Li, Z. Z. (2002) Stochastic Ecosystem Resilience and Productivity: Seeking a Relationship. *Ecological Modelling* 156(2–3): 143–52.

Yohe, G., and Tol, R. S. J. (2002) Indicators for Social and Economic Coping Capacity: Moving Toward a Working Definition of Adaptive Capacity. *Global Environmental Change* 12: 25–40.

Young, O. (1999) *The Effectiveness of International Environmental Regimes: Causal Connections and Behavioral Mechanisms.* Cambridge, MA: MIT Press.

Zadeh, L. (1965) Fuzzy Sets. *Information and Control* 8: 338–53.

Zarin, D., Ducey, M. J., Tucker, J. M., and Salas ,W. A. (2001) Potential Biomass Accumulation in Amazonian Regrowth Forests. *Ecosystems* 4: 658–68.

Zarin, D., Alavapati, J., Putz, F. E., and Schmink, M. (eds.) (2002) *Working Forests in the Tropics: Conservation through Sustainable Management?* New York: Columbia University Press.

Zerbe, R. O., Jr., and Dively, D. D. (1994) *Benefit-Cost Analysis in Theory and Practice.* New York: Harper-Collins.

Zhang, P., Shao, G., Zhao, G., et al. (2000) China's Forest Policy for the 21st Century. *Science* 288(23): 2135–6.

Zimmerer, K. S. (1994) Human Geography and the "New Ecology": The Prospect and Promise of Integration. *Annals of the Association of American Geographers* 84(1): 108–25.

Zipperer, W. C., Wu, J., Pouyat, R. V., and Pickett, S. T. A. (2000) The Application of Ecological Principles to Urban and Urbanizing Landscapes. *Ecological Applications* 10: 685–8.

Index